Historical Journals

"Historical Journals"

A HANDBOOK FOR WRITERS AND REVIEWERS

Dale R. Steiner

ABC-Clio

Santa Barbara, California

Oxford, England

Library of Congress Cataloging in Publication Data

Steiner, Dale R.
    Historical Journals.

    Includes bibliographies and index.
    1. History—Periodicals—Directories. 2. History—Authorship.
3. Book reviewing. I. Title.
Z6205.S73 [D10]   808'.02   80–26215
ISBN 0–87436–312–8

ABC-Clio, Inc.
Riviera Campus
2040 Alameda Padre Serra, Box 4397
Santa Barbara, California 93103

Clio Press Ltd.
Woodside House, Hinksey Hill
Oxford, OX1 5BE, England

Manufactured in the United States of America

Contents

Acknowledgments

I am indebted to all of the journal editors who cooperated with this project by furnishing information about their publications. No less appreciated were the advice and the expressions of encouragement offered by a considerable number. Several of my friends and colleagues deserve thanks for the suggestions which they made and for reading the manuscript. Most notable in that regard are Jacqueline Barnhart and Joseph Conlin. Special recognition is due Nancy Riley who labored tirelessly for many months, editing and typing, without ever losing her sense of humor. I am grateful for all her help. Barbara Corchero assisted with the typing. My wife Christine, with limitless quantities of patience and support, provided the inspiration to see the *Handbook* through to its completion.

Introduction

Scope

Historical Journals: A Handbook for Writers and Reviewers is designed to help would-be authors penetrate the mystique of publishing their work in historical periodicals. It draws no distinction between amateur and professional historians, between academics and laymen. The *Handbook* simply proceeds from the premise that you have researched and planned a historical article which you would like to publish. If you are uncertain of how to accomplish that goal, the following pages can assist you in several ways. First, the *Handbook* offers general suggestions on the preparation and submission of manuscripts. Second, it contains a Directory which lists more than three hundred and fifty journals published in the United States and Canada, and provides specific information on the editorial standards and publishing policies of each. These two tools should help you maximize the chances of having a manuscript accepted for publication.

There is, of course, no guarantee of success, even if you follow all of the suggestions to the letter. The fact that journal editors—the men and women who decide what is published—furnished the advice and information on the succeeding pages makes the *Handbook* valuable to authors. The *Handbook* should also prove useful to editors by promoting the submission of manuscripts that are consistent with the needs and standards of their publications.

The *Handbook* is not a comprehensive catalog of historical periodicals published in the United States and Canada. Some editors chose not to respond to several appeals for information; others requested, for a variety of reasons, that their publications be omitted from the *Handbook*. But with well over three hundred and fifty detailed entries covering a broad spectrum of fields, interests, and eras, and ranging from highly specialized scholarly journals to avowedly amateur local publications, the *Handbook* offers historians numerous outlets for satisfying their creative urges.

An additional feature of the *Handbook* is a section which discusses the purposes and techniques of book reviewing. The *Handbook*'s Directory section includes information on the reviewing needs and policies of individual journals.

Organization

The information contained in the Directory of Journals is the product of a questionnaire completed by editors of historical journals. The format of the listings reflects the questionnaire. Although the listings are for the most part readily understandable, a few explanatory remarks are in order.

Under the heading "Manuscripts," are the subheadings "Query" and "Abstract." Journal editors were asked whether queries or abstracts were required before a publication decision could be reached. The negative answer does not imply that queries or abstracts are unwelcome, but that an article submitted without an initial query or without a summarizing abstract would nevertheless be considered.

The only abbreviations which the Directory employs are those denoting the various style guides used by journals.

GPO United States Government Printing Office, *Style Manual*

MFW Kate L. Turabian, *A Manual for Writers of Term Papers, Theses, and Dissertations* (fourth edition)

MLA Modern Language Association, *The MLA Style Sheet* (second edition)

MOS University of Chicago Press, *A Manual of Style* (twelfth edition)

SAGE Sage Publications, *Journal Editorial Style*

Individual Directory entries note other style guides where appropriate.

The subheading "Notes" gave the editors an opportunity to state their preference for the placement of notes in articles published in their journal. "Blind referee" indicates whether the journal conceals the identity of an article's author from the reviewers who comment on the work. "Foreign languages" indicates languages other than English which are acceptable for publication.

The Directory of Journals is organized alphabetically by journal title. Journals known by titles in more than one language are listed under the English title.

Advice on Articles

WRITING AN ARTICLE

What Editors Look For

All prospective authors should be aware of the various factors that influence an editor to publish or reject a manuscript. These factors should be considered carefully throughout the composition of an article and especially when deciding which journal to submit it to. While the order of importance may vary from periodical to periodical, the most significant factors are an article's suitability to the journal's readership, its quality of presentation, and the degree to which it conforms to the journal's requirements of space and style.

Suitability means that the subject of a manuscript falls within the focus of the journal and that it is aimed at that journal's readership. The editor of a journal dealing with African history is unlikely to consider an article on American expansion across the Great Plains. Similarly, an extremely technical piece of great interest to professional historians would be unwelcome at a journal geared to enthusiasts or the general public. *Quality* refers to the accuracy and credibility of a manuscript as well as to the clarity with which it is presented. An article which is well-written and easily understood stands a far better chance of acceptance than one that is not. The physical form of a manuscript is also important—it should be neat and clean. *Conformity* involves the amount of work an editor must perform to bring an article into alignment with his journal's particular needs and standards. Confronted by a manuscript a half dozen pages too long, an editor may, understandably, opt for a shorter piece, in preference to reducing the longer manuscript himself. Likewise an article which observes the same rules of style, punctuation, and note form and placement as are used by a journal is more likely to receive a favorable response from the editor.

Seek Criticism

Before your article is in final form, tighten it up as well as you can. This should by no means be a solitary process. Discuss your ideas with colleagues and knowledgable friends; invite them to read your rough draft. If you belong to a historical society or club, arrange to present your ideas as a paper at a meeting. Academics should take advantage of existing speakers' series or organize their own colloquium if their department lacks such a program. The point is to test your premises, research, and conclusions on an objective audience. Nothing is lost in the process and the possible rewards include useful criticism, a better article, and improved chances of publication.

Literary Style

The proper medium for your article is clear, formal English (not stiff, merely correct). Avoid slang at all costs; most editors detest it. Professional jargon is scarcely more welcome, unless you happen to be writing for a narrow, highly specialized readership. *The Elements of Style* by William Strunk and E. B. White is a good place to turn for assistance. Questions of proper spelling and word division should be settled by consulting *Webster's Third International Dictionary,* a volume recommended by a substantial number of editors.

Introduction/title

Pay particular attention to the first few paragraphs, which persuade readers that the article is worth reading. Editors realize that readers often skim the introduction before deciding to read an article in its entirety and therefore look for manuscripts which have strong openings. One editor observed that "Too many articles simply 'die' in the first paragraph through bad writing, or by taking the reader for granted, i.e., simply assuming that the topic is as of great interest to him as it is to the author." The introduction should indicate what your article is about and tell why that topic is important. This should be done in an implicit, rather than an explicit, manner.

The title of your article is also important. It should be informative, and if possible, intriguing. It should also be short; lengthy titles sometimes create space problems for journals. Editors are grateful for any effort that your foresight spares them.

SELECTING A JOURNAL

What to Consider

Submitting your manuscript to the right journal greatly enhances the possibility of publication. Considerable care should therefore be exercised. Begin by making a list of the journals whose focus of interest coincides with that of your article. Then consider the descriptions of their readership. Narrow your list down to those periodicals whose readership is compatible with the level of the ideas and language contained in your article. Other factors to weigh include the size of the journal's circulation, its rate of acceptance, the length of time needed to reach a decision, and whether or not any payment is made to contributors. For most journals listed in the *Handbook,* payment consists of a few reprints of your article or several copies of the issue in which your work appears. Only a handful offer monetary payment. Another consideration is prestige. Certainly acceptance by some journals represents more of a distinction than does publication by others. But as prestige is rather an intangible and subjective factor, the *Handbook* can offer no direction on this point.

If a particular journal has previously published an article of yours, you should not assume that your chances are improved in submitting a second article to the same journal. In fact, the opposite is probably true; lightning rarely strikes twice in the same place. Furthermore, publication in more than one journal should strengthen your reputation as a writer since it conveys an impression of breadth.

Your final decision on a journal should not be made until you have perused a copy or two of each of the journals to which you have narrowed your choice. Make certain that your assumptions are correct, that your article really *is* suited to those journals. Eliminating uncertainty on this point is worth the trip to the library.

Query

If any of the *Handbook* entries for the journals you are considering indicate a query is in order, send a letter to the editor, describe the theme of your article, mention the major sources you consulted, and indicate why you believe the article is suited to that particular periodical and whether it makes an original or unique contribution to the literature on the subject. Be sure to include a self-addressed, stamped envelope with your letter of inquiry. Although you should never submit your article to more than one journal at a time, there is no reason to limit your inquiries in such a manner. Waiting to send a second query until the first one is answered will only delay your quest for publication, should your initial inquiry receive a negative response.

Before sending a query to an editor in another country you should read the section "Mailing/postage" and "Foreign history journals."

Style Guides

If the journal in question publishes its own style sheet, it is imperative that you write for a copy (again, include a self-addressed, stamped envelope with your request). This may be done in conjunction with a query. In fact, even if the journal from which you request a style sheet does not demand a query, you might as well send one, since you are writing the editor anyway. It may give you encouragement or spare you a later rejection.

PREPARING YOUR MANUSCRIPT

Typing

All manuscripts submitted to journals should be typed. Use any standard, high quality, white bond paper, 8½ by 11 inches. Do not use erasable, onionskin, or second-copy paper. Before beginning to type, clean the keys of your typewriter and replace the ribbon if it is at all worn. A pica typeface is preferable to either elite or script, which are more difficult to read. Double-space the entire manuscript, including footnotes and quotations. This facilitates editing as well as typesetting. One or two brief handwritten corrections per page are acceptable, provided they are done legibly and in ink.

Neatness is extremely important throughout. Carelessly typed or otherwise messy manuscripts create unfavorable impressions and are less likely to be judged on the merits of the ideas they present or their contributions to knowledge.

By showing consideration of editors, they will be more favorably disposed toward your work (or at least less prejudiced against it). This can be done not only by double-spacing, but also by providing generous margins, both of which make room for editorial notations and corrections. The left side margin should be at least 1½ inches wide; all others should be at least 1 inch.

Construct your paper in the editorial style of the journal to which you are submitting it. If no specific guide is listed in the *Handbook,* use either the twelfth edition of the University of Chicago's *A Manual of Style* or the second edition of the *MLA Style Sheet.*

Illustrations

All tables, graphs, charts, or maps which you draw (or have drawn for you) should conform to the journal's standard format. Usually that means they should each be on a separate sheet of paper, labeled properly, and cite the source of the information they convey. Be certain to indicate the correct location of all such material in your manuscript. Pictorial illustrations should be similarly labeled and identified. Make sure that you have obtained permission for their use from any copyright holders.

Identification

Reviewers who evaluate a manuscript for publication without knowledge of the author's identity are known as blind referees. The obvious advantage of this system is that the article will be judged on its own merits rather than by the name or reputation of the author. If you are sending your article to a journal which utilizes a blind referee you should omit your name from the manuscript (including the title page). Be certain, however, that your paper is fully identifiable by including your name and your article's title in your accompanying cover letter (see "Cover letter/abstract"). Some of the journals listed in the *Handbook* as not using blind referees in fact do so, but prefer to delete authors' names themselves before forwarding manuscripts for review.

SUBMITTING YOUR MANUSCRIPT

Single Submission

Multiple submissions (i.e., sending articles to more than one journal at a time) are unethical and can prove embarrassing should you be found out (many individuals referee manuscripts for more than one periodical) or if two journals accept the article. More to the point, you might seriously damage your chances of future publication in some journals. Admittedly, sticking to a policy of single submission can be both frustrating and time-consuming if your article is rejected a few times, but as noted before, considerate treatment of editors is in your best interest.

Copies
You should always send the original typescript of your article. This assures editors that you do not have your manuscript under consideration elsewhere. If more than one copy of the article is desired, accompany the original with clean carbon copies or photocopies (see "Mailing/postage" for exceptions).

Cover letters/abstract
A cover letter which briefly introduces your article to an editor is not a requirement, but is useful, particularly if you are not submitting an abstract. The letter should briefly explain what your article is about, why it is suited to that particular journal, and how it enlarges the understanding of history. An abstract is a brief (one or two pages) but concise summary, which outlines your thesis, argument, and conclusion.

Mailing/postage
Do not fold your manuscript. Mail it flat in a sturdy envelope. Leave the pages loose; do not staple them or secure them with a paper clip or in a binder. Include a self-addressed envelope to facilitate the return of your manuscript if it is rejected or in need of revision. Include sufficient postage to guarantee return but do not attach the stamps to the envelope; they may be returned if the article is accepted. Failure to include a return envelope and postage represents a real imposition and may adversely influence an editor. It may also result in your article being thrown out rather than returned.

Growing numbers of editors are willing to be flexible about return postage and the original typescript in an age of rising postal rates and decreasing duplication costs. The return postage for three copies of a thirty-page article may run considerably more than the expense of photocopying. In view of this, it may be advisable to send copies instead of the original and forego return postage, provided you carefully explain in your cover letter that you are submitting disposable copies for the convenience of all concerned.

This particularly makes sense if you send the article to a journal in another country, because the return postage must be of that country's issue. Canadian editors are frequently frustrated by well-intentioned authors in the United States who include return postage in United States stamps. A Canadian editor who was only half-joking described this practice as "cultural imperialism, deliberate or not." One way to handle this problem is to purchase and send International Reply Coupons, available at any post office in the United States for 42 cents (45 cents in Canada).

These can be exchanged by editors in other countries for the correct stamps at the rate of one coupon per ounce. Another way to address this situation (in a manner that is more convenient for the editor) is to send him the proper postage stamps. United States residents can obtain Canadian stamps by writing any Canadian post office. Pay with a money order made out to Receiver-General of Canada. Make sure you include a self-addressed envelope and payment for return postage with your order.

United States postage may be obtained by writing any United States post office. Make the money order payable to Postmaster. First class rates will insure the quickest delivery of your manuscript. Speed may not be your primary consideration, but it is important to remember that the longer your manuscript is in transit, the more hazards it is exposed to.

WHAT HAPPENS NEXT

Review/decision
Describing the process by which articles are reviewed is difficult; policies vary from journal to journal. Generally speaking, when a manuscript is received it is screened by an editor or two, or perhaps by an editorial board. If the article is outside the focus of the journal, a negative decision is quickly reached and the manuscript returned. Sometimes, particularly in the case of smaller journals oriented toward local, amateur historians or buffs, the editor decides without reference to anyone else whether to accept or reject submitted material. In other instances, as with many scholarly journals aimed at professional historians, editors enlist the services of reviewers or referees (one or two or more). The referees are selected for their expertise in the field in which the article is written. They evaluate the manuscript and make recommendations to the editor. After weighing the referees' remarks, the editor decides whether or not to publish the article.

Time
Obviously, the more people involved in this process the more drawn out it becomes. This seems to be especially true for scholarly periodicals. Referees are, after all, engaged in their own research and writing, meeting classes, or whatever; despite their good intentions they sometimes take longer in their reviewing than intended. During the summer, decisions tend to come even more slowly because so many scholars employed as reviewers depart the campus. If three months pass without a decision (unless the *Handbook* entry indicates a longer period is standard for the journal in question), you are certainly within your rights to send a polite letter of inquiry to the editor. This should in no way affect the decision on your manuscript, if done diplomatically.

ACCEPTANCE AND REJECTION

Acceptance

If your article is accepted as is, you deserve congratulations. Sometimes articles are returned, with their ultimate acceptance contingent upon certain revisions. In such cases complete the revisions as promptly as possible. Even after acceptance important work remains to be done. Galley proofs are sent the author in many cases; it is your responsibility to read them quickly yet carefully, noting any errors. Since it is possible that your original manuscript will not be returned to you, it is imperative that you retain a copy, against which you can check the galleys.

Rejection

At least as far as the more prestigious journals are concerned, rejection of manuscripts is a considerably more common experience than acceptance. It does not hurt, therefore, to be prepared for it. Perhaps the most important thing to remember is not to be discouraged. Rejection of your manuscript does not necessarily mean that it is valueless or that you are a failure as a historian. Sometimes editors or their referees will explain why they decided against your article, but more frequently you are left in the frustrating position of not knowing what they found objectionable in your work. You are therefore on your own in deciding whether or not to revise it.

Simply because one or two editors decided against publication of your manuscript does not mean it is unworthy of publication. Their opinions are only subjective, after all, and may not be shared by the editor or reviewers at another journal. So reconsider your article carefully and honestly, and if you still believe it to be historically sound and well-written, send it out again without revision. And send it without delay. The natural response to rejection is discouragement, but do not let it immobilize you. In fact, even as you send your manuscript off initially, you should have a second journal in mind in case the article is rejected.

Revision

If you would like to make *some* changes in your article without undertaking a full-scale revision, the most profitable course of action would be to rewrite the first paragraph or two. Even though you may have already given the introduction a great deal of attention, you should be able to strengthen it further. The importance of the introduction cannot be stressed enough (see "Introduction/title," above).

While you should not be devastated by rejection, you should not disregard it either. It means that a person or people with some expertise in history detected what appeared to be flaws in your work. You must seriously consider the possibility that, in its existing form, your article is not very good. If that is indeed the case, you will have to undertake major revisions to improve it. If your manuscript was returned with negative comments, the logical way to begin is to address those criticisms. Without benefit of the reviewers' comments, you should seek out criticism in the fashion described earlier. One major change that might prove beneficial is shortening your manuscript. Just as lengthy titles can create space problems, long articles may pose a challenge to editors. Paring your manuscript down may make it more acceptable to an editor wrestling with a shortage of space.

Resubmission

As a general rule it is unwise to resubmit your article to a journal which has already rejected it, unless the editor has urged you to do so. This is true even if you have revised it extensively along the lines suggested by the journal's referees.

OTHER POSSIBILITIES

United States and Canada

History is the mother of many disciplines. It is not surprising, therefore, that there are hundreds of journals in the United States and Canada which publish articles by historians, even though their primary orientation is in other directions. Literary reviews, for example, frequently have a broader scope; they publish not only poetry, fiction, and literary criticism, but are often interested in the culture which produces those artistic forms. Contemporary affairs magazines accept historical articles as a means for broadening perceptions of current events. Publications on political science, economics, social science, and other fields are frequently receptive to articles by historians. Travel magazines, including those published by automobile clubs and airlines, represent another market which views historical articles with favor. Failure to find a listing in the *Handbook* which coincides with your particular interest is by no means cause for giving up.

Foreign History Journals

History is appreciated, studied, and written about throughout the world, so another possibility to consider is publication in a foreign journal. For several reasons, including language, the United Kingdom is the most logical overseas outlet for Americans and Canadians. In Great Britain there are an enormous number of historical publications dealing with every conceivable era, place, and subject. A partial list indicates the thoroughness of the coverage.

Agricultural History Review
Antiquity
The Economic History Review
The English Historical Review
French Studies
Greece and Rome

The Historical Journal
History
History of Science
The Journal of African History
The Journal of Hellenic Studies
Journal of Historical
    Geography

Journal of Latin American
    Studies
The Journal of Modern African
    Studies
The Journal of Peasant Studies
The Journal of Roman Studies

Middle Eastern Studies
Modern Asian Studies
Past and Present
Social History
Studies in the History and
    Philosophy of Science

English-language periodicals are published in many other nations, including some where English is not the official language. The following list gives only the barest indication of that outlet.

International Review of History and Political Science (India)
International Review of Social History (the Netherlands)
Irish Historical Studies (Ireland)
Journal of Asian and African Studies (the Netherlands)
Journal of Asian History (Germany)
The Journal of Pacific History (Australia)
Journal of Southeast Asian Studies (Singapore)

For those capable of composing their work in other languages, the possibilities are even more extensive.

Dealing with journals in other countries can involve the expenditure of time and money which often vary in inverse proportion. Saving time costs money and vice versa. Surface mail takes an inordinately long time. It would not be unusual, for instance, for a query or a manuscript to take three months traveling from the United States to Germany. It goes without saying that a reply would take just as long. While air mail is quicker, the expense is enormous. International Reply Coupons are an absolute necessity for transacting business with an overseas journal (see "Mailing/postage"). Before deciding to send your manuscript overseas, carefully weigh the importance of time and money spent in quest of publication.

FOR ADDITIONAL ADVICE

Barzun, Jacques, and Graff, Henry F. *The Modern Researcher.* Rev. ed. New York: Harcourt Brace Jovanovich, 1970.

Bernstein, Theodore M. *The Careful Writer: A Modern Guide to English Usage.* New York: Atheneum, 1965.

Cortada, James W. "Publishing American Scholarship in Europe." *Scholarly Publishing,* vol. 5, no. 2 (January, 1974), 173–78.

Felt, Thomas E. *Researching, Writing, and Publishing Local History.* Nashville: American Association for State and Local History, 1976.

Forscher, Bernard K. "The Role of the Referee." *Scholarly Publishing,* vol. 11, no. 2 (January, 1980), 165–69.

Harman, Eleanor. "On Seeking Permission." *Scholarly Publishing,* vol. 1, no. 2 (January, 1970), 188–92.

Kent, Sherman. *Writing History.* 2nd ed. New York: Meredith, 1967.

Lottinville, Savoie. *The Rhetoric of History.* Norman: University of Oklahoma Press, 1976.

MacGregor, A. J. "Graphics Simplified: Choosing Illustrations." *Scholarly Publishing,* vol. 9, no. 3 (April, 1978), 270–79.

Marston, Doris. *A Guide to Writing History.* Cincinnati: Writer's Digest, 1976.

Mitchell, John H. *Writing for Professional and Technical Journals.* New York: John Wiley and Sons, 1968.

Modern Language Association of America. *MLA Handbook for Writers of Research Papers, Theses, and Dissertations.* New York: Modern Language Association, 1977.

———. *The MLA Style Sheet.* 2nd ed. New York: Modern Language Association, 1970.

Mullins, Carolyn J. *A Guide to Writing and Publishing in the Social and Behavioral Sciences.* New York: John Wiley and Sons, 1977.

Rodman, Hyman. "Some Practical Advice for Journal Contributors." *Scholarly Publishing,* vol. 9, no. 3 (April, 1978), 235–41.

Rodman, Hyman, and Mancini, Jay A. "Editors, Manuscripts, and Equal Treatment." *Research in Higher Education,* vol. 7 (1977), 369–74.

Skillin, Marjorie E., Gay, Robert M., and others. *Words Into Type.* 3rd ed. Englewood Cliffs, N.J.: Prentice-Hall, 1974.

Strunk, William, Jr., and White, E. B. *The Elements of Style.* 3rd ed. New York: Macmillan, 1979.

Turabian, Kate L. *A Manual for Writers of Term Papers, Theses, and Dissertations.* 4th ed. Chicago: University of Chicago Press, 1973.

United States Government Printing Office. *Style Manual.* Rev. ed. Washington, D.C.: United States Government Printing Office, 1973.

University of Chicago Press. *A Manual of Style.* 12th ed., revised. Chicago: University of Chicago Press, 1969.

van Leunen, Mary-Claire. *A Handbook for Scholars.* New York: Alfred A. Knopf, 1978.

Westwood, John. *Typing for Print.* London: Pitman, 1976.

Advice on Book Reviewing

WHY REVIEW?

Writing a book (or film or tape) review is, generally speaking, a more readily accomplished alternative to authoring an article. While some review essays attain the length of a full-size manuscript, most book reviews run three pages or less. Obviously an eight hundred word composition represents a considerable savings in time and effort compared to one running eight thousand words. Instead of conducting research in a variety of sources, the book reviewer need only read and reflect upon one volume.

The relative ease with which a book review can be written is by no means the only reason for reviewing, but it is a significant one. The college instructor who is too burdened by classes, the demands of students, and committee assignments to research and write an article (let alone a book) can nonetheless demonstrate continuing intellectual activity by regularly writing reviews. Amateur historians can satisfy creative urges in a similar manner without encroaching upon their other interests.

Reviewing books is also a means for expanding a personal library. Customarily, volumes which are sent to an individual for review become that person's property. Some reviewers see this activity as a means of imposing a degree of discipline upon their reading habits. Without the obligation to read and report upon books, they fear becoming too busy to remain well-read in their fields.

Book reviews benefit not only their authors, they also serve the interests of readers. Obviously reviews assist readers in deciding to spend time or money on a book. They also provide a means for keeping abreast of the latest literature, an otherwise impossible task, considering the vast number of newly published books. What's more, a good review can be read and appreciated for its own sake by someone who has no intention of ever picking up the book in question. Such a review is, in its own way, as informative and valuable as a much lengthier article.

BECOMING A REVIEWER

Some journals only publish reviews written by members of their staffs, but many historical journals maintain files of reviewers to whom they periodically assign books. As a quick look through the *Handbook*'s Directory will indicate, many journals are constantly seeking to expand their reviewer files. Becoming part of a file is, therefore, quite easy. Simply consult the Directory entry for a journal you are interested in and see whether a special information or application form is required. If so, address a letter to the book review editor, indicate your interest in reviewing for the journal, and request an information form. In a majority of instances, though, no such form is needed; a letter will suffice. The Directory indicates the information each journal seeks from prospective reviewers—be certain to provide what is required. Some journals may never contact you, others may require your services immediately and often. Be sensible and selective in offering your services. Special interest journals which focus on specific subjects often only review books which deal with those subjects. So if you are not interested or competent in maritime history, you should not become a reviewer for a journal which concentrates on that subject.

WRITING A REVIEW

A good book review must be interesting. It is, after all, a creative composition. A review should be neither a transcription of the book's table of contents nor a thinly disguised summary of its dustcover remarks. The conscientious reviewer attempts, in a few brief paragraphs, to bring a much longer work into focus through the application of his understanding of the subject of the book. The result is informative, whether the review itself is critical or laudatory. Since informing readers is the principal purpose of a review, you should bear in mind their interests and levels of expertise. They are more interested in a thoughtful evaluation of a book than they are in a display of the reviewer's cleverness, vitriol, or overstatement. Remember, too, as reviewer you should be as accountable as the authors you comment upon—indicate the page numbers of any passages you quote in your review.

POINTS TO COVER

Describe the author's purpose in writing the book and indicate the extent to which it was fulfilled. Assess the book's strengths and weaknesses and note whether one category overshadows others. While a book can be analyzed merely on its own merits, placing it in the context of other works on the same subject helps to establish its significance (or lack thereof). Similarly, a few words about the author may be in order—what are his qualifications in the field? Has he written on the same subject before? How biased is he? Comment, as well, on the book's utility to the readership you represent.

If you are reviewing a new edition of an old work, discuss the extent to which the book has been revised from previous editions. Indicate whether the book is of continuing significance.

Spot-check the book for accuracy. Is the author correct on basic facts? Are quotations accurate, citations proper? If there is a bibliography, is it comprehensive, or were some important sources overlooked? What about the physical appearance of the book? Is the editing sloppy? Are illustrations reproduced clearly?

REVIEW FORM

Book reviewers whose services are solicited are usually instructed by the journals they write for as to the form they should use for heading and signature. Those who are not given directions and authors of unsolicited reviews should check a copy of the journal in question for the desired form. An example of a standard heading is:

AUTHOR NAME (capitalized). <u>Title</u> (underlined to denote italic in print). Place of publication: publisher, year. Number of pages. Price.

Some journals require more information: mention any foreword, introduction, acknowledgments, notes, appendixes, bibliography, indexes; list the type and number of illustrations; whether the book is cloth or paperback. To know exactly what is desired, look at reviews in the journal in question.

The reviewer's signature is even more standardized:

<u>Institutional affiliation</u>   REVIEWER'S NAME
(underlined to denote italic in print)   (capitalized)

A FINAL NOTE

Try to conform to the length limitation imposed by the journal. Equally important is the need to observe the deadline for submitting your review. Usually only a few weeks are allowed between receipt of a book and the due date for its review. It may seem hypocritical that journals which take months to consider articles allow only weeks for the review of books, but the timeliness of a book review often determines its value. Most journals strive to minimize the lag between the appearance of a book and the publication of a review. Since other factors are fixed, the logical way to save time is by pressuring reviewers.

FOR ADDITIONAL ADVICE

Becker, Carl H. "The Reviewing of Historical Books." *Annual Report of the American Historical Association for the Year 1912.* Washington: 1914, 127–36.

Clark, G. N. "Historical Reviewing." *Essays in History Presented to Reginald Lane Pool.* Edited by H. W. C. Davis. Freeport, N.Y.: Books for Libraries Press, 1967.

Hoge, James O., and West, James L. W., III. "Academic Book Reviewing: Some Problems and Suggestions." *Scholarly Publishing,* vol. 11, no. 1 (October, 1979), 35–41.

Jones, Llewellyn. *How to Criticize Books.* New York: W. W. Norton and Co., 1928.

Kamerman, Sylvia E., ed. *Book Reviewing: A Guide to Writing Book Reviews for Newspapers, Magazines, Radio, and Television.* Boston: Writer, 1978.

Lichtman, Allan J., and French, Valerie. *Historians and the Living Past.* Arlington Heights, Ill.: AHM, 1978, 244–48.

Lottinville, Savoie. *The Rhetoric of History.* Norman: University of Oklahoma Press, 1976. See chapter on "Criticism," 169–82.

Mullins, Carolyn J. *A Guide to Writing and Publishing in the Social and Behavioral Sciences.* New York: John Wiley and Sons, 1977, 231–37.

Wolper, R. S. "'A Grass-Blade': On Academic Reviewing." *Scholarly Publishing,* vol. 10, no. 4 (July, 1979), 325–28.

Woodcock, George. "The Critic as Mediator." *Scholarly Publishing,* vol. 4, no. 3 (April, 1973), 201–9.

Directory of Journals

ACADIENSIS: JOURNAL OF THE HISTORY OF THE ATLANTIC REGION

Focus: the Atlantic region of Canada
Institutional affiliation: University of New Brunswick
Editor: P. A. Buckner
Book review editor: same
Address: Campus House
University of New Brunswick
Fredericton, N.B. E3B 5A3
Canada
Frequency: 2/year
Circulation: 900–1,000
Pages/issue: 170
Readership: academics

Manuscripts

Query: no
Abstract: no
Style guide: MOS
Preferred length: open
Number of copies: 1
Notes: end of manuscript
Blind referee: no
Time to consider manuscript: 2–4 months
Illustrations accepted: camera-ready tables, graphs, charts, pictures
Foreign languages: French

Reviews

Seeking reviewers: yes
Unsolicited reviews accepted: rarely
How to apply: letter
Include in application: professional degrees, institutional affiliation, areas of expertise, published works
Materials reviewed: books
Length of review: most are review articles

AEROSPACE HISTORIAN

Focus: international aerospace
Institutional affiliation: Air Force Historical Foundation
Editor: Carol A. Williams
Book review editor: Robin Higham
Address: Eisenhower Hall
Kansas State University
Manhattan, KS 66506
Frequency: 4/year
Circulation: 4,000
Pages/issue: 60–70
Readership: general public, military, institutions

Manuscripts

Query: no
Abstract: no
Style guide: MLA
Preferred length: 20 pages maximum
Number of copies: 3
Notes: end of manuscript
Blind referee: no
Time to consider manuscript: 2–4 months
Illustrations accepted: captioned tables, graphs, charts, pictures (photos should be black-and-white glossies)
Foreign languages: no

Reviews

Unsolicited reviews accepted: no
How to apply: letter
Include in application: professional degrees, institutional affiliation, areas of expertise, published works
Materials reviewed: books
Length of review: 250 words

Additional notes

Include brief vita with submission.

AFRICA TODAY

Focus: contemporary Africa
Institutional affiliation: University of Denver
Editor: Edward A. Hawley
Book review editor: George Kalule
Address: Graduate School of
International Studies
University of Denver
Denver, CO 80208
Frequency: 4/year
Circulation: 1,950
Pages/issue: 96–112
Readership: academics, students, others interested in Africa

Manuscripts
Query: no
Abstract: no
Style guide: MOS
Preferred length: 2,000–6,000 words
Number of copies: 2
Notes: end of manuscript
Blind referee: yes
Time to consider manuscript: 3–9 months
Proportion of manuscripts accepted: 1/5–1/4
Illustrations accepted: tables, graphs, charts, occasionally pictures
Foreign languages: no

Reviews
Seeking reviewers: yes
Unsolicited reviews accepted: occasionally
How to apply: letter
Include in application: professional degrees, institutional affiliation, areas of expertise, published works
Materials reviewed: books, films
Length of review: 850 words; 2,700 words or less for multiple title review or review article

Additional notes
Historical articles will be considered, but only if they have relevance to understanding modern Africa.

AFRICAN URBAN STUDIES

Focus: urbanization in Africa
Institutional affiliation: African Studies Center, Michigan State University
Editor: Ruth Sims Hamilton
Address: African Studies Center
Michigan State University
East Lansing, MI 48824
Frequency: 3/year
Pages/issue: 80–100
Readership: academics

Manuscripts
Query: no
Abstract: no
Style guide: MOS
Preferred length: 30 pages maximum
Number of copies: 2
Notes: end of manuscript
Blind referee: no
Time to consider manuscript: 2 months minimum
Proportion of manuscripts accepted: 3/5
Illustrations accepted: tables and camera-ready graphs, charts, line illustrations
Foreign languages: French (occasionally)

Reviews
Seeking reviewers: no
Unsolicited reviews accepted: yes
How to apply: letter
Include in application: professional degrees, institutional affiliation, areas of expertise, published works
Materials reviewed: books, films
Length of review: 5 pages maximum

AFRO-AMERICANS IN NEW YORK LIFE AND HISTORY

Focus: interdisciplinary scholarly articles that pertain to title
Institutional affiliation: Afro-American Historical Association of the Niagara Frontier
Editor: Melvin Watkins
Book review editor: Lillian Williams
Address: P.O. Box 1663
Buffalo, NY 14216
Frequency: 2/year
Circulation: 500
Pages/issue: 100
Readership: general public

Manuscripts
Query: no
Style guide: MLA
Preferred length: 30 pages maximum
Number of copies: 2
Notes: end of manuscript
Blind referee: no
Time to consider manuscript: 4 weeks
Proportion of manuscripts accepted: high
Illustrations accepted: not usually
Foreign languages: no

Reviews
Seeking reviewers: yes
Unsolicited reviews accepted: occasionally
How to apply: letter
Include in application: professional degrees, institutional affiliation, areas of expertise, published works, current research
Materials reviewed: books
Length of review: 5 pages maximum

AGRICULTURAL HISTORY

Focus: agriculture (broadly conceived) at any time in the past, anywhere on the globe
Editor: J.H. Shideler
Book review editor: same
Address: Agricultural History Center
University of California
Davis, CA 95616
Frequency: 4/year
Circulation: 1,700
Pages/issue: 144
Readership: academics

Manuscripts
Query: no
Abstract: no
Style guide: MOS
Preferred length: 20–30 pages
Number of copies: 2
Notes: end of manuscript
Blind referee: no
Time to consider manuscript: 3–6 months
Proportion of manuscripts accepted: 1/3
Illustrations accepted: tables, graphs, charts on separate pages
Foreign languages: no

Reviews
Seeking reviewers: yes
Unsolicited reviews accepted: no
How to apply: letter
Include in application: areas of expertise, current research
Materials reviewed: books, films
Length of review: 300–700 words

Additional notes
Brief author identifications are desired either on a separate sheet or as an unnumbered first footnote. Avoid subheadings within a paper; introductory and transitional sentences can serve the same purpose.

THE ALABAMA BAPTIST HISTORIAN

Focus: Baptist history, mainly within Alabama
Institutional affiliation: Alabama Baptist Historical Society; Alabama Baptist State Convention
Editor: F. Wilbur Helmbold
Address: Samford University
Birmingham, AL 35209
Frequency: 2/year
Pages/issue: 24–25
Readership: Alabama Baptists; Society members

Manuscripts

Query: no
Abstract: no
Style guide: MOS
Preferred length: 4–20 pages (occasionally longer)
Number of copies: 1
Notes: end of manuscript
Blind referee: no
Time to consider manuscript: 4–6 months
Proportion of manuscripts accepted: 3/4
Illustrations accepted: tables, graphs, charts, pictures if appropriate
Foreign languages: no

Reviews

Seeking reviewers: no
Unsolicited reviews accepted: no
Materials reviewed: books

ALABAMA HISTORICAL QUARTERLY

Focus: Alabama and the Southeast
Institutional affiliation: Alabama Department of Archives and History
Editor: Milo B. Howard, Jr.
Book review editor: same
Address: Department of Archives and History
624 Washington Ave.
Montgomery, AL 36104
Frequency: 4/year
Circulation: 1,000
Pages/issue: 130
Readership: academics, buffs

Manuscripts

Query: no
Abstract: no
Style guide: MOS
Preferred length: 10–25 pages
Number of copies: 1
Notes: end of manuscript
Blind referee: no
Time to consider manuscript: 3 months
Proportion of manuscripts accepted: 3/4
Illustrations accepted: tables, graphs, charts, photographs
Foreign languages: no

Reviews

Seeking reviewers: yes
Unsolicited reviews accepted: no
How to apply: letter
Include in application: institutional affiliation, areas of expertise, published works, current research
Materials reviewed: books
Length of review: 500–600 words

ALABAMA REVIEW

Focus: Alabama and culture
Institutional affiliation: University of Alabama
Editor: Sarah W. Wiggins
Book review editor: same
Address: History Department
University of Alabama
University, AL 35486
Frequency: 4/year
Circulation: 1,800
Pages/issue: 80
Readership: academics, general public

Manuscripts
Query: no
Abstract: no
Style guide: MOS
Number of copies: 2
Notes: end of manuscript
Blind referee: no
Time to consider manuscript: 6–8 months
Proportion of manuscripts accepted: 1/10
Foreign languages: no

Reviews
Seeking reviewers: yes
Unsolicited reviews accepted: no
How to apply: letter
Include in application: professional degrees, institutional affiliation, areas of expertise, published works, current research
Materials reviewed: books
Length of review: 600 words

THE ALASKA JOURNAL

Focus: past, contemporary life and issues, art and artists (including photographers) of Alaska and northern Canada
Institutional affiliation: Alaska Northwest Publishing Company
Editor: Marty Loken
Book review editor: same
Address: Box 4-EEE
Anchorage, AK 99509
Frequency: 4/year
Circulation: 12,000
Pages/issue: 96
Readership: general public

Manuscripts
Query: yes
Abstract: no
Style guide: MOS
Preferred length: variable
Number of copies: 1
Notes: end of manuscript
Blind referee: no
Time to consider manuscript: 4 weeks
Illustrations accepted: tables, graphs, charts, photographs, 35mm color transparencies (Kodachrome or Ektachrome) and 8 x 10 black-and-white glossies
Foreign languages: no

Reviews
Seeking reviewers: no
Unsolicited reviews accepted: no
How to apply: letter
Materials reviewed: books
Length of review: variable

ALBERTA HISTORY

Focus: Alberta, Canada
Institutional affiliation: Historical Society
of Alberta
Editor: Hugh A. Dempsey
Book review editor: same
Address: 95 Holmwood Avenue, NW
Calgary, Alberta T2K 2G7
CANADA
Frequency: 4/year
Circulation: 2,600
Pages/issue: 40
Readership: academics, libraries,
general public

Manuscripts
Query: no
Abstract: no
Style guide: MOS
Preferred length: 3,500–8,000 words
Number of copies: 1
Notes: end of manuscript
Blind referee: no
Time to consider manuscript: 3 months
**Proportion of manuscripts
accepted:** 2/5
Illustrations accepted: graphs,
photographs
Foreign languages: no

Reviews
Seeking reviewers: no
Unsolicited reviews accepted: no
How to apply: letter
Include in application: areas of expertise
Materials reviewed: books
Length of review: 300–700 words

ALBION

Focus: British studies in all time periods,
including politics and literature with a
historical orientation
Institutional affiliation: Conference on
British Studies
Editor: Michael J. Moore
Address: Department of History
Appalachian State University
Boone, NC 28608
Book review editor: R.J.Q.
Adams
Address: Department of History
Texas A & M University
College Station, TX 77843
Frequency: 4/year
Circulation: 1,100
Pages/issue: 150
Readership: academics

Manuscripts
Query: no
Abstract: no
Style guide: MOS
Preferred length: 8,500 words
Number of copies: 2
Notes: end of manuscript
Blind referee: yes
Time to consider manuscript: 3 months
**Proportion of manuscripts
accepted:** 1/4
Illustrations accepted: tables,
camera-ready graphs, charts,
photographs, glossy illustrations
Foreign languages: no

Reviews
Seeking reviewers: yes
Unsolicited reviews accepted: no
How to apply: letter or vita
Include in application: professional
degrees, areas of expertise,
published works, current research
Materials reviewed: books
Length of review: 450–600 words

Additional notes
Albion publishes in abstract proceedings
of Conference on British Studies meetings.
It is the only quarterly journal concerned
with the whole of British studies published
in North America, and as 80% of its readers
are CBS members it brings articles directly
to colleagues in the field. Its publication
time from acceptance has averaged nine
months.

THE ALLEN COUNTY REPORTER

Focus: Allen County, Ohio
Institutional affiliation: Allen County Historical Society
Editor: Lee A. Williams, Jr.
Address: 620 West Market Street
Lima, OH 45801
Frequency: 4/year
Circulation: 650
Pages/issue: 28
Readership: Society members, general public

Manuscripts
Query: yes
Abstract: no
Style guide: MOS
Preferred length: open
Number of copies: 1
Notes: bottom of page
Blind referee: no
Time to consider manuscript: 1 month
Proportion of manuscripts accepted: 9/10
Illustrations accepted: tables, graphs, charts, pictures
Foreign languages: no

AMERASIA JOURNAL

Focus: Asian Americans; sociological or literary perspectives; empirical or theoretical case studies
Institutional affiliation: Asian-American Studies Center, UCLA
Editor: Russell Leong
Book review editor: John Liu
Address: Asian-American Studies Center
3232 Campbell Hall
University of California
Los Angeles, CA 90024
Frequency: 2/year
Circulation: 1,000
Pages/issue: 180
Readership: academics, general public

Manuscripts
Query: no
Abstract: no
Style guide: MOS; style sheet sent upon request
Preferred length: 30 pages maximum
Number of copies: 3
Notes: end of manuscript
Blind referee: yes
Illustrations accepted: maximum of 3 tables, graphs, charts, photographs
Foreign languages: no

Reviews
Seeking reviewers: yes
Unsolicited reviews accepted: yes
How to apply: letter
Include in application: professional degrees, institutional affiliation, areas of expertise, published works, foreign languages, current research
Materials reviewed: books
Length of review: 4 pages maximum

THE AMERICAN ARCHIVIST

Focus: management of archives and manuscript collections
Institutional affiliation: Society of American Archivists
Editor: Virginia C. Purdy
Book review editor: Mary Elizabeth Ruwell
Address: National Archives, Room 100 Washington, DC 20408
Frequency: 4/year
Circulation: 3,500
Pages/issue: 132
Readership: archivists, librarians, historians

Manuscripts
Query: no
Abstract: no
Style guide: MOS
Preferred length: 5,000 words
Number of copies: 2
Notes: end of manuscript
Blind referee: yes
Time to consider manuscript: 3 months
Proportion of manuscripts accepted: 2/5
Illustrations accepted: tables, graphs, charts, pictures, 8 x 10 glossy photographs, professionally-drawn illustrations to scale, about twice the size of final copy (illustrations will be returned on request)
Foreign languages: no

Reviews
Seeking reviewers: yes
Unsolicited reviews accepted: yes
How to apply: letter
Include in application: professional degrees, institutional affiliation, areas of expertise, published works, foreign languages, current research
Materials reviewed: books
Length of review: 500–750 words

Additional notes
In addition to full-length articles, there are "Shorter Features," unfootnoted articles of approximately 500 words, describing a specific process or experience or raising an issue. Concise, tightly-written articles based on careful research are preferred.

AMERICAN HERITAGE

Focus: America
Editor: Geoffrey C. Ward
Book review editor: Barbara Klaw
Address: 10 Rockefeller Plaza New York, NY 10020
Frequency: 6/year
Circulation: 130,000
Pages/issue: 112
Readership: general public

Manuscripts
Query: yes
Abstract: yes
Style guide: none
Preferred length: 3,000–6,000 words
Number of copies: 1
Notes: end of manuscript
Blind referee: no
Time to consider manuscript: 2 weeks
Illustrations accepted: pictures
Foreign languages: no

Reviews
Seeking reviewers: no
Unsolicited reviews accepted: no

AMERICAN HISTORICAL REVIEW

Focus: all fields
Institutional affiliation: American Historical Association
Editor: Otto Pflanze
Address: Ballantine Hall 721
Indiana University
Bloomington, IN 47405
Frequency: 5/year
Circulation: 15,150
Pages/issue: 360
Readership: academics, general public

Manuscripts
Query: no
Abstract: no
Style guide: MOS
Preferred length: 25–35 pages
Number of copies: 2
Notes: end of manuscript
Blind referee: yes
Time to consider manuscript: 1–3 months
Proportion of manuscripts accepted: 1/10
Illustrations accepted: tables, graphs, charts, photographs
Foreign languages: no

Reviews
Seeking reviewers: yes
Unsolicited reviews accepted: no
How to apply: write for form
Include in application: professional degrees, institutional affiliation, areas of expertise, published works, foreign languages, current research
Materials reviewed: books
Length of review: 500–600 words

AMERICAN HISTORY ILLUSTRATED

Focus: America, 1492 to the Korean War
Institutional affiliation: The National Historical Society
Editor: Elizabeth O. Rodda
Book review editor: same
Address: P.O. Box 1831
Harrisburg, PA 17105
Frequency: 10/year
Circulation: 160,000
Pages/issue: 50
Readership: academics, general public

Manuscripts
Query: yes
Abstract: no
Style guide: own
Preferred length: 3,000–5,000 words
Number of copies: 1
Notes: end of manuscript
Blind referee: no
Time to consider manuscript: 4–6 weeks
Illustrations accepted: Illustrations, maps, or hints on where to get them
Foreign languages: no

Reviews
Seeking reviewers: no
Unsolicited reviews accepted: no
How to apply: letter
Include in application: areas of expertise, published works, current research
Materials reviewed: books, galleys from forthcoming books
Length of review: 350–500 words

Additional notes
Reviews are done in-house. Articles should be more popular than scholarly in style. Although articles are published without bibliographical footnotes, informal source annotations on each manuscript are required. The bibliography need not be complete, but it should recommend a few books for interested readers.

AMERICAN JEWISH HISTORY

Focus: American Jewish experience in broadest sense
Institutional affiliation: American Jewish Historical Society
Editor: Bernard Wax
Book review editor: Stephen Whitfield
Address: 2 Thornton Road
Waltham, MA 02154
Frequency: 4/year
Circulation: 3,500
Pages/issue: 128
Readership: academics, buffs, general public

Manuscripts

Query: no
Abstract: no
Style guide: MLA
Preferred length: 20–30 pages
Number of copies: 2
Notes: end of manuscript
Blind referee: no
Time to consider manuscript: 2–3 months
Proportion of manuscripts accepted: 1/4–2/5
Illustrations accepted: tables, graphs, charts, pictures
Foreign languages: generally not

Reviews

Seeking reviewers: yes
Unsolicited reviews accepted: no
How to apply: letter
Include in application: professional degrees, institutional affiliation, areas of expertise, current research
Materials reviewed: books
Length of review: variable

AMERICAN JOURNAL OF ANCIENT HISTORY

Focus: ancient Greek and Roman history
Editor: E. Badian
Address: Robinson Hall
Harvard University
Cambridge, MA 02138
Frequency: 2/year
Circulation: about 500
Pages/issue: 96
Readership: academics

Manuscripts

Query: no
Abstract: no
Style guide: none
Preferred length: none
Number of copies: 2
Notes: end of manuscript
Blind referee: yes
Time to consider manuscript: varies
Proportion of manuscripts accepted: 3/10–4/10
Illustrations accepted: camera-ready tables, graphs, charts, pictures
Foreign languages: French, German (but delays probable)

Additional notes

The pedantic use of Greek and Latin should be avoided, but the languages may be used where needed. No indication of the author's identity should appear on the typescript. The name and address should be on a separate page. References to the author's own work should be in the same style as references to the work of others.

AMERICAN JOURNAL OF ARCHAEOLOGY

Focus: archaeology relating to the Classical World (Mediterranean and the Near East)
Institutional affiliation: Archaeological Institute of America
Editor: Brunilde S. Ridgeway
Address: Thomas Library
Bryn Mawr College
Bryn Mawr, PA 19010
Book review editor: Patricia N. Boulter
Address: Department of Classics
University of Cincinnati
Cincinnati, OH 45221
Frequency: 4/year
Circulation: 4,500
Pages/issue: 140
Readership: scholars, libraries

Manuscripts
Query: no
Abstract: yes
Style guide: own (see "Note for Contributors and Abbreviations," Winter 1978, 3–10)
Preferred length: 20 pages
Number of copies: 1 (2 preferred)
Notes: end of manuscript
Blind referee: author's choice
Time to consider manuscript: 1–3 months
Proportion of manuscripts accepted: 1/3
Illustrations accepted: tables, graphs, charts, pictures
Foreign languages: French, German, Russian

Reviews
Seeking reviewers: yes
Unsolicited reviews accepted: no
How to apply: letter
Include in application: professional degrees, institutional affiliation, areas of expertise, published works, foreign languages, current research
Materials reviewed: books
Length of review: 500–750 words

Additional notes
Shorter items are published under the heading "Archaeological Notes."

THE AMERICAN JOURNAL OF LEGAL HISTORY

Focus: American or English law
Institutional affiliation: Temple University
Editor: Erwin C. Surrency
Address: Law Library
University of Georgia
Athens, GA 30602
Book review editor: Sue Sheridan Walker
Address: History Department
Northeastern Illinois University
5500 N. St. Louis Avenue
Chicago, IL 60625
Frequency: 4/year
Circulation: 1,300
Pages/issue: 96
Readership: academics

Manuscripts
Query: no
Abstract: no
Preferred length: 20–25 pages
Number of copies: 1
Notes: end of manuscript
Blind referee: no
Time to consider manuscript: 3–5 months
Illustrations accepted: very limited
Foreign languages: no

Reviews
Seeking reviewers: yes
Unsolicited reviews accepted: no
How to apply: letter
Include in application: professional degrees, institutional affiliation, areas of expertise, published works
Materials reviewed: books

AMERICAN NEPTUNE

Focus: maritime history
Editor: Philip Chadwick Smith
Book review editor: same
Address: Peabody Museum of Salem
East India Marine Hall
Salem, MA 01970
Frequency: 4/year
Circulation: 800
Pages/issue: 50
Readership: academics, libraries,
museums

Manuscripts
Query: yes
Style guide: own
Preferred length: 45 pages maximum
Number of copies: 1
Notes: bottom of page
Blind referee: no
Time to consider manuscript: 8–10
weeks
Illustrations accepted: tables, graphs,
charts, photographs (give locations of
prints, paintings, or other items to be
reproduced)
Foreign languages: no

Reviews
Seeking reviewers: no
Unsolicited reviews accepted: no

AMERICAN QUARTERLY

Focus: social, intellectual, and literary
history of the United States
Institutional affiliation: University of
Pennsylvania, American Studies
Association
Editor: Leila Zenderland
Address: Van Pelt Library CH
3420 Walnut Street
University of Pennsylvania
Philadelphia, PA 19104
Book review editor: Leo
Ribuffo
Address: George Washington University
Washington, D.C. 20006
Frequency: 5/year
Circulation: 5,500
Pages/issue: 128
Readership: academics, academic
libraries, general public

Manuscripts
Query: no
Abstract: no
Style guide: MLA
Preferred length: 30–35 pages
Number of copies: 2
Notes: no preference
Blind referee: yes
Time to consider manuscript: 3 months
**Proportion of manuscripts
accepted:** 1/25
Illustrations accepted: tables, graphs,
charts, photographs; no color
Foreign languages: no

Reviews
Seeking reviewers: no
**Unsolicited reviews
accepted:** occasionally
How to apply: letter
Include in application: professional
degrees, institutional affiliation, areas
of expertise, published works, current
research
Length of review: 10–15 pages, or essay
review of several books

AMERICAN REVIEW OF CANADIAN STUDIES

Focus: interdisciplinary Canadian Studies
Institutional affiliation: Association for Canadian Studies in the United States
Editor: William Metcalfe
Address: History Department
Wheeler House
University of Vermont
Burlington, VT 05401
Book review editor: Ronald Tallman
Address: Canadian Studies
University of Maine
Orono, ME 04473
Frequency: 2/year
Circulation: 500
Pages/issue: 150
Readership: academics, high school teachers, Association members

Manuscripts
Query: no
Abstract: yes
Style guide: MLA
Preferred length: 25 pages maximum
Number of copies: 2
Notes: end of manuscript
Blind referee: no
Time to consider manuscript: 2 months
Proportion of manuscripts accepted: 1/3
Illustrations accepted: tables, graphs, charts
Foreign languages: French

Reviews
Seeking reviewers: yes
Unsolicited reviews accepted: no
How to apply: letter
Include in application: professional degrees, institutional affiliation, areas of expertise, foreign languages, current research
Materials reviewed: books
Length of review: variable

AMERICAN STUDIES

Focus: American culture and society; the literature, sociology, anthropology, and fine arts of the United States
Institutional affiliation: Midcontinent American Studies Association, Stephens College, University of Kansas
Editor: Stuart Levine
Book review editor: same
Address: University of Kansas
Lawrence, KS 66045
Frequency: 2/year
Circulation: 1,000
Pages/issue: 120
Readership: scholars

Manuscripts
Query: no
Abstract: yes, 2 copies
Style guide: MLA
Preferred length: 25 pages
Number of copies: 2
Notes: end of manuscript
Blind referee: yes
Time to consider manuscript: 1–5 months
Proportion of manuscripts accepted: 1/20
Illustrations accepted: tables, graphs, charts, pictures (authors pay part of the cost of printing up to $30)
Foreign languages: no

Reviews
Seeking reviewers: yes
Unsolicited reviews accepted: no
Materials reviewed: books
Length of review: 50–100 words

THE AMERICAN WEST

Focus: the heritage of the trans–Mississippi West
Institutional affiliation: Western History Association
Editor: Mae Reid-Bills
Book review editor: same
Address: American West Publishing Co.
20380 Town Center Lane, Suite 160
Cupertino, CA 95014
Frequency: 6/year
Circulation: 22,000
Pages/issue: 64
Readership: general public, scholars

Manuscripts
Query: preferred
Style guide: MOS
Preferred length: 2,500–4,000 words
Number of copies: 1
Notes: none included
Blind referee: no
Time to consider manuscript: 6–8 weeks
Illustrations accepted: good quality black-and-white glossy historical photographs considered
Foreign languages: no

Reviews
Seeking reviewers: yes
Unsolicited reviews accepted: no
How to apply: letter
Include in application: professional degrees, institutional affiliation, areas of expertise
Materials reviewed: books
Length of review: variable

Additional notes
Neither scholarly dissertations nor superficial rewrites of well-known stories common to popular interpretations of the West are desired. Submissions accompanied by suitable high-quality black-and-white illustrations have an increased probability of acceptance. If this is not possible, the author should recommend sources for such illustrations. A bibliographic note mentioning major sources should also be included. Payment for feature articles ranges from $150 minimum; for book reviews, from $20 to $40 and a complimentary copy of the book.

AMERICANA MAGAZINE

Focus: the American past as used and enjoyed today; historic preservation, collecting, architecture, decorating, crafts, gardening, and cooking
Editor: Michael Durham
Book review editor: Sandra Wilmot
Address: 475 Park Avenue South, 28th Floor
New York, NY 10016
Frequency: 6/year
Circulation: 250,000
Pages/issue: 96
Readership: general public

Manuscripts
Query: yes

THE AMERICAS

Focus: inter-American cultural, colonial, and modern history and related areas such as literature, ethnohistory, and ethnology
Institutional affiliation: Academy of American Franciscan History
Editor: Antonine S. Tibesar, O.F.M.
Book review editor: James Denson Riley
Address: P.O. Box 34440
Washington, DC 20034
Frequency: 4/year
Circulation: 1,100
Pages/issue: 142
Readership: academics

Manuscripts

Query: no
Abstract: no
Style guide: MOS
Preferred length: 25–30 pages
Number of copies: 2
Notes: bottom of page
Blind referee: no
Time to consider manuscript: 1 month
Proportion of manuscripts accepted: 1/4
Illustrations accepted: tables, graphs, charts, pictures
Foreign languages: no

Reviews

Seeking reviewers: yes
Unsolicited reviews accepted: sometimes
How to apply: letter
Include in application: professional degrees, institutional affiliation, areas of expertise
Materials reviewed: books
Length of review: 400–600 words

THE ANCIENT WORLD

Focus: Mediterranean history and archaeology
Editors: Ladislaus J. Bolchazy, A.L.N. Oikonomides
Address: Ares Publishers, Inc.
Suite 216
612 N. Michigan Ave.
Chicago, IL 60611
Frequency: 4/year
Circulation: 1,000
Pages/issue: 32–40 pages
Readership: scholars

Manuscripts

Query: no
Abstract: no
Style guide: *American Journal of Archaeology* and *American Philological Association Proceedings*
Preferred length: open
Number of copies: 2
Notes: end of manuscript
Blind referee: yes
Time to consider manuscript: 1 month
Proportion of manuscripts accepted: 2/3
Illustrations accepted: tables, graphs, charts, pictures
Foreign languages: yes, although English preferred

Reviews

Seeking reviewers: yes
Unsolicited reviews accepted: no
How to apply: letter
Include in application: professional degrees, institutional affiliation, areas of expertise, published works, current research
Materials reviewed: books
Length of review: open

Additional notes

No transliteration of Greek. Typesetting possible in Cyrillic, Greek, Coptic, and other alphabets.

THE ANNALS OF IOWA

Focus: Midwest and Iowa
Institutional affiliation: Iowa State
    Historical Department
Editor: Judith Gildner
Book review editor: Michael D. Gibson
Address: Historical Building
    East 12th and Grand
    Des Moines, IA 50319
Frequency: 4/year
Circulation: 2,000
Pages/issue: 80
Readership: academics, general public

Manuscripts

Query: no
Abstract: no
Style guide: MOS or MLA
Preferred length: 15–30 pages
Number of copies: 1
Notes: end of manuscript
Blind referee: no
Time to consider manuscript: 6–8
    weeks
**Proportion of manuscripts
    accepted:** 1/2
Illustrations accepted: tables, graphs,
    charts, photographs
Foreign languages: no

Reviews

Seeking reviewers: yes
Unsolicited reviews accepted: no
How to apply: letter
Include in application: professional
    degrees, institutional affiliation, areas
    of expertise, published works
Materials reviewed: books, trade books
Length of review: 300–600 words

ANNALS OF WYOMING

Focus: Wyoming and the West
Institutional affiliation: Wyoming State
    Archives
Editor: Katherine A. Halverson
Address: State Archives, Museums and
    Historical Department
    Barrett Building
    Cheyenne, WY 82002
Frequency: 2/year
Circulation: 1,400
Pages/issue: 150
Readership: Society members,
    academics

Manuscripts

Query: no
Abstract: no
Style guide: MOS
Preferred length: variable
Number of copies: 1
Notes: no preference
Blind referee: no
Time to consider manuscript: 2–3
    months
**Proportion of manuscripts
    accepted:** 1/2
Illustrations accepted: tables, graphs,
    charts, pictures, which add to the
    presentation of the subject
Foreign languages: no

Reviews

Seeking reviewers: yes
Unsolicited reviews accepted: yes
How to apply: letter
Include in application: institutional
    affiliation, areas of expertise
Materials reviewed: books
Length of review: 500 words

APPALACHIAN JOURNAL: A REGIONAL STUDIES REVIEW

Focus: politics, literature, and culture of Appalachia
Institutional affiliation: Appalachian State University
Editor: J. W. Williamson
Book review editor: same
Address: Appalachian State University
Boone, NC 28608
Frequency: 4/year
Circulation: 600
Pages/issue: 80 pages
Readership: academics, general public

Manuscripts
Query: no
Abstract: no
Style guide: MOS or MLA
Preferred length: 20–30 pages
Number of copies: 1
Notes: end of manuscript
Blind referee: yes
Time to consider manuscript: 1 month
Proportion of manuscripts accepted: 1/8
Illustrations accepted: tables, graphs, charts, sharp quality photographs
Foreign languages: no

Reviews
Seeking reviewers: yes
Unsolicited reviews accepted: rarely
How to apply: letter
Include in application: areas of expertise, current research
Materials reviewed: all media
Length of review: 1,000 words (up to 5,000 words for review essays)

Additional notes
Preference given to interdisciplinary articles.

ARCHIVARIA

Focus: all types of archival media; research articles, projects, reviews, opinion
Institutional affiliation: Association of Canadian Archivists
Editor: Gordon Dodds
Book review editor: same
Address: Public Archives of Canada
Room 349
395 Wellington Street
Ottawa, Ontario K1A 0N3
CANADA
Frequency: 2/year
Circulation: 800
Pages/issue: 224
Readership: archivists, academics, librarians

Manuscripts
Query: no
Abstract: yes
Style guide: MOS
Preferred length: 10,000 words
Number of copies: 2
Notes: end of manuscript
Blind referee: no
Time to consider manuscript: 6 weeks
Proportion of manuscripts accepted: moderate-high
Illustrations accepted: tables, graphs, charts, photographs (8 x 10 glossies preferred)
Foreign languages: French

Reviews
Seeking reviewers: no
Unsolicited reviews accepted: rarely
Materials reviewed: books, films, tapes, manuals, reports
Length of review: variable

Additional notes
Articles should deal principally with research of archival materials or the study of archival sources, in any media. Priority is given to articles dealing with Canadian materials.

ARIZONA AND THE WEST

Focus: trans–Mississippi West
Institutional affiliation: University of Arizona
Editor: Harwood P. Hinton
Book review editor: same
Address: University of Arizona Library
Room 310
Tucson, AZ 85721
Frequency: 4/year
Circulation: 1,300
Pages/issue: 120
Readership: academics, buffs, general public

Manuscripts

Query: no
Abstract: no
Style guide: MOS
Preferred length: 16–30 pages
Number of copies: 1
Notes: end of manuscript
Blind referee: no
Time to consider manuscript: 1–2 months
Proportion of manuscripts accepted: 1/10
Illustrations accepted: photographs
Foreign languages: no

Reviews

Seeking reviewers: yes
Unsolicited reviews accepted: no
How to apply: letter
Include in application: professional degrees, institutional affiliation, published works, current research
Materials reviewed: books
Length of review: 500–600 words

ARKANSAS HISTORICAL QUARTERLY

Focus: Arkansas
Editor: Walter L. Brown
Book review editor: same
Address: Department of History
University of Arkansas
Fayetteville, AR 72701
Frequency: 4/year
Circulation: 1,300
Pages/issue: 100
Readership: general public

Manuscripts

Query: no
Abstract: no
Style guide: MFW
Preferred length: 25–30 pages
Number of copies: 1
Notes: end of manuscript
Blind referee: no
Time to consider manuscript: 6 months
Illustrations accepted: tables, graphs, charts, black-and-white photographs
Foreign languages: no

Reviews

Seeking reviewers: no
Unsolicited reviews accepted: no
How to apply: letter
Include in application: professional degrees, institutional affiliation, areas of expertise, published works, current research
Length of review: 500 words

ARMY MUSEUM NEWSLETTER

Focus: military museums and their activities; technical and theoretical matters concerning museums
Institutional affiliation: United States Army Center of Military History
Editor: Joseph H. Ewing
Address: United States Army Center of Military History
Forrestal Building
Washington, DC 20314
Frequency: irregular, but usually 2/year
Circulation: 1,200
Pages/issue: 40
Readership: civilian and Army museum personnel, historians, librarians, buffs

Manuscripts
Query: yes
Abstract: no
Style guide: MOS
Preferred length: 1,500–2,000 words
Number of copies: 1
Notes: end of manuscript
Blind referee: no
Time to consider manuscript: 1 month
Illustrations accepted: tables, graphs, charts, pictures
Foreign languages: no

ASIAN AFFAIRS, AN AMERICAN REVIEW

Focus: United States policy toward Asia (Japan to Afghanistan), politics, economics, and international relations of Asian countries
Institutional affiliation: American-Asian Education Exchange
Editor: William Henderson, II
Address: Suite 2-L
88 Morningside Drive
New York, NY 10027
Frequency: 6/year
Circulation: 1,000
Pages/issue: 72
Readership: general public

Manuscripts
Query: no
Abstract: no
Preferred length: 4,000–6,000 words
Number of copies: 1
Notes: end of manuscript
Blind referee: no
Time to consider manuscript: 6 weeks
Illustrations accepted: tables, graphs, charts, photographs (Keep to a minimum because of expense)
Foreign languages: no

Reviews
Seeking reviewers: no
Unsolicited reviews accepted: no

Additional notes
Honorarium of $250 for accepted full-length manuscripts.

ASIAN SURVEY

Focus: contemporary Asian affairs
Institutional affiliation: University of
California Press
Editors: Leo E. Rose, Robert A. Scalapino
Address: University of California Press
Berkeley, CA 94720
Frequency: 12/year
Circulation: 3,400
Pages/issue: 100
Readership: academics, general public

Manuscripts

Query: no
Abstract: no
Style guide: MOS
Preferred length: 30 pages
Number of copies: 2
Notes: bottom of page
Blind referee: yes
Time to consider manuscript: 6–8
weeks
**Proportion of manuscripts
accepted:** 4/10–5/10
Illustrations accepted: camera-ready
tables, graphs, charts, photographs;
line copy only, no halftones

ATTAKAPAS GAZETTE

Focus: genealogy, landmarks, folklore of
southern Louisiana
Institutional affiliation: University of
Southwestern Louisiana
Editor: Gertrude C. Taylor
Book review editor: same
Address: P.O. Box 40831
University of Southwestern
Louisiana
Lafayette, LA 70504
Frequency: 4/year
Circulation: 500
Pages/issue: 48
Readership: academics, general public,
preservationists

Manuscripts

Query: no
Abstract: no
Style guide: MOS
Preferred length: 20–25 pages
Number of copies: 1
Notes: end of manuscript
Blind referee: yes
Time to consider manuscript: 1 month
**Proportion of manuscripts
accepted:** 4/5
Illustrations accepted: tables, graphs,
charts, photographs
Foreign languages: short items in French

Reviews

Seeking reviewers: no
Unsolicited reviews accepted: no
Materials reviewed: books
Length of review: 300–500 words

BAPTIST HISTORY AND HERITAGE

Focus: heritage of Baptists in all parts of the world
Institutional affiliation: Historical Commission of Southern Baptist Convention
Editor: Lynn E. May, Jr.
Book review editor: same
Address: 127 9th Ave., N.
Nashville, TN 37234
Frequency: 4/year
Circulation: 2,500
Pages/issue: 64
Readership: academics, denominational leaders, pastors

Manuscripts
Query: no
Abstract: no
Preferred length: 5,000 words maximum
Number of copies: 2
Notes: bottom of page
Blind referee: no
Time to consider manuscript: 2 months
Proportion of manuscripts accepted: good
Illustrations accepted: tables, graphs, charts, pictures
Foreign languages: no

Reviews
Seeking reviewers: yes
Unsolicited reviews accepted: yes
How to apply: letter
Include in application: professional degrees, institutional affiliation, areas of expertise, published works, foreign languages, current research
Materials reviewed: books
Length of review: 300 words

Additional notes
Use a subhead for approximately every 50 to 75 lines. Should the break in subject matter come before 50 lines or after 75, put a subhead at the proper place in the material. Do not number the subheads. Cap and lower-case subheads and center them on the page.

B.C. HISTORICAL NEWS

Focus: British Columbia
Editor: Patricia Roy
Book review editor: same
Address: P.O. Box 1738
Victoria, B.C., V8W 2Y3
CANADA
Frequency: 4/year
Circulation: 1,200
Pages/issue: 40
Readership: general public

Manuscripts
Query: no
Abstract: no
Style guide: none
Preferred length: 10–20 pages
Number of copies: 1
Notes: end of manuscript
Blind referee: no
Time to consider manuscript: a few weeks
Proportion of manuscripts accepted: 1/2
Illustrations accepted: tables, graphs, charts, pictures, glossy prints (an article requiring more than one or two tables, graphs, or charts will probably not be accepted)

Reviews
Seeking reviewers: no
Unsolicited reviews accepted: no
Materials reviewed: books
Length of review: 500 words

THE BRANDING IRON

Focus: the West
Institutional affiliation: The
    Westerners—Los Angeles Corral
Editor: Ernest Marquez
Book review editor: same
Address: 24213 Hamlin Street
         Canoga Park, CA 91307
Frequency: 4/year
Circulation: 3,000
Pages/issue: 16
Readership: general public

Manuscripts

Query: yes
Abstract: no
Style guide: MOS
Preferred length: 8 pages
Number of copies: 1
Notes: bottom of page
Blind referee: no
Time to consider manuscript: 1 month
Proportion of manuscripts
    accepted: 4/5
Illustrations accepted: tables, graphs,
    charts, pictures
Foreign languages: no

Reviews

Seeking reviewers: no
Unsolicited reviews accepted: no
Materials reviewed: books
Length of review: 2 pages

LE BRAYON: REVUE DE LA SOCIETE HISTORIQUE DU MADAWASKA

Focus: regional; Madawaska, New
    Brunswick, Canada
Institutional affiliation: La Société
    Historique du Madawaska
Editor: La Société Historique du
    Madawaska
Address: C.P. 474
        Edmundston, N.B.
        CANADA
Frequency: 4/year
Circulation: 300
Pages/issue: 30
Readership: general public, researchers,
    students

Manuscripts

Query: yes
Abstract: no
Style guide: none
Preferred length: 2–25 pages
Number of copies: 2
Notes: end of manuscript
Blind referee: sometimes
Time to consider manuscript: 2–3
    weeks
Illustrations accepted: tables, graphs,
    charts, pictures
Foreign languages: French

Reviews

How to apply: letter

THE BRONX COUNTY HISTORICAL SOCIETY JOURNAL

Focus: the Bronx, New York, and its people
Institutional affiliation: The Bronx County Historical Society
Editor: Lloyd Ultan
Book review editor: same
Address: 3266 Bainbridge Avenue
Bronx, NY 10467
Frequency: 2/year
Circulation: 1,500
Pages/issue: 60–70
Readership: academics, general public

Manuscripts
Query: no
Abstract: no
Style guide: any generally accepted guide
Preferred length: 10–15 pages
Number of copies: 1
Notes: end of manuscript
Blind referee: no
Time to consider manuscript: 6–12 months
Proportion of manuscripts accepted: 9/10
Illustrations accepted: tables, graphs, charts, pictures, camera-ready photographs (8 x 10 black-and-white glossies preferred)
Foreign languages: no

Reviews
Seeking reviewers: yes
Unsolicited reviews accepted: no
How to apply: letter
Include in application: professional degrees, institutional affiliation, areas of expertise, published works, current research, knowledge of the Bronx
Materials reviewed: books
Length of review: 250–500 words

Additional notes
Please enclose, on a separate sheet, a one-paragraph short biography highlighting the author's background and expertise, which will be published in the same issue in which the author's article appears.

BULLETIN DU CENTRE DE RECHERCHE EN CIVILISATION CANADIENNE-FRANÇAISE

Focus: French-Canadian culture; news from the archives
Institutional affiliation: Universite d'Ottawa
Editor: Leopold Lanctôt o.m.i.
Address: Editions de l'Universite d'Ottawa
65 av. Hastey
Ottawa, Ontario K1N 6N5
CANADA
Frequency: 2/year
Circulation: 1,200
Pages/issue: 32
Readership: general public

Manuscripts
Query: no
Abstract: no
Style guide: MLA
Preferred length: 5–7 pages
Number of copies: 2
Notes: end of manuscript
Blind referee: no
Time to consider manuscript: 4 months
Proportion of manuscripts accepted: 7/10
Illustrations accepted: tables, graphs, charts
Foreign languages: French only

Reviews
Seeking reviewers: yes
Unsolicited reviews accepted: yes

BULLETIN OF CONCERNED ASIAN SCHOLARS

Focus: Asia and imperialism
Editor: Bryant Avery
Address: P.O. Box W
    Charlemont, MA 01339
Frequency: 4/year
Circulation: 2,100
Pages/issue: 72
Readership: academics, libraries

Manuscripts

Query: no
Abstract: no
Style guide: own; when in doubt consult MOS
Number of copies: 3
Notes: end of manuscript
Blind referee: no
Time to consider manuscript: 3–6 months
Proportion of manuscripts accepted: 1/2
Illustrations accepted: tables, graphs, pictures
Foreign languages: no

Reviews

Seeking reviewers: yes
Unsolicited reviews accepted: yes
Materials reviewed: books, films, audio
Length of review: variable

BULLETIN OF HISTORIC SITES AND PROPERTIES

Focus: Florida anthropology and archaeology
Institutional affiliation: Florida Department of State
Editor: Tom Llewellyn
Address: Bureau of Publications, Archives
    R. A. Gray Building
    Tallahassee, FL 32301
Frequency: 1/year
Circulation: 3,000
Pages/issue: 60–100
Readership: scholars

Manuscripts

Query: no
Abstract: no
Style guide: MOS
Number of copies: 1
Notes: end of manuscript
Blind referee: no
Time to consider manuscript: 3 months
Illustrations accepted: tables, graphs, charts, pictures (publication size is 8½ x 11)
Foreign languages: no

THE BULLETIN OF THE HISTORICAL SOCIETY OF MONTGOMERY COUNTY (PENNSYLVANIA)

Focus: events, personalities, trends in Montgomery County or adjacent areas of southeast Pennsylvania, from colonial to present times
Institutional affiliation: Historical Society of Montgomery County
Editor: William T. Parsons
Address: P.O. Box 92
Collegeville, PA 19426
Frequency: 2/year
Circulation: 1,200
Pages/issue: 96
Readership: general public

Manuscripts
Query: no
Abstract: no
Style guide: MOS preferred
Preferred length: 1,500–5,000 words
Number of copies: 2
Notes: end of manuscript
Blind referee: no
Time to consider manuscript: 5 weeks to 3 months
Proportion of manuscripts accepted: 1/7–1/5
Illustrations accepted: tables, graphs, charts, but not necessary
Foreign languages: no

Additional notes
The Bulletin is abstracted and has titles listed in major publications. Historical narrative or genealogical approach are equally valid. It tries to publish one previously unpublished author each issue.

THE BULLETIN OF THE MISSOURI HISTORICAL SOCIETY

Focus: St. Louis, Missouri, and the trans–Mississippi West
Institutional affiliation: Missouri Historical Society
Editor: Frances H. Stadler
Book review editor: same
Address: Jefferson Memorial Building
St. Louis, MO 63112
Frequency: 4/year
Circulation: 3,000
Pages/issue: 50–60
Readership: Society members, academics, libraries, scholars

Manuscripts
Query: no
Abstract: no
Style guide: MOS
Preferred length: 20–30 pages
Number of copies: 1
Notes: end of manuscript
Blind referee: no
Time to consider manuscript: 3 months
Proportion of manuscripts accepted: varies
Illustrations accepted: tables, graphs, charts, pictures (glossy prints if possible)
Foreign languages: no

Reviews
Unsolicited reviews accepted: occasionally
How to apply: letter
Include in application: professional degrees, institutional affiliation, areas of expertise, published works, current research
Materials reviewed: current works on history
Length of review: 2–3 pages (500–800 words)

BUSINESS HISTORY REVIEW

Focus: business enterprise throughout the world and its interaction with society

Institutional affiliation: Harvard Business School

Editor: Albro Martin

Book review editor: same

Address: 215 Baker Library
Soldiers Field
Boston, MA 02163

Frequency: 4/year

Circulation: 2,500

Pages/issue: 150

Readership: academics, business executives, government officials

Manuscripts

Query: no

Abstract: no

Style guide: MOS; also see *BHR*, Vol. XLIII (Autumn, 1969), 388–91.

Preferred length: 20–30 pages

Number of copies: 1 (3 preferred)

Notes: end of manuscript

Blind referee: yes

Time to consider manuscript: 2–3 months

Proportion of manuscripts accepted: 1/5–1/6

Illustrations accepted: camera-ready visuals; tables accepted only if vital to text

Foreign languages: no

Reviews

Seeking reviewers: yes

Unsolicited reviews accepted: no

How to apply: letter

Include in application: professional degrees, institutional affiliation, areas of expertise

Materials reviewed: books

Length of review: 400–600 words

BYZANTINE STUDIES

Focus: art, archaeology, religion, literature, etc., of the Byzantine Empire

Institutional affiliation: Arizona State University

Editor: Charles Schlacks, Jr.

Address: Arizona State University
Russian and East European Publications
120 B McAllister Office Complex
Tempe, AZ 85281

Book review editor: Dale Kinney

Address: Department of Art History
Bryn Mawr College
Bryn Mawr, PA 19010

Frequency: 2–4/year

Circulation: 400

Pages/issue: 128–160

Readership: academics

Manuscripts

Query: no

Abstract: no

Style guide: MLA

Preferred length: 20–30 pages

Number of copies: 3

Notes: end of manuscript

Blind referee: no

Time to consider manuscript: 3 months

Illustrations accepted: tables, graphs, charts, pictures

Foreign languages: French, German, Russian

Reviews

Seeking reviewers: yes

Unsolicited reviews accepted: no

How to apply: letter

Include in application: areas of expertise

Materials reviewed: books

Length of review: 600–800 words

Additional notes

Byzantine Studies is the only scholarly journal published in North America devoted exclusively to the Byzantine Empire.

LES CAHIERS: LA SOCIETE HISTORIQUE ACADIENNE

Focus: Acadians
Institutional affiliation: La Société Historique Acadienne
Editor: Leon Thériault
Book review editor: same
Address: C.P. 2263, Succursale "A" Moncton, N.B., E1C 8J3 CANADA
Frequency: 4/year
Circulation: 600
Pages/issue: 60
Readership: academics, scholars, general public

Manuscripts

Query: no
Abstract: no
Style guide: none
Preferred length: 20 pages
Number of copies: 3
Notes: bottom of page
Blind referee: no
Time to consider manuscript: one year
Proportion of manuscripts accepted: 1/2
Illustrations accepted: tables, graphs, charts, pictures
Foreign languages: mostly French, only a few articles in English

Reviews

Seeking reviewers: no
Unsolicited reviews accepted: yes
How to apply: letter
Include in application: professional degrees, institutional affiliation, areas of expertise, published works, current research
Materials reviewed: books
Length of review: 1 page

CALIFORNIA HISTORY

Focus: California from pre-Columbian to modern times
Institutional affiliation: California Historical Society
Editor: Marilyn Ziebarth
Book review editor: Charles Wollenberg
Address: California Historical Society 2090 Jackson Street San Francisco, CA 94109
Frequency: 4/year
Circulation: 8,000
Pages/issue: 96
Readership: academics, general public

Manuscripts

Query: no
Abstract: no
Style guide: MOS
Preferred length: 8,000 words maximum
Number of copies: 2
Notes: end of manuscript
Blind referee: no
Time to consider manuscript: 2 months
Illustrations accepted: tables, graphs, charts, pictures
Foreign languages: no

Reviews

Seeking reviewers: yes
Unsolicited reviews accepted: no
How to apply: letter
Include in application: professional degrees, institutional affiliation, areas of expertise, published works, current research
Materials reviewed: books
Length of review: 500 words

CANADA AND THE WORLD

Focus: history and current events of interest to Canadian high school students
Editor: Rupert J. Taylor
Address: Maclean Hunter, Ltd.
481 University Ave.
Toronto, Ontario M5W 1A7
CANADA
Frequency: monthly (September to May)
Circulation: 45,000
Pages/issue: 24
Readership: Canadian high school students

Manuscripts
Query: yes
Abstract: no
Style guide: none
Preferred length: 1,500 words
Number of copies: 1
Notes: end of manuscript
Blind referee: no
Time to consider manuscript: 2 weeks
Illustrations accepted: charts, pictures
Foreign languages: no

Additional notes
Each issue has a theme and articles are assigned. Unsolicited articles or story ideas are unlikely to be published.

CANADIAN-AMERICAN REVIEW OF HUNGARIAN STUDIES

Focus: Hungarian studies
Editor: N. F. Dreisziger
Book review editor: same
Address: History Department
Royal Military College of Canada
Kingston, Ontario
CANADA
Frequency: 2/year
Circulation: 500
Pages/issue: 80
Readership: scholars

Manuscripts
Query: no
Abstract: no
Style guide: MOS
Preferred length: 30 pages
Number of copies: 3
Notes: end of manuscript
Blind referee: no
Time to consider manuscript: 3 months
Proportion of manuscripts accepted: 1/2
Illustrations accepted: tables, pictures
Foreign languages: possibly French

Reviews
Seeking reviewers: yes
Unsolicited reviews accepted: yes
How to apply: letter
Include in application: professional degrees, institutional affiliation, areas of expertise, published works, foreign languages, current research
Materials reviewed: books
Length of review: 4 pages

CANADIAN-AMERICAN SLAVIC STUDIES

Focus: humanities and social sciences devoted to Russian/Soviet and East European area studies
Institutional affiliation: Arizona State University
Editor: Charles Schlacks, Jr.
Book review editors: Allan Simel, Robert North
Address: Arizona State University
120 B McAllister
Tempe, AZ 85281
Frequency: 4/year
Circulation: 1,000
Pages/issue: 150
Readership: academics

Manuscripts

Query: no
Abstract: no
Style guide: MLA
Preferred length: 20–40 pages
Number of copies: 3
Notes: end of manuscript
Blind referee: no
Time to consider manuscript: 3 months
Illustrations accepted: camera-ready tables, graphs, charts, pictures
Foreign languages: French, German, Russian

Reviews

Seeking reviewers: yes
Unsolicited reviews accepted: yes
How to apply: letter
Include in application: areas of expertise, published works, foreign languages
Materials reviewed: books
Length of review: 600 words

CANADIAN ETHNIC STUDIES ETUDES ETHNIQUES AU CANADA

Focus: interdisciplinary studies of ethnicity, immigration, intergroup relations, and the cultural life of ethnic groups in Canada
Institutional affiliation: Research Centre for Canadian Ethnic Studies, University of Calgary
Editors: James Frideres, Anthony Raspovich
Book review editor: Herman Ganzevoort
Address: University of Calgary
Calgary, Alberta T2N 1N4
CANADA
Frequency: 2–3/year
Circulation: 975
Pages/issue: 250
Readership: academics, scholars, librarians, high school teachers, administrators

Manuscripts

Query: yes
Abstract: yes
Style guide: MLA
Preferred length: 15–20 pages
Number of copies: 2–3
Notes: end of manuscript
Blind referee: no
Time to consider manuscript: 4–6 months
Proportion of manuscripts accepted: 1/3
Illustrations accepted: tables, graphs, charts, pictures
Foreign languages: French

Reviews

Seeking reviewers: yes
Unsolicited reviews accepted: yes
How to apply: letter
Include in application: areas of expertise, foreign languages, current research
Materials reviewed: books, films, novels, translations
Length of review: 750 words maximum

CANADIAN HISTORIC SITES

Focus: Canadian architectural, military, and social history; historic period and underwater archaeology
Institutional affiliation: National Historic Parks and Sites Branch, Parks Canada
Editor: John H. Rick
Address: Chief, Research Division
National Historic Parks and
Sites Branch, Parks Canada
Department of the Environment
Ottawa, Ontario K1A 0H4
CANADA
Frequency: 3/year average
Pages/issue: 180
Readership: scholars

Manuscripts
Query: yes
Abstract: yes
Style guide: own
Preferred length: minimum of 30 pages
Number of copies: 1
Notes: end of manuscript
Blind referee: no
Proportion of manuscripts accepted: 1/7
Illustrations accepted: tables, graphs, charts, pictures
Foreign languages: French

Additional notes
Due to a large backlog of unpublished material, *Canadian Historic Sites* is not prepared to consider any unsolicited material for the next three or four years.

CANADIAN HISTORICAL REVIEW

Focus: Canada; related imperial and American history
Institutional affiliation: University of Toronto Press
Editors: Robert Bothwell, David Bercuson
Book review editors: same
Address: University of Toronto Press
5201 Dufferin St.
Downsview, Ontario M5S 1A6
CANADA
Frequency: 4/year
Circulation: about 4,000
Pages/issue: 144
Readership: academics, general public

Manuscripts
Query: no
Abstract: yes
Style guide: none
Preferred length: 25–30 pages
Number of copies: 2
Notes: end of manuscript
Blind referee: no
Time to consider manuscript: 6 weeks–2 months
Proportion of manuscripts accepted: 1/8
Illustrations accepted: tables, graphs, charts
Foreign languages: French

Reviews
Seeking reviewers: yes
Unsolicited reviews accepted: no
How to apply: special form
Materials reviewed: books
Length of review: variable

Additional notes
The oldest historical periodical in Canada with the largest circulation.

CANADIAN JOURNAL OF AFRICAN STUDIES

Focus: African studies for specialists
Institutional affiliation: Universities of Guelph and Laval
Editors: B. Jewsiewicki, G. D. Killam
Book review editor: Bonny Campbell
Address: English Department
University of Guelph
Guelph, Ontario N1G 2W1
CANADA
Frequency: 3/year
Circulation: 1,000
Pages/issue: 250
Readership: academics

Manuscripts
Query: no
Abstract: yes, in the language opposite that in which article is written, that is, either French or English
Style guide: noted on back page of each issue
Preferred length: 5,000 words
Number of copies: 3
Notes: bottom of page
Blind referee: no
Time to consider manuscript: 2 months
Proportion of manuscripts accepted: 1/2
Illustrations accepted: camera-ready tables, graphs, charts, pictures
Foreign languages: French

Reviews
Seeking reviewers: yes
Unsolicited reviews accepted: no
How to apply: letter
Include in application: professional degrees, institutional affiliation, areas of expertise, published works, foreign languages (especially French), current research
Materials reviewed: books
Length of review: 500 words

CANADIAN JOURNAL OF HISTORY ANNALES CANADIENNES D'HISTOIRE

Focus: all history except Canadian
Institutional affiliation: University of Saskatchewan
Editor: Christopher Kent
Book review editor: same
Address: University of Saskatchewan
Saskatoon, Saskatchewan
S7N 0W0
CANADA
Frequency: 3/year
Circulation: 750
Pages/issue: 175
Readership: academics

Manuscripts
Query: no
Abstract: no
Style guide: MLA
Preferred length: 30 pages
Number of copies: 2
Notes: end of manuscript
Blind referee: yes
Time to consider manuscript: 3 months
Proportion of manuscripts accepted: 1/5
Illustrations accepted: tables, camera-ready graphs and charts
Foreign languages: French

Reviews
Seeking reviewers: yes
Unsolicited reviews accepted: no
How to apply: letter
Include in application: professional degrees, institutional affiliation, areas of expertise, published works, foreign languages, current research
Materials reviewed: books
Length of review: 900 words

Additional notes
Articles which embody substantial original research preferred.

CANADIAN JOURNAL OF HISTORY OF SPORT AND PHYSICAL EDUCATION

Focus: sport and physical education
Institutional affiliation: University of Windsor
Editors: Michael A. Salter, Alan Metcalfe
Address: Faculty of Human Kinetics
University of Windsor
Windsor, Ontario N9B 3P4
CANADA
Frequency: 2/year
Circulation: 500
Pages/issue: 100
Readership: academics

Manuscripts
Query: no
Abstract: no
Style guide: MOS
Preferred length: 20–25 pages
Number of copies: 2
Notes: bottom of page
Blind referee: yes
Time to consider manuscript: 3 months
**Proportion of manuscripts
accepted:** 1/2
Illustrations accepted: tables, graphs, charts
Foreign languages: French

Reviews
Seeking reviewers: yes
**Unsolicited reviews
accepted:** occasionally
How to apply: letter
Include in application: institutional affiliation, areas of expertise, published works, current research
Materials reviewed: books
Length of review: 2–3 pages

CANADIAN REVIEW OF AMERICAN STUDIES

Focus: interdisciplinary analysis of the culture of the United States; intercultural relations between the United States and Canada
Institutional affiliation: Canadian Association for American Studies
Editors: John J. Teunissen, Bruce C. Daniels
Address: Department of English
University of Manitoba
Winnipeg, Manitoba R3T 2N2
CANADA
Frequency: 3/year
Circulation: 600
Pages/issue: 132
Readership: academics

Manuscripts
Query: no
Abstract: no
Style guide: MLA
Preferred length: 20–40 pages
Number of copies: 2
Notes: end of manuscript
Blind referee: no
Time to consider manuscript: 3 months maximum
**Proportion of manuscripts
accepted:** 1/10
Illustrations accepted: tables, graphs, charts, pictures
Foreign languages: French

Reviews
Seeking reviewers: yes
Unsolicited reviews accepted: no
How to apply: letter
Include in application: professional degrees, institutional affiliation, areas of expertise, published works, current research
Materials reviewed: books
Length of review: 10 or more pages

CANADIAN REVIEW OF STUDIES IN NATIONALISM

Focus: topical and theoretical studies of nationalism
Institutional affiliation: University of Prince Edward Island
Editor: Thomas Spira
Address: University of Prince Edward Island
Charlottetown, Prince Edward Island C1A 4P3
CANADA
Book review editor: Keith Cassidy
Address: Guelph University
Guelph, Ontario
CANADA
Frequency: 2/year
Circulation: 500
Pages/issue: 150
Readership: academics

Manuscripts
Query: preferred
Abstract: no
Style guide: MOS
Preferred length: 25–35 pages
Number of copies: 2
Notes: end of manuscript
Blind referee: yes
Time to consider manuscript: 2 months
Proportion of manuscripts accepted: 1/4
Illustrations accepted: limited number of tables, graphs, charts
Foreign languages: French, German, Spanish

Reviews
Seeking reviewers: yes
Unsolicited reviews accepted: yes
How to apply: letter
Include in application: professional degrees, institutional affiliation, areas of expertise, published works, foreign languages, current research
Materials reviewed: books
Length of review: 3 pages

Additional notes
Articles must represent original research, be written in essay style, and be free of polemics.

CANADIAN SLAVONIC PAPERS

Focus: Soviet Union and Eastern Europe
Institutional affiliation: Canadian Association of Slavists
Editor: R. C. Elwood
Book review editor: J. L. Black
Address: 256 Paterson Hall
Carleton University
Ottawa, Ontario K1S 5B6
CANADA
Frequency: 4/year
Circulation: 1,000
Pages/issue: 150
Readership: academics

Manuscripts
Query: no
Abstract: yes, after acceptance
Style guide: own
Preferred length: 35 pages maximum
Number of copies: 2
Notes: end of manuscript
Blind referee: no
Time to consider manuscript: 3 months
Proportion of manuscripts accepted: 1/4
Illustrations accepted: camera-ready, if possible; tables, graphs, charts
Foreign languages: French

Reviews
Seeking reviewers: yes
Unsolicited reviews accepted: no
How to apply: write for form
Include in application: institutional affiliation, areas of expertise, foreign languages
Materials reviewed: books
Length of review: 500 words

CATHOLIC HISTORICAL REVIEW

Focus: Christianity, the Catholic Church
Institutional affiliation: Catholic University of America Press
Editor: Reverend Robert Trisco
Book review editor: same
Address: 620 Michigan Ave., NE
Washington, DC 20064
Frequency: 4/year
Circulation: 2,121
Pages/issue: 170
Readership: academics

Manuscripts

Query: no
Abstract: no
Style guide: MOS
Preferred length: 30 pages maximum
Number of copies: 1
Notes: end of manuscript
Blind referee: no
Time to consider manuscript: 3 months
Proportion of manuscripts accepted: 1/5
Illustrations accepted: tables, graphs, charts, pictures
Foreign languages: no

Reviews

Seeking reviewers: yes
Unsolicited reviews accepted: no
How to apply: form
Include in application: professional degrees, institutional affiliation, published works, foreign languages, current research
Materials reviewed: books
Length of review: 400–500 words

CENTERPOINT: A JOURNAL OF INTERDISCIPLINARY STUDIES

Focus: interdisciplinary articles in sciences, social sciences, and humanities
Institutional affiliation: CUNY Graduate School and Queens College Press
Editor: Akiva Kaminsky
Book review editor: Toni Kamins
Address: 33 West 42nd St.
New York, NY 10036
Frequency: 2–4/year
Circulation: 500
Pages/issue: 96
Readership: scholars, libraries

Manuscripts

Query: yes
Abstract: on acceptance
Style guide: MLA or MOS
Preferred length: 8–12 pages
Number of copies: 3 preferred
Notes: end of manuscript
Blind referee: no
Time to consider manuscript: 3–6 months
Proportion of manuscripts accepted: 1/7–1/5
Illustrations accepted: tables, graphs, charts, pictures
Foreign languages: Spanish, French, German, Italian

Reviews

Seeking reviewers: yes
Unsolicited reviews accepted: no
How to apply: letter
Include in application: professional degrees, institutional affiliation, areas of expertise, published works, foreign languages, current research
Materials reviewed: books, films, audio
Length of review: 300 words

CENTRAL EUROPEAN HISTORY

Focus: German-speaking Central Europe, all periods
Institutional affiliation: Conference Group for Central European History
Editor: Douglas Unfug
Book review editor: same
Address: Department of History
Emory University
Atlanta, GA 30322
Frequency: 4/year
Circulation: 1,400
Pages/issue: 100
Readership: academics

Manuscripts
Query: no
Abstract: no
Style guide: MOS
Preferred length: 15–20 pages
Number of copies: 2
Notes: end of manuscript
Blind referee: no
Time to consider manuscript: 4 months
Proportion of manuscripts accepted: 1/5–1/4
Illustrations accepted: tables, graphs, charts, pictures (not encouraged)
Foreign languages: will consider German

Reviews
Seeking reviewers: yes
Unsolicited reviews accepted: no
How to apply: letter
Include in application: professional degrees, institutional affiliation, areas of expertise, published works, foreign languages, current research
Materials reviewed: books established by the editor; all are review articles
Length of review: established by the editor; all are review articles

CHICAGO HISTORY

Focus: Chicago and environs
Institutional affiliation: Chicago Historical Society
Editor: Fannia Weingartner
Book review editor: Gail Farr Casterline
Address: Chicago Historical Society
Clark Street at North Avenue
Chicago, IL 60614
Frequency: 4/year
Circulation: 7,500
Pages/issue: 64
Readership: academics, general public

Manuscripts
Query: preferred
Abstract: no
Style guide: MOS
Preferred length: 4,500 words maximum
Number of copies: 1
Notes: end of manuscript
Blind referee: no
Time to consider manuscript: 2–4 months
Proportion of manuscripts accepted: 1/4
Illustrations accepted: pictures (see Additional notes)
Foreign languages: no

Reviews
Seeking reviewers: yes
Unsolicited reviews accepted: no
How to apply: letter
Include in application: areas of expertise, published works, current research
Materials reviewed: books, films, audio

Additional notes
The Society's editorial office provides illustrations for each article if they exist in the Society's collections. Authors are free to submit their own illustrations or ideas on where to find them. *Chicago History* pays an honorarium of $250 for full-length articles and a prorated amount for shorter ones. Payment is made after the author has accepted the edited copy.

THE CHRONICLES OF OKLAHOMA

Focus: Oklahoma culture and environment; the West
Institutional affiliation: Oklahoma Historical Society
Editor: Kenny A. Franks
Book review editor: Bob L. Blackburn
Address: 2100 North Lincoln
Oklahoma City, OK 73105
Frequency: 4/year
Circulation: 3,000
Pages/issue: 140
Readership: academics, general public

Manuscripts
Query: no
Abstract: no
Style guide: MOS
Preferred length: 15–25 pages
Number of copies: 1
Notes: end of manuscript
Blind referee: no
Time to consider manuscript: 6 months
Proportion of manuscripts accepted: 1/10
Illustrations accepted: three to five photos per article increase chances of acceptance
Foreign languages: no

Reviews
Seeking reviewers: yes
Unsolicited reviews accepted: no
How to apply: letter
Include in application: professional degrees, institutional affiliation, areas of expertise, published works, current research
Materials reviewed: books
Length of review: 1–3 pages

CHURCH HISTORY

Focus: religion during the past 2,000 years, specifically Christianity
Institutional affiliation: American Society of Church History
Editors: Martin E. Marty, Robert Grant, Jerald Brauer
Address: Swift Hall
University of Chicago
Chicago, IL 60637
Frequency: 4/year
Circulation: about 3,000
Pages/issue: 125
Readership: academics

Manuscripts
Query: no
Abstract: no
Style guide: MOS
Preferred length: 25 pages maximum
Number of copies: 2
Notes: end of manuscript
Blind referee: no
Time to consider manuscript: 5–6 months
Proportion of manuscripts accepted: 1/10
Illustrations accepted: tables, graphs, charts
Foreign languages: no

Reviews
Seeking reviewers: no
Unsolicited reviews accepted: no
How to apply: letter
Materials reviewed: books
Length of review: 150–450 words, depending on the book

Additional notes
Articles should be based on primary source materials and should constitute original contributions to scholarship. Book reviewers must be members of the American Society of Church History.

CINCINNATI HISTORICAL SOCIETY BULLETIN

Focus: cultural, economic, political, and social aspects of Cincinnati, the Miami Valley, the old Northwest Territory
Institutional affiliation: Cincinnati Historical Society
Editor: Dottie L. Lewis
Address: Eden Park
Cincinnati, OH 45202
Frequency: 4/year
Circulation: 2,400
Pages/issue: 72
Readership: academics, general public

Manuscripts
Query: no
Abstract: no
Preferred length: 20–26 pages
Number of copies: 1
Notes: end of manuscript
Blind referee: no
Time to consider manuscript: 6–8 weeks
Illustrations accepted: tables, graphs, charts, pictures
Foreign languages: no

Reviews
Seeking reviewers: no
Unsolicited reviews accepted: no

CIVIL WAR HISTORY

Focus: United States, Civil War era, 1820–1880
Institutional affiliation: Kent State University
Editor: John T. Hubbell
Book review editor: same
Address: Department of History
Kent State University
Kent, OH 44242
Frequency: 4/year
Circulation: 1,700
Pages/issue: 96
Readership: academics, buffs

Manuscripts
Query: no
Abstract: no
Style guide: MOS
Preferred length: 20 pages
Number of copies: 1
Notes: bottom of page
Blind referee: yes
Time to consider manuscript: 6–8 weeks
Proportion of manuscripts accepted: 1/5
Illustrations accepted: tables, graphs
Foreign languages: no

Reviews
Seeking reviewers: yes
Unsolicited reviews accepted: no
How to apply: letter
Include in application: professional degrees, institutional affiliation, areas of expertise, published works, current research
Materials reviewed: books, anthologies
Length of review: 350–1,000 words

CIVIL WAR ROUND TABLE DIGEST

Focus: Civil War, battlefield preservation, contemporary activities inspired by Civil War interest
Editor: Jerry L. Russell
Book review editor: same
Address: P.O. Box 7388
Little Rock, AR 72217
Frequency: 12/year
Circulation: 1,000
Pages/issue: 16
Readership: buffs

Manuscripts
Query: yes
Style guide: MLA
Preferred length: 500–1,000 words
Number of copies: 1
Blind referee: no
Time to consider manuscript: 2 months
Illustrations accepted: tables, graphs, charts, pictures
Foreign languages: no

Reviews
Seeking reviewers: no
Unsolicited reviews accepted: yes
How to apply: letter
Include in application: professional degrees, institutional affiliation, areas of expertise, published works, current research
Materials reviewed: books
Length of review: 200–500 words

Additional notes
The *Digest* is a newsletter.

CIVIL WAR TIMES ILLUSTRATED

Focus: Civil War, 1861–1865
Institutional affiliation: Historical Times, Inc.
Editor: John E. Stanchak (assistant)
Book review editor: same
Address: P.O. Box 1831
Harrisburg, PA 17105
Frequency: 10/year
Circulation: 100,000
Pages/issue: 50
Readership: buffs

Manuscripts
Query: yes
Abstract: no
Style guide: own
Preferred length: 3,000–5,000 words
Number of copies: 1
Notes: end of manuscript
Blind referee: no
Time to consider manuscript: 6–8 weeks
Illustrations accepted: illustrations, maps, or hints on where to get them
Foreign languages: no

Reviews
Seeking reviewers: no
Unsolicited reviews accepted: no
How to apply: letter
Include in application: professional degrees, institutional affiliation, areas of expertise, published works, current research
Materials reviewed: books
Length of review: 300–500 words

Additional notes
$200 to $350 paid for full-length manuscripts. Articles should be based on sound research, but written in a style that is popular rather than scholarly—authoritative enough to satisfy historians and readable enough to fascinate beginning enthusiasts. Although articles are published without bibliographical footnotes, informal source annotations for each manuscript are required.

THE CLASSICAL JOURNAL

Focus: classical philology and literature, ancient history, the teaching of Latin and Greek
Institutional affiliation: Classical Association of the Middle West and South, Inc.
Editor-in-chief: Hunter R. Rawlings, III
Book review editors: Harold D. Evjen, E. Christian Kopff
Address: Department of Classics
University of Colorado
Boulder, CO 80309
Frequency: 4/year
Circulation: 3,200
Pages/issue: 96
Readership: academics

Manuscripts
Query: no
Abstract: no
Style guide: MLA
Preferred length: under 25 pages
Number of copies: 2 preferred
Notes: end of manuscript
Blind referee: yes
Time to consider manuscript: 1–3 months
Proportion of manuscripts accepted: 1/12
Illustrations accepted: tables, charts, pictures
Foreign languages: no

Reviews
Seeking reviewers: no
Unsolicited reviews accepted: no
Materials reviewed: books
Length of review: under 5 pages

CLASSICAL PHILOLOGY

Focus: languages, literature, and life of ancient Greece and Rome
Institutional affiliation: University of Chicago
Editor: Stewart Irvin Oost
Book review editor: same
Address: Box I, Faculty Exchange
University of Chicago
Chicago, IL 60637
Frequency: 4/year
Circulation: 1,400
Pages/issue: 96
Readership: academics

Manuscripts
Query: no
Abstract: no
Style guide: MOS; see inside front cover of recent issue
Preferred length: 50 pages maximum
Number of copies: 1
Notes: bottom of page
Time to consider manuscript: varies
Proportion of manuscripts accepted: 1/7
Illustrations accepted: clear and uncluttered tables, graphs, charts, pictures
Foreign languages: all major Western European languages—English, French, German, Italian, Latin

Reviews
Seeking reviewers: no
Unsolicited reviews accepted: no
How to apply: letter
Include in application: institutional affiliation, areas of expertise, foreign languages
Materials reviewed: books, general works
Length of review: variable

THE CLASSICAL WORLD

Focus: all phases of Greek and Roman antiquity
Institutional affiliation: Classical Association of the Atlantic States
Editor: Jerry Clack
Book review editor: Gerald Quinn
Address: Department of Classics
Duquesne University
Pittsburgh, PA 15219
Frequency: 7/year
Circulation: 3,000
Pages/issue: 64
Readership: academics

Manuscripts

Query: no
Abstract: no
Style guide: MLA
Preferred length: open
Number of copies: 1
Notes: end of manuscript
Blind referee: yes
Time to consider manuscript: 3 months
Illustrations accepted: tables, graphs, charts, pictures (author pays additional expenses)
Foreign languages: no

Reviews

Seeking reviewers: yes
Unsolicited reviews accepted: no
How to apply: letter
Include in application: professional degrees, institutional affiliation, areas of expertise, published works, foreign languages
Materials reviewed: books
Length of review: 300–600 words

CLIO

Focus: literature, history, and philosophy of history
Institutional affiliation: Indiana University–Purdue University
Editor: Frederick T. Kirchoff
Book review editor: Andrew McLean
Address: Indiana University–Purdue University
Fort Wayne, IN 46805
Frequency: 3/year
Circulation: 550
Pages/issue: 170
Readership: academics

Manuscripts

Query: no
Abstract: yes
Style guide: MLA
Preferred length: 20–25 pages
Number of copies: 2
Notes: end of manuscript
Blind referee: no
Time to consider manuscript: 3 months
Proportion of manuscripts accepted: 1/20
Illustrations accepted: usually not accepted due to printing costs
Foreign languages: no

Reviews

Seeking reviewers: yes
Unsolicited reviews accepted: no
How to apply: letter
Include in application: professional degrees, institutional affiliation, areas of expertise
Materials reviewed: books
Length of review: 1,000 words

THE COLORADO MAGAZINE

Focus: Colorado and the Rocky Mountain West
Institutional affiliation: Colorado Historical Society
Editor: Cathryne Johnson
Book review editor: same
Address: Colorado Heritage Center
1300 Broadway
Denver, CO 80203
Frequency: 4/year
Circulation: 4,200
Pages/issue: 112
Readership: academics, general public

Manuscripts

Query: no
Abstract: no
Style guide: MOS
Preferred length: 30 pages
Number of copies: 1
Notes: end of manuscript
Blind referee: no
Time to consider manuscript: 6–8 weeks
Proportion of manuscripts accepted: 1/2
Illustrations accepted: tables, pictures (illustrations should be black-and-white glossies)
Foreign languages: no

Reviews

Seeking reviewers: yes
Unsolicited reviews accepted: no
How to apply: letter
Include in application: professional degrees, institutional affiliation, areas of expertise, current research
Materials reviewed: books
Length of review: 3 pages

Additional notes

Generally, genealogical studies are not accepted. Originality, documentation, significance, and presentation determine suitability for publication.

COMPARATIVE FRONTIER STUDIES

Focus: the frontier as focal point for social, political, and economic change
Institutional affiliation: Departments of History, Anthropology, and Geography, University of Oklahoma
Editor: William W. Savage, Jr.
Address: Department of History
University of Oklahoma
455 West Lindsey, Room 406
Norman, OK 73019
Frequency: 3–4/year
Circulation: 1,000
Pages/issue: 4
Readership: academics

Manuscripts

Query: no
Abstract: no
Preferred length: 4–6 pages
Number of copies: 1
Notes: end of manuscript
Blind referee: no
Time to consider manuscript: 2–4 weeks
Proportion of manuscripts accepted: 4/5
Illustrations accepted: camera-ready tables, graphs, charts, pictures
Foreign languages: no

Reviews

Seeking reviewers: no
Unsolicited reviews accepted: yes
Materials reviewed: books
Length of review: 2–3 pages

Additional notes

Comparative Frontier Studies, a newsletter, is the only interdisciplinary publication for frontier studies. An average of three brief articles or research notes appear in each issue.

LA CONFLUENCIA

Focus: the American Southwest
Editors: Karl Kopp, Susan Dewitt
Book review editors: same
Address: P.O. Box 409
　　　　　Albuquerque, NM 87103
Frequency: 4/year
Circulation: 300
Pages/issue: 60
Readership: scholars, general public

Manuscripts
Query: no
Abstract: no
Preferred length: 3,000 words
Number of copies: 1
Notes: bottom of page
Blind referee: no
Time to consider manuscript: 1 month
**Proportion of manuscripts
　　accepted:** 1/5
Illustrations accepted: tables, graphs,
　　charts, pictures
Foreign languages: Spanish

Reviews
Seeking reviewers: yes
Unsolicited reviews accepted: no
How to apply: letter
Include in application: areas of expertise
Materials reviewed: books
Length of review: 250–500 words

Additional notes
La Confluencia is geared to the
multi-cultural diversity of the American
Southwest. It publishes material of current
as well as historical interest, but with an
emphasis on the current, the
contemporary, and the future of this region.
The fewer footnotes, the better.

THE CONNECTICUT ANTIQUARIAN

Focus: historic preservation, art,
　　architecture, decorative arts,
　　antiques, restoration
Institutional affiliation: The Antiquarian
　　and Landmarks Society, Inc., of
　　Connecticut
Editor: Richard N. Ford
Book review editor: Arthur W.
　　Leibundguth
Address: 394 Main Street
　　Hartford, CT 06103
Frequency: 2/year
Circulation: 2,000
Pages/issue: 32
Readership: Society members

Manuscripts
Query: yes
Abstract: no
Style guide: MOS preferred
Preferred length: 5–6 pages
Number of copies: 1
Notes: end of manuscript
Blind referee: no
Time to consider manuscript: varies
Illustrations accepted: tables, graphs,
　　charts, pictures
Foreign languages: no

Reviews
Seeking reviewers: no
Unsolicited reviews accepted: no
Materials reviewed: books

Additional notes
Reviews are done in-house.

CONTEMPORARY FRENCH CIVILIZATION

Focus: multidisciplinary perspectives on modern francophone societies
Institutional affiliation: Montana State University
Editor: Bernard Quinn
Book review editor: Pierre Aubéry
Address: Department of Language
University of South Alabama
Mobile, AL 36688
Frequency: 3/year
Circulation: 750–1,000
Pages/issue: 175
Readership: academics

Manuscripts
Query: no
Abstract: no
Style guide: MLA
Preferred length: 15–20 pages
Number of copies: 3
Notes: end of manuscript
Blind referee: no
Time to consider manuscript: 2–3 months
Proportion of manuscripts accepted: 1/4
Illustrations accepted: tables
Foreign languages: French

Reviews
Seeking reviewers: yes
Unsolicited reviews accepted: yes
How to apply: letter
Include in application: professional degrees, institutional affiliation, areas of expertise, foreign languages
Materials reviewed: books, films, audio
Length of review: 4–8 pages

Additional notes
Articles of purely linguistic or literary perspective are not considered for publication.

COUNCIL ON ABANDONED MILITARY POSTS PERIODICAL

Focus: military or historical matters concerning posts, camps, or stations; preservation of posts
Institutional affiliation: Council on Abandoned Military Posts (CAMP)
Editor: Dan L. Thrapp
Address: 4970 North Camino Antonio
Tucson, AZ 85718
Frequency: 4/year
Circulation: 1,500
Pages/issue: 56
Readership: military personnel, buffs

Manuscripts
Query: yes
Abstract: no
Style guide: own
Preferred length: 3,000–4,000 words
Number of copies: 2
Notes: end of manuscript
Time to consider manuscript: 3 weeks
Illustrations accepted: tables, graphs, charts, 8 x 10 pictures
Foreign languages: no

Additional notes
Writers should be thoroughly versed in their subject and remember that they are writing for an intelligent, professional, informed audience. *CAMP Periodical* pays about $2 a page on publication.

CROSS AND COCKADE

Focus: World War I aviation
Editor: Lonnie Raidor
Book review editor: same
Address: 10443 S. Memphis Avenue
Whittier, CA 90604
Frequency: 4/year
Circulation: 2,500
Pages/issue: 96
Readership: general public

Manuscripts

Query: yes
Abstract: yes
Preferred length: 20 pages maximum
Number of copies: 1
Notes: bottom of page
Blind referee: no
Time to consider manuscript: 6 months
or longer
**Proportion of manuscripts
accepted:** good
Illustrations accepted: tables, graphs,
charts, pictures
Foreign languages: no

Reviews

Seeking reviewers: yes
Unsolicited reviews accepted: yes
How to apply: letter
Materials reviewed: books
Length of review: 1/2 page maximum

CURRENT HISTORY

Focus: political science, economics,
current events
Editor: Carol L. Thompson
Book review editor: E. P. Thompson
Address: RR1, Box 132
Furlong, PA 18925
Frequency: 10/year
Circulation: 30,000
Pages/issue: 48
Readership: academics

Manuscripts

Query: yes
Abstract: no
Style guide: MOS
Preferred length: 5,000 words
Number of copies: 1
Notes: bottom of page
Blind referee: no
Illustrations accepted: tables, graphs,
charts
Foreign languages: no

Reviews

Seeking reviewers: no
Unsolicited reviews accepted: no

Additional notes

No unsolicited manuscripts. Prospective
authors should either telephone or write.

DAEDALUS

Focus: scholarship and public affairs
Institutional affiliation: The American Academy of Arts and Sciences
Editor: William H. Brubeck
Address: 7 Linden Street
Cambridge, MA 02138
Frequency: 4/year
Circulation: 36,000
Pages/issue: 224
Readership: academics

Manuscripts
Query: yes
Abstract: no
Style guide: MOS
Preferred length: 7,500 words
Number of copies: 3
Notes: end of manuscript
Blind referee: no
Time to consider manuscript: 6–10 weeks
Foreign languages: only by prior agreement

Reviews
Seeking reviewers: no
Unsolicited reviews accepted: no

Additional notes
Because *Daedalus* issues result from a lengthy process of planning seminars and author conferences, unsolicited manuscripts are only infrequently accepted. Prior inquiry is essential.

DAUGHTERS OF THE AMERICAN REVOLUTION MAGAZINE

Focus: the American Revolution
Institutional affiliation: National Society, Daughters of the American Revolution
Address: 1776 D Street NW
Washington, DC 20006
Frequency: 10/year
Circulation: 55,000
Pages/issue: 108
Readership: historians, genealogists, general public, Society members

Manuscripts
Query: no
Abstract: no
Style guide: MLA
Preferred length: 5,000 words
Number of copies: 1
Notes: end of manuscript
Blind referee: no
Time to consider manuscript: 3 months
Illustrations accepted: pictures

DETROIT IN PERSPECTIVE: A JOURNAL OF REGIONAL HISTORY

Focus: Detroit, Southeastern Michigan, Southern Ontario
Institutional affiliation: Department of History, Wayne State University and Detroit Historical Society
Editor: Kermit L. Hall
Book review editor: same
Address: Department of History
Wayne State University
Detroit, MI 48202
Frequency: 3/year
Circulation: 2,500
Pages/issue: 75–85
Readership: Society members, academics

Manuscripts
Query: no
Abstract: no
Style guide: MOS
Preferred length: 15–30 pages
Number of copies: 1
Notes: end of manuscript
Blind referee: no
Time to consider manuscript: 6 weeks
Proportion of manuscripts accepted: 7/10
Illustrations accepted: tables, graphs, charts, pictures, glossy photographs

Reviews
Seeking reviewers: yes
Unsolicited reviews accepted: no
How to apply: letter
Include in application: professional degrees, institutional affiliation, areas of expertise, published works, current research
Materials reviewed: books
Length of review: 350–1,200 words

DIGGIN'S

Focus: Butte County, California, particularly stories of everyday life, old families, personal memories
Institutional affiliation: Butte County Historical Society
Editor: Gertrude N. Bartley
Address: 134 Riverview Drive
Oroville, CA 95965
Frequency: 4/year
Circulation: 750
Pages/issue: 25
Readership: general public, historians, California historical societies

Manuscripts
Query: yes
Abstract: no
Preferred length: variable
Number of copies: 1
Notes: end of manuscript
Blind referee: no
Time to consider manuscript: 1 month
Illustrations accepted: pictures
Foreign languages: no

DIPLOMATIC HISTORY

Focus: American foreign policy, all periods
Institutional affiliation: Society for Historians of American Foreign Relations
Editor: Warren I. Cohen
Address: Department of History
Michigan State University
East Lansing, MI 48824
Frequency: 4/year
Circulation: 950
Pages/issue: 100–110
Readership: Society members, libraries

Manuscripts
Query: no
Abstract: no
Style guide: MLA
Preferred length: 30 pages maximum
Number of copies: 3
Notes: end of manuscript
Blind referee: yes
Time to consider manuscript: 3–4 months
Proportion of manuscripts accepted: 1/5
Illustrations accepted: tables, charts; maps will be considered
Foreign languages: no

Reviews
Seeking reviewers: no
Unsolicited reviews accepted: yes
Materials reviewed: books
Length of review: 10–15 pages; all are review essays

Additional notes
Date form: day month year (e.g., 12 December 1950).

EAST CENTRAL EUROPE

Focus: humanities and social sciences pertaining to the German Democratic Republic, Poland, Czechoslovakia, Hungary, the Habsburg Empire
Institutional affiliation: Arizona State University
Editor: Charles Schlacks, Jr.
Book review editor: same
Address: Arizona State University
Russian and East European Publications
120 B McAllister Office Complex
Tempe, AZ 85281
Frequency: 2–4/year
Circulation: 500
Pages/issue: 128–160
Readership: academics, diplomats

Manuscripts
Query: no
Abstract: no
Style guide: MLA
Preferred length: 20–30 pages
Number of copies: 3
Notes: end of manuscript
Blind referee: no
Time to consider manuscript: 3 months
Illustrations accepted: tables, graphs, charts, pictures
Foreign languages: French, German, Russian

Reviews
Seeking reviewers: yes
Unsolicited reviews accepted: no
How to apply: letter
Include in application: areas of expertise
Materials reviewed: books
Length of review: 600–800 words

Additional notes
Frequent contributions by scholars from East Central Europe.

EAST EUROPEAN QUARTERLY

Focus: East European civilization, politics, and economics
Institutional affiliation: University of Colorado
Editor: Stephen Fischer-Galati
Book review editor: same
Address: University of Colorado
Boulder, CO 80309
Frequency: 4/year
Circulation: 800
Pages/issue: 128
Readership: academics, scholars, general public

Manuscripts
Query: no
Abstract: no
Style guide: any standard form
Preferred length: 15–25 pages
Number of copies: 1
Notes: either bottom of page or end of manuscript
Blind referee: no
Time to consider manuscript: 4 weeks
Proportion of manuscripts accepted: 3/5
Illustrations accepted: tables, graphs, charts, pictures
Foreign languages: French, German, Italian

Reviews
Seeking reviewers: yes
Unsolicited reviews accepted: yes
How to apply: letter
Include in application: professional degrees, institutional affiliation, areas of expertise, foreign languages
Materials reviewed: books
Length of review: 1,000–1,500 words maximum

EAST TENNESSEE HISTORICAL SOCIETY PUBLICATIONS

Focus: Tennessee
Institutional affiliation: Knoxville–Knox County Public Library
Editor: William J. MacArthur
Address: Lawson McGhee Library
Knoxville, TN 37902
Frequency: 1/year
Circulation: 1,000
Pages/issue: 170
Readership: scholars, general public

Manuscripts
Query: no
Abstract: no
Style guide: MOS
Preferred length: 30 pages
Number of copies: 1
Notes: end of manuscript
Blind referee: no
Time to consider manuscript: 4 months
Proportion of manuscripts accepted: 1/2
Illustrations accepted: tables, graphs, charts, pictures
Foreign languages: no

Reviews
Seeking reviewers: no
Unsolicited reviews accepted: no

ECHOES

Focus: Ohio and museum news
Editor: Nancy Summers Pollack
Address: Ohio Historical Society
I-71 and 17th Avenue
Columbus, OH 43211
Frequency: 12/year
Circulation: 12,000
Pages/issue: 8
Readership: Society members

Manuscripts

Query: no
Abstract: no
Style guide: MOS
Preferred length: 5 pages
Number of copies: 2
Notes: notes not desired
Blind referee: no
Time to consider manuscript: 1 month
**Proportion of manuscripts
accepted:** 1/2
Illustrations accepted: charts
Foreign languages: no

Additional notes

Echoes is a newsletter which occasionally
features articles of general historical
interest, emphasizing local and regional
history.

EIGHTEENTH-CENTURY STUDIES

Focus: all aspects of the eighteenth
century
Institutional affiliation: University of
California, Davis
Editor: Max Byrd
Book review editor: Paul Alkon
Address: Department of English
University of California
Davis, CA 95616
Frequency: 4/year
Circulation: 3,800
Pages/issue: 150
Readership: academics, members of the
American Society of
Eighteenth-Century Studies

Manuscripts

Query: no
Abstract: no
Style guide: MLA
Preferred length: 6,000 words maximum
Number of copies: 1
Notes: end of manuscript
Blind referee: yes
Time to consider manuscript: 6 months
**Proportion of manuscripts
accepted:** 1/10
Illustrations accepted: camera-ready
tables, graphs, charts, pictures
Foreign languages: no

Reviews

Length of review: variable

THE EIGHTEENTH CENTURY: THEORY AND INTERPRETATION

Focus: 1660–1800, interdisciplinary topics, literary and historiographical theory
Institutional affiliation: Texas Tech University
Editors: Jeffrey Smitten, Joel Weinsheimer
Book review editors: same
Address: P.O. Box 4530
Texas Tech University
Lubbock, TX 79409
Frequency: 3/year
Circulation: 600
Pages/issue: 96
Readership: academics

Manuscripts
Query: no
Abstract: no
Style guide: MOS
Preferred length: 20–25 pages
Number of copies: 2
Notes: end of manuscript
Blind referee: no
Time to consider manuscript: 3 months
Proportion of manuscripts accepted: 1/20
Illustrations accepted: tables, graphs, charts, pictures
Foreign languages: no

Reviews
Seeking reviewers: yes
Unsolicited reviews accepted: yes
How to apply: letter
Include in application: published works
Materials reviewed: books
Length of review: 20–25 pages; review essays

Additional notes
The Eighteenth Century discourages essays that convey information without apparent significance and favors those that possess methodological self-consciousness.

EIRE-IRELAND: A JOURNAL OF IRISH STUDIES

Focus: Ireland and the Irish influence worldwide
Editor: Eoin McKiernan
Book review editor: Henry Beechhold
Address: 683 Osceola Ave.
St. Paul, MN 55105
Frequency: 4/year
Circulation: 8,500
Pages/issue: 160
Readership: academics, general public

Manuscripts
Query: recommended
Abstract: no
Style guide: MOS
Preferred length: 5,000 words maximum
Number of copies. 1
Notes: end of manuscript
Blind referee: no
Time to consider manuscript: 2–3 months
Proportion of manuscripts accepted: 4/5
Illustrations accepted: tables, graphs, charts; no color
Foreign languages: Irish, but require abstract in English

Reviews
Seeking reviewers: yes
Unsolicited reviews accepted: occasionally
How to apply: letter
Include in application: professional degrees, institutional affiliation, areas of expertise, published works, current research
Materials reviewed: books
Length of review: seldom more than 1,500 words

ENVIRONMENTAL REVIEW

Focus: interdisciplinary studies in environmental context
Institutional affiliation: Duquesne University
Editor: John Opie
Book review editor: Kent Shifferd
Address: Department of History
Duquesne University
Pittsburgh, PA 15219
Frequency: 3/year
Circulation: 300
Pages/issue: 64
Readership: academics, policy specialists

Manuscripts
Query: no
Abstract: no
Style guide: depends on discipline
Preferred length: 20 pages
Number of copies: 2
Notes: end of manuscript
Blind referee: no
Time to consider manuscript: 6 months
Proportion of manuscripts accepted: 2/5
Illustrations accepted: tables, graphs, charts, pictures
Foreign languages: no

Reviews
Seeking reviewers: yes
Unsolicited reviews accepted: yes
How to apply: letter
Include in application: professional degrees, institutional affiliation, areas of expertise, current research
Materials reviewed: books
Length of review: 500–1,000 words

EL ESCRIBANO

Focus: northeastern Florida
Institutional affiliation: St. Augustine Historical Society
Editor: Mark E. Fretwell
Address: St. Augustine Historical Society
271 Charlotte St.
St. Augustine, FL 32084
Frequency: 4/year
Circulation: 450
Pages/issue: 80
Readership: Society members, academics, buffs

Manuscripts
Query: no
Abstract: no
Preferred length: 1,500–6,000 words
Number of copies: 1
Illustrations accepted: pictures
Foreign languages: no

Additional notes
Reviews written in-house.

ESSEX INSTITUTE HISTORICAL COLLECTIONS

Focus: Essex County, Massachusetts
Institutional affiliation: Essex Institute, Salem, Massachusetts
Editor: Bryant F. Tolles, Jr.
Address: 132 Essex Street
Salem, MA 01970
Frequency: 4/year
Circulation: 1,350
Pages/issue: 90–100
Readership: Institute members, scholars, libraries, academic institutions

Manuscripts

Query: no
Abstract: no
Style guide: MOS
Preferred length: 20 pages
Number of copies: 2
Notes: bottom of page
Blind referee: no
Time to consider manuscript: 6 weeks
Proportion of manuscripts accepted: 1/3
Illustrations accepted: carefully captioned tables, graphs, charts, pictures (photographs should be black-and-white, 8 x 10 glossies)
Foreign languages: no

Reviews

Seeking reviewers: no
Unsolicited reviews accepted: no
Materials reviewed: books
Length of review: 1,000–1,500 words

ETHNOHISTORY

Focus: interdisciplinary articles emphasizing historical methods and their integration with anthropological theories
Editor: Charles A. Bishop
Address: S.U.N.Y.
Oswego, NY 13126
Book review editor: Shepard Krech, III
Address: Department of Sociology
George Mason University
Fairfax, VA
Frequency: 4/year
Circulation: 1,200
Pages/issue: 100
Readership: anthropologists, historians

Manuscripts

Query: yes
Abstract: yes
Style guide: *American Anthropologist* format
Preferred length: 25–35 pages
Number of copies: 3
Notes: end of manuscript
Blind referee: no
Time to consider manuscript: 6 months
Proportion of manuscripts accepted: 1/2
Illustrations accepted: tables, graphs, charts, pictures (originals, if possible)
Foreign languages: no

Reviews

Seeking reviewers: yes
Unsolicited reviews accepted: no
How to apply: letter
Include in application: professional degrees, institutional affiliation, areas of expertise, published works, foreign languages, current research
Materials reviewed: books, films
Length of review: 400 words

EUROPA: A JOURNAL OF INTERDISCIPLINARY STUDIES

Focus: European society, past and present; interdisciplinary approaches to humanities and social sciences
Institutional affiliation: Inter-University Centre for European Studies, Montreal, Canada
Editor: Pierre H. Boulle
Address: CIEE
C. P. 8888
Montreal H3C 3P8, Quebec
CANADA
Frequency: 2/year
Circulation: 700
Pages/issue: 100–125
Readership: academics

Manuscripts

Query: no
Abstract: yes
Style guide: MOS
Preferred length: 20–30 pages
Number of copies: 2
Notes: end of manuscript
Blind referee: yes
Time to consider manuscript: 3 months
Proportion of manuscripts accepted: 3/10
Illustrations accepted: tables, graphs, charts, pictures, camera-ready illustrations (glossies)
Foreign languages: French

Additional notes

Articles must be of interest to specialists in more than one discipline, either because of the subject or because of the methodology which they exemplify. Shorter pieces (10 pages) are also published under the rubrics "Forum" or "Debate," which focus on problems of methodology and interpretation. Such pieces are also published under "Research Notes" when they report on new avenues of research in interdisciplinary studies.

EUROPEAN STUDIES NEWSLETTER

Focus: European studies; social science
Institutional affiliation: Columbia University
Editor: Marion A. Kaplan
Book review editor: same
Address: International Affairs
Columbia University
New York, NY 10027
Frequency: 6/year
Circulation: 1,100
Pages/issue: 30
Readership: academics, government and nongovernment agencies

Manuscripts

Query: yes
Abstract: yes
Style guide: MOS
Preferred length: 12 pages maximum
Number of copies: 2
Notes: end of manuscript
Blind referee: no
Time to consider manuscript: 3 months
Proportion of manuscripts accepted: varies
Illustrations accepted: no
Foreign languages: no

Reviews

Seeking reviewers: yes
Unsolicited reviews accepted: yes
How to apply: letter
Include in application: professional degrees, institutional affiliation, areas of expertise, foreign languages
Materials reviewed: books, films, audio, newsletters, journals
Length of review: 2 pages

EXPLORATIONS IN ECONOMIC HISTORY

Focus: all aspects of economic change, all periods, all geographical locales
Institutional affiliation: Washington State University
Editors: Gary M. Walton, James F. Shepherd
Address: College of Business and Economics
Washington State University
Pullman, WA 99163
Frequency: 4/year
Pages/issue: 110
Readership: academics

Manuscripts
Query: no
Abstract: no
Style guide: own
Preferred length: 25 pages maximum
Number of copies: 2
Notes: end of manuscript
Blind referee: yes
Time to consider manuscript: 2–3 months
Illustrations accepted: tables, graphs, charts, pictures
Foreign languages: no

Reviews
Seeking reviewers: yes
Unsolicited reviews accepted: yes
How to apply: letter
Include in application: institutional affiliation, areas of expertise
Materials reviewed: books, articles
Length of review: 2–3 pages

Additional notes
All artwork should be numbered in order of appearance (with Arabic numerals) and should have short descriptive captions. All figure captions should be typed in order, double-spaced on a separate page.

Line drawings must be originals in black India ink on white paper. Lettering should be uniform and large enough to be legible after reduction of fifty to sixty percent. Halftone artwork should be camera-ready glossy prints. The author should consider the proportions of the printed page in planning artwork (a maximum size of.5 x 7 inches is desirable).

All tabular material should be numbered in order of appearance in text (with Arabic numerals). Descriptions should be typed double-spaced on a separate page. Each page should have a short descriptive title typed above it. Footnotes to the table (indicated by superscript lower-case letters) should be typed at the bottom of the table.

FEMINIST STUDIES

Focus: women's studies, feminist theory
Institutional affiliation: University of
  Maryland
Editor: Claire Moses
Book review editor: same
Address: Women's Studies Program
        University of Maryland
        College Park, MD 20742
Frequency: 3/year
Circulation: 5,000
Pages/issue: 200
Readership: academics, general public

Manuscripts
Query: no
Abstract: yes
Style guide: MOS
Preferred length: 15–25 pages
Number of copies: 2
Notes: end of manuscript
Blind referee: no
Time to consider manuscript: 3 months
Illustrations accepted: tables, graphs,
  charts, pictures
Foreign languages: no

Reviews
Seeking reviewers: yes
Unsolicited reviews accepted: yes
How to apply: letter
Include in application: professional
    degrees, institutional affiliation, areas
    of expertise, published works, foreign
    languages, current research
Materials reviewed: books
Length of review: 1,500–2,500 words

FIDES ET HISTORIA

Focus: all subjects, Christian orientation
Institutional affiliation: Conference on
  Faith and History
Editor: Ronald A. Wells
Address: History Department
        Calvin College
        Grand Rapids, MI 49506
Book review editor: Robert D. Linder
Address: Kansas State University
        Manhattan, KS 66506
Frequency: 2/year
Circulation: 850
Pages/issue: 100
Readership: academics, clergy, general
  public

Manuscripts
Query: helpful
Abstract: no
Style guide: MOS
Preferred length: 10,000 words
  maximum
Number of copies: 2
Notes: end of manuscript
Blind referee: no
Time to consider manuscript: 3–6
  months
**Proportion of manuscripts
  accepted:** 1/8
Illustrations accepted: tables, graphs,
  charts
Foreign languages: no

Reviews
Seeking reviewers: yes
Unsolicited reviews accepted: yes
How to apply: letter
Include in application: professional
    degrees, institutional affiliation, areas
    of expertise, published works, current
    research
Materials reviewed: books
Length of review: 600 words

(continued on next page)

FIDES ET HISTORIA
(continued)

Additional notes

Conference on Faith and History is an organization of historians, mostly in the United States and Canada, but also in Britain and other foreign countries. Members are Christians of all denominations, so the Conference is not sectarian in any way. Nevertheless, the members seek to have their faith commitment inform their historical work, or be reflected in it in some way.

FILM AND HISTORY

Focus: film and television; classroom applications for the teaching of history
Institutional affiliation: The Historians Film Committee (an affiliated society of the American Historical Association)
Editors: Martin A. Jackson, John E. O'Connor
Book review editors: same
Address: c/o History Faculty
New Jersey Institute of Technology
Newark, NJ 07102
Frequency: 4/year
Circulation: 400–500
Pages/issue: 24
Readership: teachers, archivists, researchers, scholars

Manuscripts

Query: no
Abstract: no
Style guide: MOS
Preferred length: 2,500–3,500 words
Number of copies: 2
Notes: end of manuscript
Blind referee: no
Time to consider manuscript: 6–10 weeks
Proportion of manuscripts accepted: 1/3
Illustrations accepted: tables, graphs, charts, pictures
Foreign languages: no

Reviews

Seeking reviewers: yes (film)
Unsolicited reviews accepted: no
How to apply: letter
Include in application: professional degrees, institutional affiliation, areas of expertise, published works, foreign languages, current research
Materials reviewed: books, films, audio
Length of review: 300 words

Additional notes

The editors of this journal seek articles in which the critical tools and traditional resources of historical scholarship are applied to the study of film and television. Film reviews should include comment on and possible suggestions for use of the film in teaching history.

THE FILSON CLUB HISTORY QUARTERLY

Focus: Kentucky
Institutional affiliation: The Filson Club
Editor: Nelson L. Dawson
Book review editor: same
Address: 118 W. Breckinridge Street
    Louisville, KY 40203
Frequency: 4/year
Circulation: 3,500
Pages/issue: 96
Readership: Club members, scholars

Manuscripts

Query: no
Abstract: no
Style guide: MOS
Preferred length: 15–30 pages
Number of copies: 1
Notes: end of manuscript
Blind referee: no
Time to consider manuscript: 1 month
**Proportion of manuscripts
    accepted:** 1/2
Illustrations accepted: tables, graphs,
    charts, pictures
Foreign languages: no

Reviews

Seeking reviewers: yes
Unsolicited reviews accepted: no
How to apply: letter
Include in application: professional
    degrees, institutional affiliation, areas
    of expertise, published works
Materials reviewed: books
Length of review: 500–1,000 words

FLASHBACK

Focus: Washington County, Arkansas
Institutional affiliation: Washington
    County Historical Society
Editor: Ellen Shipley
Address: Washington County Historical
    Society
    118 East Dickson
    Fayetteville, AR 72701
Frequency: 4/year
Circulation: 840
Pages/issue: 40
Readership: general public

Manuscripts

Query: advised
Abstract: no
Style guide: none
Preferred length: 10–12 pages
Number of copies: 2 preferred
Notes: end of manuscript
Blind referee: no
Time to consider manuscript: 3 months
**Proportion of manuscripts
    accepted:** 3/4
Illustrations accepted: tables, graphs,
    etc. (not too many)
Foreign languages: no

Reviews

Seeking reviewers: no
Unsolicited reviews accepted: yes
How to apply: letter
Include in application: nothing required,
    but any information helpful
Materials reviewed: books
Length of review: 250–300 words

Additional notes

Flashback publishes articles about the
history of local businesses, organizations,
families, individuals, etc.; old marriage and
circuit court records; old letters and diaries
about Washington County or by residents
of Washington County, Arkansas.

FLORIDA HISTORICAL QUARTERLY

Focus: Florida, from the discovery to the present
Institutional affiliation: Florida Historical Society
Editor: Samuel Proctor
Book review editor: same
Address: Box 14045
University Station
Gainesville, FL 32604
Frequency: 4/year
Circulation: 2,000
Pages/issue: 130
Readership: general public, historians

Manuscripts
Query: no
Abstract: no
Style guide: MOS
Preferred length: 20–25 pages
Number of copies: 1
Notes: end of manuscript
Blind referee: no
Time to consider manuscript: 1–3 months
Proportion of manuscripts accepted: 2/5
Illustrations accepted: tables, graphs, charts, pictures
Foreign languages: no

Reviews
Seeking reviewers: yes
Unsolicited reviews accepted: no
How to apply: letter
Include in application: professional degrees, institutional affiliation, areas of expertise, published works, foreign languages, current research
Materials reviewed: books
Length of review: 500–600 words

FOUNDATIONS

Focus: Baptist history and theology
Institutional affiliation: American Baptist Historical Society
Editor: Joseph R. Sweeny
Book review editor: same
Address: 18 Putnam Road
Arlington, MA 02174
Frequency: 4/year
Circulation: 800
Pages/issue: 96
Readership: Baptist ministers, scholars, lay persons, libraries

Manuscripts
Query: helpful
Abstract: no
Style guide: own (see Additional notes)
Preferred length: 20–30 pages
Number of copies: 1
Notes: end of manuscript
Blind referee: no
Proportion of manuscripts accepted: 7/8
Foreign languages: no

Reviews
Seeking reviewers: yes
Unsolicited reviews accepted: yes
How to apply: letter
Include in application: professional degrees, institutional affiliation, areas of expertise, published works
Materials reviewed: books
Length of review: 500 words

Additional notes
Place the title, with your name below it, on the first page, followed by the first paragraph of the text. Leave a two-inch margin at the bottom of the first page, with about an inch margin on all sides of subsequent pages.

As a general rule, all relevant material arguments, etc. should be in the body of the article rather than in the notes.

FRANKLIN COUNTY HISTORICAL REVIEW

Focus: Franklin County, Tennessee
Institutional affiliation: Franklin County Historical Society
Editor: Virginia McKown Brock
Address: P.O. Box 128
Cowan, TN 37318
Frequency: 2/year
Circulation: 750
Pages/issue: 60
Readership: general public

Manuscripts
Query: no
Abstract: no
Style guide: MOS
Preferred length: 10–12 pages
Number of copies: 3
Notes: end of manuscript
Blind referee: no
Time to consider manuscript: 3 months
Proportion of manuscripts accepted: 1/2
Illustrations accepted: tables, charts, pictures (photographs must be black-and-white glossies), camera-ready graphs and maps

FRANKLIN FLYER

Focus: Franklin County and southeast Washington history
Institutional affiliation: Franklin County Historical Society
Editor: Walter A. Oberst
Book review editor: same
Address: Box 1033
Pasco, WA 99301
Frequency: 4/year
Circulation: 750
Pages/issue: 12
Readership: general public, libraries

Manuscripts
Query: yes
Preferred length: open
Notes: no notes
Illustrations accepted: pictures
Foreign languages: no

Additional notes
Franklin Flyer prefers articles of interest to the general public, to pioneers, and their descendants; and especially such articles as reflect and depict pioneer conditions, events, and social and cultural aspects of early days. It does not publish material that is purely genealogical in content.

FRENCH HISTORICAL STUDIES

Focus: France, especially since the medieval period
Institutional affiliation: Ohio State University, College of Humanities
Editor: John Rothney
Address: Department of History
Ohio State University
230 West 17th Avenue
Columbus, OH 43210
Frequency: 2/year
Circulation: 1,500
Pages/issue: 200
Readership: academic libraries, historians

Manuscripts
Query: no
Abstract: no
Style guide: MOS
Preferred length: 30 pages
Number of copies: 2
Notes: end of manuscript
Blind referee: yes
Time to consider manuscript: 2–3 months
Proportion of manuscripts accepted: 1/6–1/7
Illustrations accepted: tables, graphs, charts (professionally prepared, if more is involved than a simple table)
Foreign languages: occasionally French

FRONTIER TIMES

Focus: events and lives on the western frontier, preferably 1840–1905
Editor: Pat Wagner
Address: P.O. Box 3338
Austin, TX 787C-
Frequency: 6/year
Circulation: 68,000
Pages/issue: 64
Readership: general public

Manuscripts
Query: yes
Abstract: no
Style guide: own
Preferred length: 1,500–4,000 words
Number of copies: 1
Notes: no notes; list sources separate from text
Time to consider manuscript: 6 weeks
Illustrations accepted: pictures
Foreign languages: no

Reviews
Seeking reviewers: no

Additional notes
Frontier Times does not use fiction based on fact, or a lot of dialogue that cannot be substantiated. Its editors are not looking for the dry textbook approach, but do insist that the material be researched and accurate. *Frontier Times* pays 2¢ a word, minimum, on acceptance, plus an allowance for pictures.

FULTON COUNTY HISTORICAL AND GENEALOGICAL SOCIETY NEWSLETTER QUARTERLY

Focus: Fulton County, Illinois
Institutional affiliation: Fulton County, Illinois, Historical and Genealogical Society
Editor: Curtis Strode
Address: Route 2
Marietta, IL 61459
Book review editor: Marjorie R. Bordner
Address: 45 North Park Drive
Canton, IL 61520
Frequency: 4/year
Circulation: 350
Pages/issue: 32
Readership: general public

Manuscripts
Query: yes
Abstract: no
Style guide: none
Preferred length: 1–2 pages
Number of copies: 1
Notes: no preference
Blind referee: optional
Time to consider manuscript: 3 months
Illustrations accepted: camera-ready tables, graphs, charts, pictures
Foreign languages: no

Reviews
Seeking reviewers: no
Unsolicited reviews accepted: yes
How to apply: letter
Include in application: professional degrees, institutional affiliation, areas of expertise, published works, current research
Materials reviewed: historical or genealogical works preferred, especially with western Illinois focus
Length of review: 1–2 pages

GENEALOGICAL JOURNAL

Focus: genealogy, family and local history (international in scope)
Institutional affiliation: Utah Genealogical Association
Editor: Kip Sperry
Address: Utah Genealogical Association
P.O. Box 1144
Salt Lake City, UT 84110
Frequency: 4/year
Circulation: 1,000
Pages/issue: 60
Readership: genealogists, historians, librarians

Manuscripts
Query: no
Abstract: no
Style guide: MOS
Preferred length: variable
Number of copies: 1
Notes: end of manuscript
Blind referee: no
Time to consider manuscript: 1–2 months
Proportion of manuscripts accepted: 9/10
Illustrations accepted: camera-ready tables, graphs, charts, pictures
Foreign languages: no

Reviews
Seeking reviewers: yes
Unsolicited reviews accepted: yes
How to apply: letter
Include in application: professional degrees, institutional affiliation, areas of expertise
Materials reviewed: books
Length of review: 1–2 pages

GEORGIA ARCHIVE

Focus: archival theory and practice
Institutional affiliation: Society of
Georgia Archivists
Editor: Elisabeth H. Breuer
Book review editor: Ellen Garrison
Address: Box 261
Georgia State University
Atlanta, GA 30303
Frequency: 2/year
Circulation: 500
Pages/issue: 85
Readership: archivists, librarians,
manuscript curators

Manuscripts
Query: no
Abstract: no
Style guide: MOS
Preferred length: 12–35 pages
Number of copies: 2
Notes: end of manuscript
Blind referee: no
Time to consider manuscript: 3 months
**Proportion of manuscripts
accepted:** solicited, 9/10; unsolicited,
1/2
Illustrations accepted: tables, graphs,
charts (only if clear, accurate, and
enhancing to the text)
Foreign languages: no

Reviews
Seeking reviewers: yes
Unsolicited reviews accepted: no
How to apply: letter
Include in application: professional
degrees, institutional affiliation, areas
of expertise, published works, current
research
Materials reviewed: books
Length of review: 1–5 pages

Additional notes
Georgia Archive has a national readership.
Articles are not limited to regional topics or
authors. Papers written from oral
presentations should be edited before
submission with careful attention to
elements of style that do not translate well
from the spoken to the written word.

GEORGIA HISTORICAL QUARTERLY

Focus: Georgia and the southern United
States
Institutional affiliation: Georgia
Historical Society
Editor: Phinizy Spalding
Address: Department of History
University of Georgia
Athens, GA 30602
Frequency: 4/year
Circulation: 2,000
Pages/issue: 100
Readership: academics, buffs, librarians

Manuscripts
Query: desired
Abstract: no
Preferred length: 15 pages maximum
Number of copies: 1
Notes: end of manuscript
Blind referee: yes
Time to consider manuscript: varies
**Proportion of manuscripts
accepted:** 1/10
Illustrations accepted: rarely
Foreign languages: no

Reviews
Seeking reviewers: yes
Unsolicited reviews accepted: no
How to apply: letter
Include in application: professional
degrees, institutional affiliation, areas
of expertise, published works, current
research
Materials reviewed: books, essays,
architectural works, historic
preservation volumes, if applicable
Length of review: 300–500 words; some
review essays

Additional notes
Firsthand accounts of events in the
twentieth century and literary-historical
interpretations are also welcome.

THE GLADES STAR

Focus: Garrett County, Maryland
Institutional affiliation: Garrett County Historical Society
Editor: Bradley A. Stewart
Book review editor: same
Address: 32 South Second Street
Oakland, MD 21550
Frequency: 4/year
Circulation: 2,500
Pages/issue: 24
Readership: general public

Manuscripts

Query: no
Abstract: no
Style guide: MOS
Preferred length: open
Number of copies: 2
Notes: end of manuscript
Blind referee: no
Time to consider manuscript: 1 month
Proportion of manuscripts accepted: 3/4
Illustrations accepted: tables, graphs, charts, pictures
Foreign languages: no

Reviews

Seeking reviewers: no
Unsolicited reviews accepted: yes
How to apply: letter
Include in application: areas of expertise, published works, current research
Materials reviewed: books, articles
Length of review: open

GOOD OLD DAYS

Focus: nostalgia, preferably 1895–1940
Editor: Evelyn Schoolcraft
Book review editor: same
Address: Folly Mill Road
Seabrook, NH 03874
Frequency: 1/month
Circulation: 150,000–175,000
Pages/issue: 64–72
Readership: general public

Manuscripts

Query: no
Abstract: no
Preferred length: 1,000–2,500 words
Number of copies: 1
Notes: end of manuscript
Blind referee: no
Time to consider manuscript: 1–6 months
Proportion of manuscripts accepted: 3/4
Illustrations accepted: charts, pictures
Foreign languages: no

Reviews

Seeking reviewers: no
Unsolicited reviews accepted: yes
How to apply: letter
Materials reviewed: nostalgia material
Length of review: 200–250 words

GREAT PLAINS JOURNAL

Focus: ten-state Great Plains
Institutional affiliation: Museum of the
    Great Plains
Editor: Steve Wilson
Book review editor: same
Address: Museum of the Great Plains
    P.O. Box 68
    Lawton, OK 73502
Frequency: 1/year
Circulation: 800
Pages/issue: 96
Readership: academics, general public

Manuscripts

Query: yes
Abstract: no
Style guide: MOS
Preferred length: 5,000–8,000 words
Number of copies: 1
Notes: end of manuscript
Blind referee: no
Time to consider manuscript: 2 months
Illustrations accepted: pictures
Foreign languages: no

Reviews

Seeking reviewers: no
Unsolicited reviews accepted: yes
How to apply: letter
Include in application: professional
    degrees, institutional affiliation, areas
    of expertise
Materials reviewed: books
Length of review: 300–500 words

THE GREATER LLANO ESTACADO SOUTHWEST HERITAGE

Focus: literary, historical and cultural arts
Institutional affiliation: Llano Estacado
    Heritage, Inc.
Editor: Orin Hatch
Address: LEHI
    P.O. Box 2446
    Hobbs, NM 88240
Book review editor: Jean Burroughs
Address: LEHI
    S. Abilene
    Portales, NM 88130
Frequency: 4/year
Circulation: 1,100
Pages/issue: 32
Readership: academics, general public

Manuscripts

Query: no
Abstract: no
Style guide: MOS
Preferred length: 2,000 words
Number of copies: 1
Notes: end of manuscript
Blind referee: no
Time to consider manuscript: 6 months
**Proportion of manuscripts
    accepted:** 3/4
Illustrations accepted: tables, graphs,
    charts, pictures
Foreign languages: no

Reviews

Seeking reviewers: yes
Unsolicited reviews accepted: no
How to apply: letter
Include in application: professional
    degrees, institutional affiliation, areas
    of expertise, brief vita
Materials reviewed: books, films, audio,
    all media and print formats
Length of review: 150–250 words

THE GREEK ORTHODOX THEOLOGICAL REVIEW

Focus: scholarly papers and reviews in Biblical studies, orthodox theology, church history, related classical, archaeological, and philosophical studies
Institutional affiliation: Holy Cross School of Theology of Hellenic College
Editor: Rev. Fr. Ilia Katre
Book review editor: Lewis J. Patsavos
Address: 50 Goodard Avenue
Brookline, MA 02146
Frequency: 4/year
Circulation: 800
Pages/issue: 90
Readership: theologians, seminary libraries, historians

Manuscripts
Query: no
Abstract: no
Style guide: MOS
Preferred length: 25–30 pages
Number of copies: 2
Notes: end of manuscript
Blind referee: no
Time to consider manuscript: 1 month
Proportion of manuscripts accepted: 1/2
Illustrations accepted: no
Foreign languages: no

Reviews
Seeking reviewers: yes
Unsolicited reviews accepted: yes
How to apply: letter
Include in application: professional degrees, institutional affiliation, areas of expertise, published works, foreign languages, current research
Materials reviewed: books
Length of review: 4 pages

GREEK, ROMAN AND BYZANTINE STUDIES

Focus: Greek, Roman and Byzantine studies
Institutional affiliation: Duke University
Editor: Kent J. Rigsby
Address: Box 4715
Duke Station
Durham, NC 27706
Frequency: 4/year
Circulation: 900
Pages/issue: 100
Readership: academics

Manuscripts
Query: no
Abstract: no
Style guide: see inside front cover of any issue
Preferred length: 5–30 pages
Number of copies: 1
Notes: end of manuscript
Blind referee: no
Time to consider manuscript: 1–3 months
Proportion of manuscripts accepted: 1/4
Illustrations accepted: tables, graphs, charts, pictures
Foreign languages: German, French

Reviews
Seeking reviewers: no
Unsolicited reviews accepted: no

Additional notes
Review articles solicited on occasion.

HARVARD JOURNAL OF ASIATIC STUDIES

Focus: pre-modern East Asia; China, Japan, Korea before 1860; modern East Asian literature
Institutional affiliation: Harvard–Yenching Institute
Editor: Donald H. Shively
Book review editor: same
Address: 2 Divinity Ave.
Cambridge, MA 02138
Frequency: 2/year
Circulation: 1,500
Pages/issue: 450–500
Readership: academics

Manuscripts
Query: helpful
Abstract: no
Style guide: MLA
Preferred length: 20–50 pages
Number of copies: 2
Notes: end of manuscript
Blind referee: no
Time to consider manuscript: 2–5 months
Illustrations accepted: tables, graphs, charts, pictures
Foreign languages: French, German, Russian

Reviews
Seeking reviewers: yes
Unsolicited reviews accepted: will consider
How to apply: letter
Include in application: professional degrees, institutional affiliation, areas of expertise, published works, foreign languages, current research
Materials reviewed: books
Length of review: variable

Additional notes
East Asian articles based upon research in the primary sources sought. Typesetting possible in Chinese, Japanese, Cyrillic, Arabic, and other alphabets.

HAYES HISTORICAL JOURNAL

Focus: the period of Rutherford B. Hayes, his family and interests
Institutional affiliation: The Rutherford B. Hayes Library and Museum
Editor: Kenneth E. Davison
Address: Spiegel Grove
1337 Hayes Avenue
Fremont, OH 43420
Frequency: 2/year
Pages/issue: 72–80
Readership: academics, general public

Manuscripts
Query: no
Abstract: no
Style guide: MLA
Preferred length: 3,000–5,000 words
Number of copies: 1
Notes: end of manuscript
Blind referee: no
Time to consider manuscript: 4–6 weeks
Illustrations accepted: tables, graphs, charts, pictures, glossy prints
Foreign languages: no

THE HIGH COUNTRY

Focus: the West, especially Southern California
Editor: Tom Hudson
Book review editor: same
Address: P.O. Box 371
Lake Elsinore, CA 92330
Frequency: 4/year
Circulation: 2,000
Pages/issue: 52
Readership: general public

Manuscripts
Query: no
Abstract: no
Preferred length: 3,000 words maximum
Number of copies: 1
Notes: bottom of page
Blind referee: no
Time to consider manuscript: 2–3 weeks
Illustrations accepted: no
Foreign languages: no

HISPANIC AMERICAN HISTORICAL REVIEW

Focus: Latin America and related topics
Institutional affiliation: Duke University Press
Editor: John Johnson
Book review editor: Edwin Lieuwen
Address: Department of History
University of New Mexico
Albuquerque, NM 87131
Frequency: 4/year
Circulation: 2,500
Pages/issue: 200
Readership: academics, academic libraries

Manuscripts
Query: no
Abstract: no
Style guide: MOS, own (see "Information for Authors," *HAHR,* 58 (August 1978), 566–69)
Preferred length: 40–45 pages
Number of copies: 2
Notes: end of manuscript
Blind referee: yes
Time to consider manuscript: 1–2 months
Proportion of manuscripts accepted: 1/5
Illustrations accepted: tables, graphs, charts
Foreign languages: will consider manuscripts in Spanish and Portuguese but, if accepted, they must be translated into English

Reviews
Seeking reviewers: yes
Unsolicited reviews accepted: no
How to apply: special form
Include in application: professional degrees, institutional affiliation, areas of expertise, published works, foreign languages
Materials reviewed: books

HISTORIA MATHEMATICA

Focus: mathematics
Institutional affiliation: City University of New York
Editor: Joseph W. Dauben
Book review editor: Judith V. Grabiner
Address: Department of History
   Lehman College, CUNY
   Bedford Park Boulevard West
   New York, NY 10468
Frequency: 4/year
Circulation: 1,250
Pages/issue: 125
Readership: academics,
   mathematicians, historians of science

Manuscripts

Query: no
Abstract: yes
Style guide: MOS
Preferred length: 20–30 pages
Number of copies: 3
Notes: end of manuscript
Blind referee: no
Time to consider manuscript: 2–3
   months
**Proportion of manuscripts
   accepted:** 1/4
Illustrations accepted: tables, graphs,
   charts, pictures
Foreign languages: no languages are
   excluded; English predominates, with
   some articles in French and German

Reviews

Seeking reviewers: yes
Unsolicited reviews accepted: no
How to apply: letter
Include in application: professional
   degrees, institutional affiliation, areas
   of expertise, published works, foreign
   languages, current research
Materials reviewed: books, films, audio,
   significant articles
Length of review: 2–3 pages

Additional notes

Historia Mathematica welcomes manuscripts on the history of all aspects of the mathematical sciences in all parts of the world and all periods, including theory and practice; computer science; statistics; cybernetics; operations research; actuarial science; mathematical technology, both hardware and software (from the abacus to the computer, algorithms, language, notation, and tables); all applications; interrelations with the natural sciences, social science, humanities, arts, and education; philosophy, psychology, and sociology of mathematics; mathematical communication, including information systems and bibliography; biography of mathematicians and historians; organizations and institutions; historiography; and the interaction between all these facets of mathematical activity and other aspects of culture and society.

Papers should involve new historical data from primary sources, analysis of known data, review of previous historical work, survey of recent mathematical or historical research, previously unpublished manuscripts, translation or reprint of inaccessible materials, annotated bibliography, critical chronology. Generalizations should be supported by argument and documentation.

THE HISTORIAN

Focus: all areas
Institutional affiliation: Phi Alpha Theta, International Honor Society in History
Editor: Gerald D. Nash
Address: University of New Mexico
Albuquerque, NM 87131
Book review editor: Phillip D. Thomas
Address: Department of History
Wichita State University
Wichita, KS 67208
Frequency: 4/year
Circulation: 10,000
Pages/issue: 200
Readership: scholars

Manuscripts

Query: no
Abstract: no
Style guide: MOS
Preferred length: 6,000 words
Number of copies: 2
Notes: end of manuscript
Blind referee: yes
Time to consider manuscript: 3–6 months
Proportion of manuscripts accepted: 1/8
Illustrations accepted: tables, graphs, charts, pictures
Foreign languages: no

Reviews

Seeking reviewers: yes
Unsolicited reviews accepted: not as a rule
How to apply: form
Materials reviewed: books
Length of review: 450–600 words

Additional notes

Articles published in *The Historian* should make a contribution to historical knowledge and be based on unpublished primary sources.

HISTORIC KERN

Focus: Kern County, California
Institutional affiliation: Kern County Historical Society
Editor: Christopher D. Brewer
Book review editor: same
Address: P.O. Box 141
Bakersfield, CA 93301
Frequency: 4/year
Circulation: 350
Pages/issue: 4
Readership: general public, local historians, libraries

Manuscripts

Query: yes
Abstract: yes
Style guide: none
Preferred length: 1,000–2,000 words
Number of copies: 3
Notes: end of manuscript
Blind referee: no
Time to consider manuscript: 3–4 months
Proportion of manuscripts accepted: 3/5
Illustrations accepted: 8 x 10 illustrations preferred; maps may be acceptable
Foreign languages: no

Reviews

Seeking reviewers: no
Unsolicited reviews accepted: if pertinent to local history
How to apply: letter
Include in application: institutional affiliation, areas of expertise, current research
Materials reviewed: books, films, audio
Length of review: 500 words

HISTORIC PRESERVATION

Focus: historic preservation, saving the built environment
Institutional affiliation: National Trust for Historic Preservation
Editor: Gail K. Wentzell
Address: 1729 H Street, N.W.
Washington, DC 20006
Frequency: 6/year
Circulation: 160,000
Pages/issue: 56
Readership: general public

Manuscripts
Query: preferred
Abstract: no
Style guide: MOS
Preferred length: 1,500–2,000 words
Number of copies: 1
Notes: none
Blind referee: no
Time to consider manuscript: 1 month
Proportion of manuscripts accepted: 1/10
Illustrations accepted: pictures, black-and-white photographs, color transparencies
Foreign languages: no

Reviews
Seeking reviewers: yes
Unsolicited reviews accepted: no
How to apply: letter
Include in application: areas of expertise, published works
Length of review: 750 words

Additional notes
Articles on broad preservation subjects preferred, rather than accounts of how a single building was restored.

HISTORICAL ARCHAEOLOGY

Focus: archaeology
Editor: Ronald L. Michael
Book review editor: Roderick Sprague
Address: Department of Anthropology
University of Idaho
Moscow, ID 83843
Frequency: 1/year
Pages/issue: 128
Readership: academics, buffs

Manuscripts
Query: no
Abstract: yes
Style guide: own
Preferred length: 3–30 pages
Number of copies: 3
Notes: no notes
Blind referee: no
Time to consider manuscript: 6 weeks
Proportion of manuscripts accepted: 2/5
Illustrations accepted: tables, graphs, charts, pictures
Foreign languages: no

Reviews
Seeking reviewers: no
Unsolicited reviews accepted: yes
How to apply: letter
Include in application: professional degrees, institutional affiliation, areas of expertise, published works
Materials reviewed: books, films
Length of review: 2–5 pages

HISTORICAL AVIATION ALBUM

Focus: aviation, aircraft, and
personalities; emphasis on American
aeronautical achievements
Editor: Paul R. Matt
Address: P.O. Box 33
Temple City, CA 91780
Frequency: 1/year
Circulation: 3,500
Pages/issue: 72
Readership: academics, model builders,
buffs

Manuscripts
Query: yes
Abstract: yes
Style guide: MOS
Preferred length: 25 pages
Number of copies: 1
Notes: end of manuscript
Blind referee: no
Time to consider manuscript: 1 month
**Proportion of manuscripts
accepted:** 1/2
Illustrations accepted: tables, graphs,
charts, pictures
Foreign languages: no

HISTORICAL MAGAZINE OF THE EPISCOPAL CHURCH

Focus: Episcopal church; American
church history; Church of England;
church history in British
Commonwealth countries;
Reformation
Institutional affiliation: Episcopalian
Editor: John F. Woolverton
Book review editor: Carlton Hayden
Address: P.O. Box 2247
Austin, TX 78767
Frequency: 4/year
Circulation: 1,400
Pages/issue: 120
Readership: academics, general public

Manuscripts
Query: no
Abstract: no
Style guide: MOS
Preferred length: 30 pages
Number of copies: 2
Notes: end of manuscript
Blind referee: no
Time to consider manuscript: 4 months
**Proportion of manuscripts
accepted:** 2/5
Illustrations accepted: tables, charts
Foreign languages: no

Reviews
Seeking reviewers: yes
Unsolicited reviews accepted: no
How to apply: letter
Include in application: professional
degrees, areas of expertise, current
research
Materials reviewed: books
Length of review: 3 pages

THE HISTORICAL MESSENGER

Focus: United Methodist Church and predecessor denominations in the Central Illinois area, especially 1800–1860
Institutional affiliation: United Methodist Church
Editor: Lynn W. Turner
Address: Box 2050
Bloomington, IL 61701
Frequency: 4/year
Circulation: 800
Pages/issue: 4
Readership: United Methodist ministers, church historians, general public

Manuscripts
Query: yes
Abstract: no
Preferred length: 3 pages maximum
Number of copies: 1
Notes: notes unnecessary
Blind referee: no
Time to consider manuscript: 1 week
Proportion of manuscripts accepted: very high
Illustrations accepted: tables, graphs, charts, pictures (small)
Foreign languages: no

HISTORICAL METHODS

Focus: social science, quantitative and computer methodology
Institutional affiliation: University of Illinois at Chicago Circle
Editor: Daniel Scott Smith
Address: Department of History
University of Illinois at Chicago Circle
Chicago, IL 60680
Frequency: 4/year
Circulation: 800
Pages/issue: 48
Readership: academics, scholars

Manuscripts
Query: no
Abstract: no
Style guide: MOS
Preferred length: 20–30 pages
Number of copies: 2
Notes: end of manuscript
Blind referee: no
Time to consider manuscript: 4 months
Proportion of manuscripts accepted: 1/5
Illustrations accepted: camera-ready tables, graphs, charts, pictures
Foreign languages: no

Reviews
Seeking reviewers: yes
Unsolicited reviews accepted: no
How to apply: letter
Materials reviewed: books
Length of review: 20–30 pages

Additional notes
Historical Methods publishes a small number of reviews (or essay reviews) on major works in historical methods.

HISTORICAL NEW HAMPSHIRE

Focus: New Hampshire
Institutional affiliation: New Hampshire
    Historical Society
Editor: R. Stuart Wallace
Book review editor: same
Address: 30 Park Street
          Concord, NH 03301
Frequency: 4/year
Circulation: 2,000
Pages/issue: 100
Readership: academics, general public

Manuscripts

Query: no
Abstract: no
Style guide: MOS
Preferred length: 2,500–6,000 words
Number of copies: 2
Notes: end of manuscript
Blind referee: no
Time to consider manuscript: 3 weeks
**Proportion of manuscripts
    accepted:** 1/10
Illustrations accepted: tables, graphs,
    charts, pictures
Foreign languages: no

Reviews

Seeking reviewers: yes
Unsolicited reviews accepted: no
How to apply: letter
Include in application: professional
    degrees, institutional affiliation, areas
    of expertise, published works, current
    research
Materials reviewed: books
Length of review: 1,000–1,200 words

HISTORICAL REFLECTIONS
REFLEXIONS HISTORIQUES

Focus: interpretive essays, from any field
    of history but of broad general interest
Institutional affiliation: Department of
    History, University of Waterloo
Editors: D. N. Baker, S. K. Johannesen,
    J. F. H. New
Address: Department of History
        University of Waterloo
        Waterloo, Ontario N2L 3G1
        CANADA
Frequency: 2/year
Circulation: 400
Pages/issue: 150
Readership: academics, scholars, buffs

Manuscripts

Query: no
Abstract: no
Style guide: MOS
Preferred length: varies
Number of copies: 1
Notes: end of manuscript
Blind referee: no
Time to consider manuscript: 6–8
    weeks
Illustrations accepted: tables, graphs,
    charts
Foreign languages: French

HISTORICAL SOCIETY OF MICHIGAN CHRONICLE

Focus: Michigan
Institutional affiliation: Historical Society of Michigan
Editor: Kristine Moore Meves
Address: Historical Society of Michigan
2117 Washtenaw Avenue
Ann Arbor, MI 48104
Frequency: 4/year
Circulation: 6,500
Pages/issue: 32
Readership: Society members, scholars, teachers, museum curators, archivists

Manuscripts
Query: yes (mention available illustrations)
Abstract: no
Style guide: none
Preferred length: 3,000 words
Number of copies: 1
Notes: end of manuscript
Blind referee: no
Time to consider manuscript: 2 months
Proportion of manuscripts accepted: 1/5
Illustrations accepted: pictures (availability of good illustrations is an important consideration in deciding whether to accept an article)
Foreign languages: no

Additional notes
Articles for the *Chronicle* should be written in a fresh, lively style that avoids both the flowery and the pedantic. The *Chronicle* does not seek scholarly dissertations, but the author of a long or scholarly work may wish to submit a shorter article on the same subject that has been rewritten in an informal style.

HISTORICALLY SPEAKING

Focus: museum and historical agency work
Institutional affiliation: Illinois State Historical Society
Editor: Blanche Burgess
Address: Illinois State Historical Library
Old State Capitol
Springfield, IL 62706
Frequency: 4/year
Circulation: 600
Pages/issue: 8
Readership: museum and historical agency personnel and volunteers

Manuscripts
Query: yes
Abstract: no
Style guide: MLA
Preferred length: 2–4 pages
Number of copies: 2
Notes: end of manuscript
Blind referee: no
Time to consider manuscript: 2–3 weeks
Proportion of manuscripts accepted: 7/10
Illustrations accepted: camera-ready tables, graphs, charts, pictures
Foreign languages: no

THE HISTORY AND SOCIAL SCIENCE TEACHER

Focus: social science teaching
Editor: G. Milburn
Address: Faculty of Education
University of Western Ontario
1137 Wetstern Road
London, Ontario N6G 1G7
CANADA
Frequency: 4/year
Circulation: 4,000
Pages/issue: 84
Readership: academics, general public

Manuscripts
Query: no
Abstract: yes
Style guide: own
Preferred length: 16 pages
Number of copies: 3
Notes: end of manuscript
Blind referee: yes
Time to consider manuscript: 6 weeks
**Proportion of manuscripts
accepted:** 3/10
Illustrations accepted: tables, graphs,
charts, pictures
Foreign languages: no

Reviews
Seeking reviewers: yes
Unsolicited reviews accepted: yes
How to apply: letter
Include in application: institutional
affiliation, areas of expertise
Materials reviewed: books, films, audio
Length of review: 400 words

Additional notes
The History and Social Science Teacher will
publish original contributions to curriculum
theory, planning, and development related
to the study of history and the social
sciences. It will also publish original
contributions to the theory and practice of
teaching and learning related to the study
of history and the social sciences.
Unsolicited manuscripts are welcomed.

The publication is intended to be a
vehicle to effect systematic communication
among professional educators. Where
possible, authors are urged to consider
developing practical examples to illustrate
their arguments.

HISTORY AND THEORY: STUDIES IN THE PHILOSOPHY OF HISTORY

Focus: theories of history; historiography;
method of history
Institutional affiliation: Wesleyan
University
Editor: Richard T. Vann
Book review editor: Richard V. Buel
Address: Wesleyan Station
Middletown, CT 06457
Frequency: 4/year
Circulation: 2,500
Pages/issue: 120
Readership: academics

Manuscripts
Query: no
Abstract: no
Style guide: own
Number of copies: 1
Notes: end of manuscript
Time to consider manuscript: 6
weeks–2 months
Illustrations accepted: tables, graphs,
charts, pictures
Foreign languages: French

Reviews
**Unsolicited reviews
accepted:** occasionally
How to apply: letter
Include in application: areas of
expertise, published works
Materials reviewed: books
Length of review: 3,000 words minimum

THE HISTORY BOOK CLUB REVIEW

Focus: all fields
Editor: Nancy R. M. Whitin
Address: 40 Guernsey St.
Stamford, CT 06904
Frequency: 13/year
Circulation: 100,000
Pages/issue: 32
Readership: scholars, professionals
(lawyers, doctors, etc.)

Reviews
Seeking reviewers: yes
Unsolicited reviews accepted: no
How to apply: letter
Include in application: professional
degrees, institutional affiliation, areas
of expertise, published works, current
research
Materials reviewed: books
Length of review: 750–1,000 words

HISTORY IN AFRICA: A JOURNAL OF METHOD

Focus: historical method, source
criticism, philosophy of history,
archives as they relate to Africa;
comparative history
Editor: David Henige
Address: Memorial Library
University of Wisconsin
Madison, WI 53706
Frequency: 1/year
Circulation: 450
Pages/issue: 380
Readership: academics

Manuscripts
Query: no
Abstract: no
Style guide: MOS
Preferred length: 12,000 words
maximum
Number of copies: 2
Notes: end of manuscript
Blind referee: yes
Time to consider manuscript: 6–8
weeks
**Proportion of manuscripts
accepted:** 3/10
Illustrations accepted: camera-ready
tables, graphs, charts, pictures
Foreign languages: French

Reviews
Seeking reviewers: no
Unsolicited reviews accepted: yes
Length of review: 2,500–6,500 words

HISTORY NEWS

Focus: historical societies, museums, grant funding, practical projects, ideas, technical leaflets, seminars
Institutional affiliation: American Association for State and Local History
Editor: Betty Doak Elder
Address: 1400 Eighth Avenue, South Nashville, TN 37203
Frequency: 1/month
Circulation: 6,000
Pages/issue: 24
Readership: historical society and museum personnel, librarians, archivists, preservationists

Manuscripts
Query: no
Abstract: helpful
Style guide: MOS
Notes: no notes
Illustrations accepted: pictures
Foreign languages: no

Reviews
Seeking reviewers: yes
Unsolicited reviews accepted: no
How to apply: letter
Include in application: areas of expertise, published works
Materials reviewed: books

HISTORY, NUMBERS, AND WAR

Focus: military; Soviet and Middle East military affairs
Editor: Gay Hammerman
Book review editor: same
Address: Historical Evaluation and Research Organization P.O. Box 157 Dunn Loring, VA 22027
Frequency: 4/year
Circulation: 200
Pages/issue: 60
Readership: military personnel, buffs; general public, Defense Department, and academic libraries

Manuscripts
Query: no
Abstract: desired
Style guide: MOS preferred
Preferred length: 30 pages
Time to consider manuscript: varies
Proportion of manuscripts accepted: 1/2
Illustrations accepted: tables, graphs, charts, pictures, line-drawing maps (see Additional notes below)
Foreign languages: no

Reviews
Seeking reviewers: yes
Unsolicited reviews accepted: yes
How to apply: letter
Include in application: professional degrees, institutional affiliation, areas of expertise, published works, current research
Materials reviewed: books
Length of review: see Additional notes

Additional notes
Provide camera-ready originals for publication. These need not be submitted with manuscript; reprographed copies will be fine for the initial submission. Line drawings are preferred to photographs, but photographs are acceptable if appropriate. Authors should provide clear, glossy prints. Length of reviews is widely variable. A good essay, up to article length, would be welcome.

HISTORY OF EDUCATION QUARTERLY

Focus: the intellectual and social history of education, of educational ideas; comparative education; analysis of educational thinkers and philosophers; studies of family and childhood
Institutional affiliation: History of Education Society
Editor: Robin Berson
Book review editor: Paul H. Mattingly
Address: 737 East Bldg.,
New York University
239 Greene Street, Washington Square
New York, NY 10003
Frequency: 4/year
Circulation: 2,000
Pages/issue: 128
Readership: scholars, educators

Manuscripts
Query: no
Abstract: no
Style guide: MOS
Preferred length: 20–25 pages
Number of copies: 2
Notes: end of manuscript
Blind referee: yes
Time to consider manuscript: 1–2 months
Proportion of manuscripts accepted: 1/10–1/7
Illustrations accepted: tables, graphs, charts, pictures
Foreign languages: if accepted by the referee process; English preferred

Reviews
Seeking reviewers: yes
Unsolicited reviews accepted: occasionally
How to apply: letter
Include in application: professional degrees, institutional affiliation, areas of expertise, published works, foreign languages, current research, HES membership
Materials reviewed: books
Length of review: 5–8 pages; 10–15 pages for essay reviews

Additional notes
Original thought is essential for acceptance.

HISTORY OF POLITICAL ECONOMY

Focus: economic thought and policy
Institutional affiliation: Duke University
Editor: Craufurd D. Goodwin
Book review editor: S. Todd Lowry
Address: Department of Economics
Duke University
Durham, NC 27706
Frequency: 4/year
Circulation: 1,500
Pages/issue: 135–140
Readership: academics, government officials

Manuscripts

Query: no
Abstract: yes
Style guide: MOS
Preferred length: 20 pages maximum
Number of copies: 2
Notes: end of manuscript
Time to consider manuscript: 2–3 months
Proportion of manuscripts accepted: 1/4
Illustrations accepted: camera-ready tables, graphs, charts, pictures
Foreign languages: no

Reviews

Seeking reviewers: yes
Unsolicited reviews accepted: no

HISTORY OF RELIGIONS

Focus: comparative and historical study of religious phenomena and traditions
Institutional affiliation: University of Chicago
Editor: Mircea Eliade
Address: Swift Hall
1025 East 58th St.
Chicago, IL 60637
Frequency: 4/year
Circulation: 2,200
Pages/issue: 100
Readership: academics

Manuscripts

Query: no
Abstract: no
Style guide: MOS
Preferred length: 30 pages
Number of copies: 1
Notes: end of manuscript (must be double-spaced)
Blind referee: no
Time to consider manuscript: 6 weeks
Illustrations accepted: camera-ready tables, graphs, charts, pictures
Foreign languages: any major language

Reviews

Seeking reviewers: no
Unsolicited reviews accepted: yes

THE HISTORY TEACHER

Focus: craft of teaching, historiography, and state of the profession
Institutional affiliation: California State University, Long Beach
Editor: Albie Burke
Book review editor: William Sater
Address: California State University,
Long Beach
Long Beach, CA 90840
Frequency: 4/year
Circulation: 3,500
Pages/issue: 240
Readership: secondary and college teachers

Manuscripts
Query: no
Abstract: no
Preferred length: 15–30 pages
Number of copies: 1
Notes: end of manuscript
Blind referee: no
Time to consider manuscript: 6–8 weeks
Proportion of manuscripts accepted: 1/10
Illustrations accepted: camera-ready tables, graphs, charts, pictures
Foreign languages: no

Reviews
Seeking reviewers: yes
Unsolicited reviews accepted: no
How to apply: letter
Include in application: professional degrees, institutional affiliation, areas of expertise, published works, foreign languages, current research
Materials reviewed: books, films
Length of review: 500 words

THE HUMANITIES ASSOCIATION REVIEW LA REVUE DE L'ASSOCIATION DES HUMANITES

Focus: all humanities, fine arts, religion; comparative and interdisciplinary studies especially welcome
Institutional affiliation: The Humanities Association of Canada
Editor: P. W. Rogers
Book review editor: same
Address: John Watson Hall
Queen's University
Kingston, Ontario
CANADA
Frequency: 4/year
Circulation: 900
Pages/issue: 96–112
Readership: Association members, academics, general public

Manuscripts
Query: no
Abstract: yes
Style guide: MLA
Preferred length: 20–30 pages
Number of copies: 2
Notes: end of manuscript
Blind referee: no
Time to consider manuscript: 6 months
Proportion of manuscripts accepted: 3/10
Illustrations accepted: tables, graphs, charts, pictures
Foreign languages: French

Reviews
Seeking reviewers: no
Unsolicited reviews accepted: no
How to apply: letter
Include in application: professional degrees, institutional affiliation, areas of expertise, published works, foreign languages, current research
Materials reviewed: books
Length of review: 800–1,000 words

HUNTSVILLE HISTORICAL REVIEW

Focus: Huntsville and Madison County, Alabama
Editor: Henry S. Marks
Book review editor: same
Address: 301–2 Terry Hutchens Bldg. Huntsville, AL 35801
Frequency: 2/year
Circulation: 200
Pages/issue: 40–50
Readership: general public

Manuscripts

Query: no
Abstract: no
Style guide: MOS
Preferred length: open
Number of copies: 1
Notes: end of manuscript
Blind referee: no
Time to consider manuscript: 1 month
Proportion of manuscripts accepted: 1/2
Illustrations accepted: tables, graphs, charts, pictures
Foreign languages: no

Reviews

Seeking reviewers: no
Unsolicited reviews accepted: no
How to apply: letter
Include in application: professional degrees, institutional affiliation, areas of expertise, published works, current research
Materials reviewed: books
Length of review: open

IDAHO YESTERDAYS

Focus: Idaho and Pacific Northwest
Institutional affiliation: Idaho State Historical Society
Editor: Judith Austin
Book review editor: same
Address: 610 North Julia Davis Drive Boise, ID 83702
Frequency: 4/year
Circulation: 1,300
Pages/issue: 32
Readership: Society members, general public, scholars, libraries

Manuscripts

Query: no
Abstract: no
Preferred length: 20 pages maximum
Number of copies: 1
Notes: bottom of page
Blind referee: no
Time to consider manuscript: 2 months
Proportion of manuscripts accepted: 4/5
Illustrations accepted: tables, graphs, charts, pictures
Foreign languages: no

Reviews

Seeking reviewers: yes
Unsolicited reviews accepted: no
How to apply: letter
Include in application: professional degrees, institutional affiliation, areas of expertise, current research
Materials reviewed: books
Length of review: 500 words

IMMIGRATION HISTORY NEWSLETTER

Focus: immigration and ethnic groups
Institutional affiliation: Immigration History Society, c/o Minnesota Historical Society
Editor: Carlton C. Qualey
Book review editor: same
Address: Minnesota Historical Society
690 Cedar Street
St. Paul, MN 55101
Frequency: 2/year
Circulation: 600
Pages/issue: 20
Readership: scholars, libraries

Manuscripts
Query: yes
Abstract: no
Style guide: MOS
Preferred length: 12 pages
Number of copies: 1
Notes: end of manuscript
Blind referee: no
Time to consider manuscript: 1 month
Proportion of manuscripts accepted: good
Foreign languages: no

Reviews
Seeking reviewers: no
Unsolicited reviews accepted: no
How to apply: letter
Include in application: institutional affiliation, areas of expertise, published works, current research
Materials reviewed: books
Length of review: 100 words

Additional notes
The *Newsletter*'s emphasis is on service to researchers and teachers. Articles should be bibliographical or historiographical or both.

INDIANA HISTORY BULLETIN

Focus: Indiana and Midwest
Institutional affiliation: Indiana Historical Bureau
Editor: Pamela J. Bennett
Address: 408 State Library and Historical Building
140 North Senate Avenue
Indianapolis, IN 46204
Frequency: 1/month
Circulation: 6,000
Pages/issue: 24
Readership: general public, members of historical societies

Manuscripts
Query: no
Abstract: no
Style guide: MOS
Preferred length: 10–20 pages
Number of copies: 1
Notes: end of manuscript
Blind referee: no
Time to consider manuscript: 3–6 months
Proportion of manuscripts accepted: 1/2–3/4
Illustrations accepted: tables, graphs, charts, pictures
Foreign languages: no

Reviews
Seeking reviewers: yes
Unsolicited reviews accepted: no
How to apply: letter
Include in application: institutional affiliation, areas of expertise, current research
Materials reviewed: books, films, audio
Length of review: 250 words

INDIANA MAGAZINE OF HISTORY

Focus: Indiana and Old Northwest
Institutional affiliation: Indiana Historical Society and History Department, Indiana University
Editor: James H. Madison
Book review editor: Lorna Lutes Sylvester
Address: Department of History
Ballantine Hall, 742
Indiana University
Bloomington, IN 47401
Frequency: 4/year
Circulation: 5,154
Pages/issue: 100
Readership: academics, general public

Manuscripts
Query: no
Abstract: no
Style guide: own
Preferred length: 20–30 pages
Number of copies: 2
Notes: end of manuscript
Blind referee: yes
Time to consider manuscript: 4–6 weeks
Proportion of manuscripts accepted: 1/4–1/5
Illustrations accepted: tables, graphs, charts, pictures, black-and-white illustrations, captioned photographs
Foreign languages: no

Reviews
Seeking reviewers: yes
Unsolicited reviews accepted: no
How to apply: letter
Include in application: professional degrees, institutional affiliation, areas of expertise, published works, current research
Materials reviewed: books
Length of review: 400–500 words

INDIANA SOCIAL STUDIES QUARTERLY

Focus: social sciences
Institutional affiliation: Ball State University and Indiana Council for the Social Studies
Editor: Richard Wires
Address: History Department
Ball State University
Muncie, IN 47306
Frequency: 4/year
Circulation: 1,250
Pages/issue: 110
Readership: academics, libraries

Manuscripts
Query: yes
Abstract: no
Style guide: MOS
Preferred length: 4,000–4,500 words
Number of copies: 3
Notes: end of manuscript
Blind referee: yes
Time to consider manuscript: 2 months
Proportion of manuscripts accepted: 1/2
Illustrations accepted: tables, graphs, charts
Foreign languages: no

Reviews
Seeking reviewers: yes
Unsolicited reviews accepted: yes
How to apply: letter
Include in application: professional degrees, institutional affiliation, areas of expertise, current research
Materials reviewed: books
Length of review: 2,000–4,500 words

Additional notes
Issues are always thematic, self-contained works. Many articles are commissioned. The only book reviews published are essays dealing with two or more related books.

INLAND SEAS

Focus: Great Lakes
Institutional affiliation: Great Lakes Historical Society
Editor: Janet Coe Sanborn
Address: 2237 Westminster Road
Cleveland Heights, OH 44118
Frequency: 4/year
Circulation: 3,000
Pages/issue: 84
Readership: general public, historians, researchers in geography, ships, and commerce

Manuscripts
Query: no
Abstract: no
Style guide: GPO
Number of copies: 1
Notes: end of manuscript
Blind referee: no
Illustrations accepted: charts, pictures
Foreign languages: no

Reviews
Seeking reviewers: no
Unsolicited reviews accepted: no

INTERNATIONAL JOURNAL

Focus: each issue is devoted to a collection of articles related by a broad theme
Institutional affiliation: Canadian Institute of International Affairs
Editors: Robert Spencer, James Eayrs
Address: Canadian Institute of
International Affairs
15 King's College Circle
Toronto, Ontario M5S 2V9
CANADA
Frequency: 4/year
Circulation: 3,200
Pages/issue: 208
Readership: academics, general public

Manuscripts
Query: recommended
Abstract: no
Style guide: MOS
Preferred length: 6,000 words maximum
Number of copies: 2 preferred
Notes: end of manuscript
Blind referee: no
Time to consider manuscript: 5–7 weeks
Proportion of manuscripts accepted: 1/3
Illustrations accepted: tables, camera-ready graphs and charts
Foreign languages: French

Reviews
Seeking reviewers: yes
Unsolicited reviews accepted: no
How to apply: letter
Include in application: institutional affiliation, areas of expertise, published works
Materials reviewed: books
Length of review: 300–400 words

Additional notes
Each issue is on a theme; themes are announced in advance on verso of title page of each journal.

INTERNATIONAL JOURNAL OF AFRICAN HISTORICAL STUDIES

Focus: Africa and archaeology
Institutional affiliation: Boston University
Editor: Norman R. Bennett
Address: African Studies Center
Boston University
Brookline, MA 02146
Frequency: 4/year
Circulation: 800
Pages/issue: 192
Readership: academics

Manuscripts
Query: no
Abstract: no
Style guide: own, based on MOS
Preferred length: no limits
Number of copies: 2
Notes: end of manuscript
Blind referee: yes
Time to consider manuscript: 3–6 months
Proportion of manuscripts accepted: 1/2
Illustrations accepted: camera-ready tables, graphs, charts, pictures
Foreign languages: French

Reviews
Seeking reviewers: yes
Unsolicited reviews accepted: occasionally
How to apply: form
Materials reviewed: books, reference works
Length of review: no limits

INTERNATIONAL JOURNAL OF ORAL HISTORY

Focus: oral history as it relates to the broad concept of social, political, and economic history, as well as anthropology; theory and method of oral history
Editor: Ronald J. Grele
Book review editor: same
Address: 615 South First Avenue
Highland Park, NJ 08904
Frequency: 3/year
Circulation: 1,000 (projected)
Pages/issue: 64–72
Readership: researchers, academics

Manuscripts
Query: advised
Abstract: useful
Style guide: own (a composite of MOS and MLA)
Preferred length: 12–15 pages
Number of copies: 2
Notes: end of manuscript
Blind referee: no
Time to consider manuscript: 2–4 weeks
Illustrations accepted: exact scale tables, graphs, charts, pictures (glossy prints)
Foreign languages: major European languages

Reviews
Seeking reviewers: yes
Unsolicited reviews accepted: no
How to apply: letter
Include in application: professional degrees, areas of expertise and interest
Materials reviewed: books, equipment (recording, transcribing)
Length of review: 4–5 pages minimum (longer for review essays)

INTERNATIONAL LABOR AND WORKING CLASS HISTORY

Focus: trade unionism, socialism, communism, and other workers' political movements; working class culture, immigration, women, and the family
Institutional affiliation: Yale University
Editor: David Montgomery
Book review editor: same
Address: Department of History
Yale University
New Haven, CT 06520
Frequency: 2/year
Circulation: 450
Pages/issue: 100
Readership: academics, general public

Reviews
Seeking reviewers: yes
Unsolicited reviews accepted: yes
How to apply: letter
Include in application: institutional affiliation, areas of expertise, current research
Materials reviewed: books, films, audio
Length of review: 1,000–2,000 words

Additional notes
International Labor and Working Class History does not publish research articles. The majority of the journal is devoted to book reviews, with some attention paid to conferences, news and announcements, and listings of current research of people working in labor and working class history.

ISIS

Focus: science and its cultural influences
Institutional affiliation: History of Science Society
Address: Department of History and Sociology of Science
University of Pennsylvania D6
215 South 34th Street
Philadelphia, PA 19104
Frequency: 5/year
Circulation: 3,000
Pages/issue: 160
Readership: academics

Manuscripts
Query: no
Abstract: no
Style guide: own
Preferred length: 5,000–8,000 words
Number of copies: 3
Notes: end of manuscript
Blind referee: yes
Time to consider manuscript: 2–4 months
Proportion of manuscripts accepted: 1/4
Illustrations accepted: tables, graphs, charts, pictures, camera-ready line drawings (glossy prints of all halftone illustrations)
Foreign languages: no

Reviews
Seeking reviewers: yes
Unsolicited reviews accepted: no
How to apply: letter
Include in application: professional degrees, institutional affiliation, areas of expertise, published works, foreign languages, current research
Materials reviewed: books, films
Length of review: 700 words

JOURNAL OF AFRICAN STUDIES

Focus: African studies
Institutional affiliation: African Studies Center, UCLA
Editor: Lorraine Gardner
Address: University of California
Los Angeles, CA 90024
Frequency: 4/year
Circulation: 600
Pages/issue: 64
Readership: academics, general public

Manuscripts
Query: no
Abstract: no
Style guide: MOS
Preferred length: 30 pages
Number of copies: 1
Notes: end of manuscript
Blind referee: no
Time to consider manuscript: 6 months to 1 year
Proportion of manuscripts accepted: 2/3
Illustrations accepted: camera-ready tables, graphs, charts, pictures
Foreign languages: no

Reviews
Seeking reviewers: yes
Unsolicited reviews accepted: yes
How to apply: letter
Include in application: institutional affiliation
Materials reviewed: books

JOURNAL OF AMERICAN CULTURE

Focus: American culture
Institutional affiliation: Bowling Green State University
Editor: Ray B. Browne
Book review editor: Pat Browne
Address: Popular Culture Center
Bowling Green State University
Bowling Green, OH 43403
Frequency: 4/year
Circulation: 1,000
Pages/issue: 200
Readership: academics

Manuscripts
Query: no
Abstract: no
Style guide: MLA
Preferred length: 12–18 pages
Number of copies: 1
Notes: end of manuscript
Blind referee: no
Time to consider manuscript: 1 month
Proportion of manuscripts accepted: 1/5
Illustrations accepted: tables, graphs, charts, pictures
Foreign languages: no

Reviews
Seeking reviewers: yes
Unsolicited reviews accepted: yes
How to apply: letter
Include in application: professional degrees, institutional affiliation, areas of expertise, current research
Materials reviewed: trade books
Length of review: 150–250 words

JOURNAL OF AMERICAN FOLKLORE

Focus: scholarly studies of current folklore theory with emphasis on analysis and interpretation
Institutional affiliation: American Folklore Society
Editor: Jan Harold Brunvand
Book review editor: W. K. McNeil
Address: University of Utah
Salt Lake City, UT 84112
Frequency: 4/year
Circulation: 2,000
Pages/issue: 125
Readership: professional folklorists

Manuscripts
Query: no
Abstract: no
Style guide: own, based on MLA
Preferred length: 40 pages
Number of copies: 2
Notes: end of manuscript
Blind referee: yes
Time to consider manuscript: 6 weeks
Proportion of manuscripts accepted: 1/10
Illustrations accepted: crisp, clear copies of tables, graphs, charts, pictures
Foreign languages: no

Reviews
Seeking reviewers: yes
Unsolicited reviews accepted: yes
How to apply: letter
Include in application: professional degrees, areas of expertise, foreign languages
Materials reviewed: books, films, audio
Length of review: concise

Additional notes
Strictly a scholarly journal interested in the work of professional or trained folklorists.

JOURNAL OF AMERICAN HISTORY

Focus: all periods and methods in American history
Institutional affiliation: Organization of American Historians
Editor: Lewis Perry
Book review editor: Stephen Vaughn
Address: 702 Ballantine Hall
Indiana University
Bloomington, IN 47405
Frequency: 4/year
Circulation: 12,500
Pages/issue: 270
Readership: academics, scholars, general public

Manuscripts
Query: no
Abstract: no
Style guide: MOS
Preferred length: 22–29 pages
Number of copies: 2
Notes: end of manuscript
Blind referee: yes
Time to consider manuscript: 12 weeks
Proportion of manuscripts accepted: 1/20
Illustrations accepted: tables, graphs, charts, pictures
Foreign languages: no

Reviews
Seeking reviewers: yes
Unsolicited reviews accepted: no
How to apply: 5" x 8" card
Include in application: professional degrees, institutional affiliation, areas of expertise, published works, foreign languages, current research
Materials reviewed: books
Length of review: 400 words, sometimes longer

THE JOURNAL OF ARIZONA HISTORY

Focus: Arizona
Institutional affiliation: Arizona Historical Society
Editor: Tracy Row
Book review editor: same
Address: Arizona Historical Society
949 East Second Street
Tucson, AZ 85719
Frequency: 4/year
Circulation: 3,800
Pages/issue: 120
Readership: academics, general public

Manuscripts
Query: no
Abstract: no
Style guide: none required; MOS generally followed
Preferred length: 20–25 pages
Number of copies: 1
Notes: end of manuscript
Blind referee: no
Time to consider manuscript: 2–3 weeks
Proportion of manuscripts accepted: 3/5
Illustrations accepted: pertinent illustrations, tables, or appendixes (photocopies are acceptable)
Foreign languages: no

Reviews
Seeking reviewers: yes
Unsolicited reviews accepted: no
How to apply: letter
Include in application: professional degrees, institutional affiliation, areas of expertise, published works
Materials reviewed: books
Length of review: 300–500 words

Additional notes
The editors prefer original and imaginative papers which are slanted toward personalities and the events created by personal action.

JOURNAL OF ASIAN STUDIES

Focus: Southern, Eastern and Northern Asia, China, inner Asia
Institutional affiliation: Association for Asian Studies
Editor: Joyce K. Kallgren
Book review editor: see Additional notes
Address: Barrows Hall
University of California
Berkeley, CA 94720
Frequency: 4/year
Circulation: 8,500
Pages/issue: 240
Readership: scholars

Manuscripts
Query: no
Abstract: yes
Style guide: MOS
Preferred length: 40 pages maximum
Number of copies: 3
Notes: end of manuscript
Blind referee: yes
Time to consider manuscript: 2–3 months
Illustrations accepted: tables, graphs, charts, pictures, within limits
Foreign languages: rarely; only for book reviews and short notes, and with a translation

Reviews
Seeking reviewers: yes
Unsolicited reviews accepted: yes
How to apply: letter
Include in application: professional degrees, institutional affiliation, areas of expertise, published works, foreign languages, current research
Materials reviewed: books; films occasionally
Length of review: 600–1,000 words

(continued on next page)

JOURNAL OF ASIAN STUDIES
(continued)

Additional notes

For an extended exposition of the *Journal*'s interests and policies, see the November 1978 issue, pages 7–9. There are five book review editors, according to geographical region.

China: Guy Alitto
  Department of History
  University of Chicago
  Chicago, IL 60680

Korea: Karl Moskowitz
  Department of East Asian
  Languages and Civilizations
  Harvard University
  Cambridge, MA 02138

Japan: Peter Duus
  Department of History
  Stanford University
  Palo Alto, CA 94305

South Asia: Barbara Metcalf
  c/o JOURNAL OF ASIAN
  STUDIES
  Barrows Hall
  University of California
  Berkeley, CA 94720

Southeast Asia: William Keyes
  Department of Anthropology
  University of Washington
  Seattle, WA 98195

JOURNAL OF BLACK STUDIES

Focus: interdisciplinary African and African–American studies
Editor: Molefi Kete Asante
Book review editor: James Pitts
Address: Department of
  African/African–American
  Studies
  SUNY-Buffalo
  Buffalo, NY 14214
Frequency: 4/year
Circulation: 3,500
Pages/issue: 120
Readership: academics

Manuscripts

Query: no
Abstract: no
Style guide: SAGE
Preferred length: 25 pages maximum
Number of copies: 2
Notes: end of manuscript
Blind referee: yes
Time to consider manuscript: 2 months
Illustrations accepted: tables, graphs, charts, pictures
Foreign languages: no

Reviews

Unsolicited reviews accepted: yes
How to apply: letter
Include in application: professional degrees, institutional affiliation, areas of expertise, foreign languages
Materials reviewed: books, films, audio
Length of review: 3 pages

JOURNAL OF BRITISH STUDIES

Focus: British studies
Institutional affiliation: University of Illinois at Chicago Circle
Editor: Bentley B. Gilbert
Address: Department of History
University of Illinois at Chicago Circle
Chicago, IL 60680
Frequency: 2/year
Circulation: 1,500
Pages/issue: 176
Readership: academics

Manuscripts
Query: no
Abstract: no
Style guide: MOS
Preferred length: 8,000 words
Number of copies: 2
Notes: bottom of page
Blind referee: no
Time to consider manuscript: 3–4 months
Proportion of manuscripts accepted: 1/10
Illustrations accepted: tables, graphs, charts
Foreign languages: no

JOURNAL OF CANADIAN STUDIES REVUE D'ETUDES CANADIENNES

Focus: Canada
Institutional affiliation: Trent University
Editor: Arlene Davis
Book review editor: John Wadland
Address: Champlain College
Trent University
Peterborough, Ontario K9J 7B8
CANADA
Frequency: 4/year
Circulation: 1,650
Pages/issue: 128
Readership: academics, academic libraries

Manuscripts
Query: no
Abstract: no
Preferred length: 2,000–10,000 words
Number of copies: 2
Notes: end of manuscript
Blind referee: no
Time to consider manuscript: 6 months
Illustrations accepted: tables, graphs, charts, pictures
Foreign languages: French

Reviews
Seeking reviewers: no

JOURNAL OF CONFLICT RESOLUTION

Focus: research on war and peace between and within nations
Institutional affiliation: Yale University
Editor: Bruce M. Russett
Address: P.O. Box 3532 Yale Station
New Haven, CT 06520
Frequency: 4/year
Circulation: 3,000
Pages/issue: 200
Readership: academics

Manuscripts
Query: no
Abstract: yes
Style guide: SAGE
Preferred length: 40 pages maximum
Number of copies: 3
Notes: end of manuscript
Blind referee: yes
Time to consider manuscript: 3 months
Proportion of manuscripts accepted: 1/6–1/5 after revisions
Illustrations accepted: tables, graphs, charts, glossy prints for artwork
Foreign languages: no

Reviews
Unsolicited reviews accepted: yes, treated as any other submitted manuscript
Materials reviewed: scholarly works
Length of review: 10–20 pages

Additional notes
The *Journal* specializes in rigorous, often quantitative research in the social sciences and is interdisciplinary. It publishes occasional reviews of a group of recent related books; and solicits reviews from well-known scholars.

JOURNAL OF DEVELOPING AREAS

Focus: Third World development
Institutional affiliation: Western Illinois University
Editor: Nicholas C. Pano
Book review editor: A. R. Longwell
Address: Western Illinois University
Macomb, IL 61455
Frequency: 4/year
Circulation: 1,650
Pages/issue: 135
Readership: academics

Manuscripts
Query: no
Abstract: no
Style guide: MOS
Preferred length: 20–30 pages
Number of copies: 3
Notes: end of manuscript
Blind referee: yes
Time to consider manuscript: 4 months
Proportion of manuscripts accepted: 1/12
Illustrations accepted: camera-ready tables, graphs, charts
Foreign languages: no

Reviews
Seeking reviewers: yes
Unsolicited reviews accepted: no
How to apply: form
Include in application: institutional affiliation, areas of expertise
Materials reviewed: books
Length of review: 500 words

JOURNAL OF ECONOMIC HISTORY

Focus: demography, econometrics, history of economic thought
Institutional affiliation: North Carolina State University
Editor: Richard Sylla
Book review editor: same
Address: Department of Business and Economics
North Carolina State University
Raleigh, NC 27650
Frequency: 4/year
Circulation: 2,500
Pages/issue: 250
Readership: academics

Manuscripts
Query: no
Abstract: only if accepted for publication
Style guide: MOS
Preferred length: 30 pages maximum
Number of copies: 3
Notes: end of manuscript
Blind referee: yes
Time to consider manuscript: 3 months
Proportion of manuscripts accepted: 1/15–1/10
Illustrations accepted: professionally drawn tables, graphs, charts, pictures
Foreign languages: French, very rarely

Reviews
Seeking reviewers: yes
Unsolicited reviews accepted: no
How to apply: form or letter
Include in application: professional degrees, institutional affiliation, areas of expertise, published works, foreign languages, current research
Materials reviewed: books
Length of review: 500 words maximum

Additional notes
Articles submitted by authors who are not members of the Economic History Association should be accompanied by the $15 submission fee.

JOURNAL OF ERIE STUDIES

Focus: northwest Pennsylvania
Institutional affiliation: Mercyhurst College
Editor: Michael McQuillen
Address: 501 East 38th Street
Erie, PA 16501
Frequency: 2/year
Circulation: 600
Pages/issue: 80
Readership: general public

Manuscripts
Query: no
Abstract: no
Preferred length: 20 pages
Number of copies: 2
Notes: end of manuscript
Blind referee: no
Time to consider manuscript: 2 months
Illustrations accepted: tables, graphs, charts, pictures
Foreign languages: no

THE JOURNAL OF ETHNIC STUDIES

Focus: interdisciplinary scholarship, opinion, and creative expression
Institutional affiliation: Western Washington University
Editor: Jesse Hiraoka
Book review editor: same
Address: College of Ethnic Studies
Western Washington State College
Bellingham, WA 98225
Frequency: 4/year
Circulation: 800
Pages/issue: 128
Readership: academics, government employees, general public

Manuscripts
Query: no
Abstract: no
Number of copies: 2
Notes: end of manuscript
Blind referee: no
Time to consider manuscript: 3 months maximum
Proportion of manuscripts accepted: 1/20–1/10
Illustrations accepted: tables, graphs, charts, pictures
Foreign languages: no

Reviews
Seeking reviewers: yes
Unsolicited reviews accepted: yes
How to apply: letter
Include in application: institutional affiliation, areas of expertise
Materials reviewed: books, fiction
Length of review: variable

Additional notes
The Journal prefers theoretical materials, articles exploring new areas and topics. Articles should not be highly specialized or limited in scope, but should state their position clearly.

JOURNAL OF FOREST HISTORY

Focus: forestry, conservation, forest industries, and man-forest relationships
Institutional affiliation: Forest History Society
Editor: Ronald J. Fahl
Book review editor: same
Address: Forest History Society
109 Coral Street
Santa Cruz, CA 95060
Frequency: 4/year
Circulation: 1,900
Pages/issue: 52–64
Readership: foresters, businessmen, scholars, general public

Manuscripts
Query: no
Abstract: no
Style guide: MOS
Preferred length: 8–30 pages
Number of copies: 2
Notes: end of manuscript
Blind referee: yes
Time to consider manuscript: 2–6 months
Proportion of manuscripts accepted: 3/10–1/2
Illustrations accepted: tables, graphs, charts, pictures
Foreign languages: no

Reviews
Seeking reviewers: yes
Unsolicited reviews accepted: no
How to apply: letter
Include in application: professional degrees, institutional affiliation, areas of expertise, published works, current research
Materials reviewed: books
Length of review: variable

(continued on next page)

JOURNAL OF FOREST HISTORY

(continued)

Additional notes

Submitted articles should concern some important aspect of North American forest and conservation history, either wholly or in relation to another subject or geographical area. The editors especially invite articles based on original research in archival and manuscript sources which contribute knowledge not previously illuminated in a published work. Articles concerning local history or minor figures should be explicitly and analytically related to broader historical themes.

The Forest History Society grants two awards annually for excellent articles in the field of forest and conservation history. The Frederick K. Weyerhaeuser Award is given to the author of the best scholarly article published in the *Journal of Forest History.* The Theodore C. Blegen Award recognizes the best scholarly article to appear in another journal.

THE JOURNAL OF HISTORICAL STUDIES

Focus: general interest
Institutional affiliation: Organization of Historical Studies, American University
Editor: Gary L. Braithwaite
Address: Department of History American University Washington, DC 20016
Frequency: intermittent
Circulation: 400
Pages/issue: 75–100
Readership: academics, academic libraries

Manuscripts

Query: no
Abstract: no
Style guide: MOS
Preferred length: 50 pages maximum
Number of copies: 2
Notes: no preference
Blind referee: yes
Time to consider manuscript: 6–9 months
Proportion of manuscripts accepted: 1/5–1/4
Illustrations accepted: tables, graphs, charts, pictures
Foreign languages: no

Additional notes

The Journal is student run and solely for students. It publishes only works by students (i.e., one must have written the article submitted while a full- or part-time student).

JOURNAL OF INTERAMERICAN STUDIES AND WORLD AFFAIRS

Focus: social, economic, political, and cultural aspects of life in Latin America
Institutional affiliation: University of Miami
Editor: John P. Harrison
Address: Box 24-8134
University of Miami
Coral Gables, FL 33124
Frequency: 4/year
Circulation: 2,000
Pages/issue: 145
Readership: scholars, interested public

Manuscripts
Query: no
Abstract: advantageous
Style guide: SAGE
Preferred length: 25 pages
Number of copies: 3
Notes: in text of manuscript
Blind referee: yes
Time to consider manuscript: 1 week to 3 months
Illustrations accepted: camera-ready tables, graphs, charts
Foreign languages: translated if accepted

Reviews
Seeking reviewers: no
Unsolicited reviews accepted: no

Additional notes
Historical articles are limited to 25 percent of each issue. Acceptance is based on quality and relevance to the contemporary scene, whether the topic is pre-Columbian population, the Brazilian experience in higher education, or Haitian historiography. Special consideration is given to diplomatic history when related to contemporary international affairs.

JOURNAL OF INTERDISCIPLINARY HISTORY

Focus: social sciences
Institutional affiliation: Massachusetts Institute of Technology
Editors: Robert I. Rotberg, Theodore K. Rabb
Book review editor: same
Address: 14N-323
Massachusetts Institute of Technology
Cambridge, MA 02139
Frequency: 4/year
Circulation: 2,000
Pages/issue: 186
Readership: academics

Manuscripts
Query: no
Abstract: no
Style guide: own (see inside back cover of any issue)
Preferred length: 30 pages
Number of copies: 2
Notes: end of manuscript
Blind referee: no
Time to consider manuscript: 1 month
Proportion of manuscripts accepted: 1/10
Illustrations accepted: camera-ready tables, graphs, charts, pictures
Foreign languages: no

Reviews
Seeking reviewers: yes
Unsolicited reviews accepted: rarely
How to apply: letter
Include in application: professional degrees, institutional affiliation, areas of expertise, published works, current research
Materials reviewed: books
Length of review: 2–3 pages

Additional notes
Interdisciplinary means explicit methodology and conscious intermarriage of history, social, and other sciences. See the explanatory material on the inside back cover of any issue of the *Journal*.

JOURNAL OF JAPANESE STUDIES

Focus: Japan area studies
Institutional affiliation: Society for Japanese Studies
Editor: Susan B. Hanley
Book review editor: Roy Andrew Miller
Address: Thomson Hall, DR-05
University of Washington
Seattle, WA 98195
Frequency: 2/year
Circulation: 1,500
Pages/issue: 235
Readership: scholars, general public

Manuscripts
Query: no
Abstract: no
Style guide: MOS, own
Preferred length: 35–40 pages
Number of copies: 3
Notes: end of manuscript
Blind referee: yes
Time to consider manuscript: 2–3 months
Proportion of manuscripts accepted: 1/7
Illustrations accepted: tables, camera-ready graphs, charts, pictures (printer can reduce)
Foreign languages: Japanese, major European languages

Reviews
Seeking reviewers: no
Unsolicited reviews accepted: no
Materials reviewed: books

Additional notes
Papers on Japan in any discipline are accepted, but they should be written for a nonspecific readership; that is, jargon should be avoided and specialized terms explained in text or footnote. Papers must also represent a contribution in their field and must be based on original research or fieldwork. Stress is put on interpretation and analysis. Translations of documents and literature are not accepted.

JOURNAL OF MEDIEVAL AND RENAISSANCE STUDIES

Focus: transition from Middle Ages to Renaissance
Institutional affiliation: Duke University
Editor: Marcel Tetel
Address: Duke Station 4666
Durham, NC 27706
Frequency: 2/year
Circulation: 550
Pages/issue: 160
Readership: academics

Manuscripts
Query: no
Abstract: no
Style guide: MLA
Preferred length: 20–30 pages
Number of copies: 1
Notes: end of manuscript
Blind referee: no
Time to consider manuscript: 2–3 months
Proportion of manuscripts accepted: 1/5–1/4
Illustrations accepted: pictures; $20 per page fee for reproduction
Foreign languages: French, Italian, German

THE JOURNAL OF MISSISSIPPI HISTORY

Focus: Mississippi area; Civil War; political and economic history, archaeology, literary figures
Institutional affiliation: Mississippi Historical Society and Department of Archives and History
Editor: Christine Wilson
Book review editor: Joseph Kiger
Address: P.O. Box 571
Jackson, MS 39205
Frequency: 4/year
Circulation: 1,737
Pages/issue: 100
Readership: academics, Society members

Manuscripts
Query: no
Abstract: no
Style guide: MOS, own
Preferred length: 10–20 pages
Number of copies: 1
Notes: end of manuscript
Blind referee: no
Illustrations accepted: tables, graphs, charts, pictures
Foreign languages: no

Reviews
Seeking reviewers: yes
Unsolicited reviews accepted: yes
How to apply: letter
Include in application: professional degrees, institutional affiliation, areas of expertise, foreign languages, current research, published works
Materials reviewed: books
Length of review: 500 words

JOURNAL OF MODERN HISTORY

Focus: Europe since 1500
Institutional affiliation: University of Chicago
Editor: William H. McNeill
Book review editor: Julius Kirshner
Address: 1126 East 59th Street
Chicago, IL 60637
Frequency: 4/year
Circulation: 4,700
Pages/issue: 192–210
Readership: academics

Manuscripts
Query: no
Abstract: upon acceptance
Style guide: MOS
Preferred length: 30–50 pages
Number of copies: 1
Blind referee: yes
Time to consider manuscript: 2 months
Proportion of manuscripts accepted: 1/10–1/7
Foreign languages: book reviews in German, French, Italian

Reviews
Seeking reviewers: yes
Unsolicited reviews accepted: no
How to apply: letter
Include in application: professional degrees, areas of expertise
Materials reviewed: books
Length of review: 600–1,000 words

JOURNAL OF NEAR EASTERN STUDIES

Focus: literature, archaeology, art, languages of ancient and medieval Near East
Institutional affiliation: University of Chicago
Editor: Robert D. Biggs
Book review editor: same
Address: 1155 E. 58th Street
Chicago, IL 60637
Frequency: 4/year
Circulation: 2,500
Pages/issue: 80
Readership: academics, general public, clergy

Manuscripts
Query: no
Abstract: no
Style guide: MOS
Preferred length: 30 pages maximum
Number of copies: 2
Notes: end of manuscript
Blind referee: no
Time to consider manuscript: 4 weeks
Proportion of manuscripts accepted: 3/10
Illustrations accepted: tables, graphs, charts, pictures (photographs not larger than 5 x 7 glossies)
Foreign languages: very brief articles in French or German

Reviews
Seeking reviewers: yes
Unsolicited reviews accepted: no
How to apply: letter
Include in application: institutional affiliation, areas of expertise, published works, foreign languages, current research
Materials reviewed: books
Length of review: 2 pages

JOURNAL OF NEGRO HISTORY

Focus: Afro-Americans and other peoples of color throughout the world
Institutional affiliation: Morehouse College
Editor: Alton Hornsby, Jr.
Address: Box 73
Morehouse College
Atlanta, GA 30314
Book review editor: E. C. Foster
Address: Jackson State University
Jackson, MS 39217
Frequency: 4/year
Circulation: 7,500
Pages/issue: 85
Readership: academics

Manuscripts
Query: no
Abstract: no
Style guide: MFW
Preferred length: 20–25 pages
Number of copies: 3
Notes: end of manuscript
Blind referee: no
Time to consider manuscript: 4–8 weeks
Proportion of manuscripts accepted: 1/5
Illustrations accepted: tables, graphs, charts, pictures
Foreign languages: no

Reviews
Seeking reviewers: yes
Unsolicited reviews accepted: yes
How to apply: form
Include in application: professional degrees, institutional affiliation, areas of expertise, published works, current research
Materials reviewed: books, documents
Length of review: 5,000 words

JOURNAL OF POPULAR CULTURE

Focus: popular culture
Institutional affiliation: Bowling Green State University
Editor: Ray P. Browne
Book review editor: Pat Browne
Address: Popular Culture Center
Bowling Green State University
Bowling Green, OH 43403
Frequency: 4/year
Circulation: 2,500
Pages/issue: 200
Readership: academics, general public

Manuscripts

Query: no
Abstract: no
Style guide: MLA
Preferred length: 12–18 pages
Number of copies: 1
Notes: end of manuscript
Blind referee: no
Time to consider manuscript: 1 month
**Proportion of manuscripts
    accepted:** 1/5
Illustrations accepted: tables, graphs, charts, pictures
Foreign languages: no

Reviews

Seeking reviewers: yes
Unsolicited reviews accepted: yes
How to apply: letter
Include in application: professional degrees, institutional affiliation, areas of expertise, current research
Materials reviewed: trade books
Length of review: 150–250 words

Additional notes

Authors should write simply, clearly, and comprehensively to inform and interest a rather broad and general audience.

JOURNAL OF PRESBYTERIAN HISTORY

Focus: the Presbyterian Church in America; the Reformation
Institutional affiliation: Presbyterian Historical Society and Historical Foundation
Editor: James H. Smylie
Book review editor: same
Address: 425 Lombard St.
Philadelphia, PA 19147
Frequency: 4/year
Circulation: 1,100
Pages/issue: 96
Readership: members of historical societies

Manuscripts

Query: no
Abstract: no
Style guide: MLA
Preferred length: 23 pages
Number of copies: 1
Notes: end of manuscript
Blind referee: no
Time to consider manuscript: 6 months
**Proportion of manuscripts
    accepted:** 3/4
Illustrations accepted: occasionally tables, graphs, charts, pictures
Foreign languages: no

Reviews

Seeking reviewers: no
**Unsolicited reviews
    accepted:** occasionally
How to apply: letter
Include in application: professional degrees, institutional affiliation, areas of expertise, published works
Materials reviewed: books
Length of review: 500 words

THE JOURNAL OF PSYCHOHISTORY

Focus: psychohistory, childhood
Institutional affiliation: The Institute for Psychohistory
Editor: David R. Beisel
Address: 2315 Broadway
New York, NY 10024
Frequency: 4/year
Circulation: 3,500
Pages/issue: 125

Manuscripts
Query: no
Abstract: no
Style guide: MOS
Number of copies: 1
Notes: end of manuscript
Blind referee: no
Time to consider manuscript: 2–6 weeks
Illustrations accepted: camera-ready tables, graphs, charts, pictures
Foreign languages: no

Reviews
Seeking reviewers: yes
Unsolicited reviews accepted: yes
How to apply: letter
Include in application: professional degrees, institutional affiliation, areas of expertise, published works, foreign languages, current research
Materials reviewed: books
Length of review: 2–4 pages

THE JOURNAL OF SAN DIEGO HISTORY

Focus: San Diego; Southern, Southwest, and Baja California, when events have a bearing on San Diego's past
Institutional affiliation: San Diego Historical Society
Editor: Thomas L. Scharf
Book review editor: Richard H. Peterson
Address: P.O. Box 81825
San Diego, CA 92138
Frequency: 4/year
Circulation: 3,000
Pages/issue: 100
Readership: academics, general public

Manuscripts
Query: yes
Abstract: no
Style guide: MOS
Preferred length: 15 pages
Number of copies: 2
Notes: end of manuscript
Blind referee: no
Time to consider manuscript: 3–4 months
Proportion of manuscripts accepted: 1/2
Illustrations accepted: tables, graphs, charts, pictures (8 x 10 black-and-white glossies)
Foreign languages: Spanish with English translation provided

Reviews
Seeking reviewers: yes
Unsolicited reviews accepted: yes
How to apply: letter
Include in application: professional degrees, institutional affiliation, areas of expertise, published works
Materials reviewed: books
Length of review: 2–3 pages

JOURNAL OF SOCIAL HISTORY

Focus: social history
Institutional affiliation: Carnegie-Mellon University
Editor: Peter N. Stearns
Address: Department of History
Carnegie-Mellon University
Pittsburgh, PA 15213
Frequency: 4/year
Circulation: 1,800
Pages/issue: 160
Readership: academics

Manuscripts

Query: no
Abstract: no
Style guide: MOS
Preferred length: 30 pages
Number of copies: 1
Notes: end of manuscript
Blind referee: no
Time to consider manuscript: 3 weeks
Proportion of manuscripts accepted: 1/5
Illustrations accepted: tables, camera-ready graphs and charts
Foreign languages: only if translation prearranged

Reviews

Seeking reviewers: yes
Unsolicited reviews accepted: yes
How to apply: letter
Include in application: institutional affiliation, areas of expertise, current research
Materials reviewed: books
Length of review: 1,000 words

JOURNAL OF SOUTHERN HISTORY

Focus: the South and related topics such as slavery, the Civil War, Reconstruction
Institutional affiliation: Southern Historical Association
Editor: Sanford W. Higginbotham
Book review editor: same
Address: Rice University
Houston, TX 77001
Frequency: 4/year
Circulation: 4,800
Pages/issue: 176–192
Readership: academics, libraries

Manuscripts

Query: no
Abstract: no
Style guide: own, based on MOS
Preferred length: 20–24 pages
Number of copies: 2 preferred
Notes: end of manuscript
Blind referee: yes
Time to consider manuscript: 6 weeks
Proportion of manuscripts accepted: 1/10–1/8
Illustrations accepted: tables, graphs, charts (see Additional notes)
Foreign languages: no

Reviews

Seeking reviewers: yes
Unsolicited reviews accepted: no
How to apply: form
Materials reviewed: books
Length of review: 500–600 words

Additional notes

Graphs and charts should be clear and easy to photograph and should conform to the dimensions of a typed page; no tip-ins or fold-ins. Tables should be clear and the arithmetic accurate. Illustrations such as maps are acceptable; others are not.

JOURNAL OF SPORT HISTORY

Focus: sport throughout the world and during all time periods
Institutional affiliation: North American Society for Sport History
Editor: Jack W. Berryman
Address: Hutchinson Hall, DX-10
University of Washington
Seattle, WA 98195
Book review editor: Lawrence Fielding
Address: Department of Physical Education
University of Louisville
Louisville, KY 40208
Frequency: 3/year
Circulation: 800–1,000
Pages/issue: 90
Readership: academics, physical educators

Manuscripts
Query: no
Abstract: no
Style guide: MOS
Number of copies: 3
Notes: end of manuscript
Blind referee: yes
Time to consider manuscript: 4–8 weeks
Proportion of manuscripts accepted: 1/5
Illustrations accepted: tables, graphs, charts, pictures (separate sheets at end of manuscript with instructions for proper placement)
Foreign languages: no

Reviews
Seeking reviewers: yes
Unsolicited reviews accepted: no
How to apply: letter
Include in application: professional degrees, institutional affiliation, areas of expertise, published works, foreign languages, current research
Materials reviewed: books

JOURNAL OF THE HISTORY OF BIOLOGY

Focus: the biological sciences from antiquity to the present with emphasis on the modern era
Editor: Everett Mendelsohn
Book review editors: Robert G. Frank, Diana Hull
Address: 235 Science Center
Harvard University
Cambridge, MA 02138
Frequency: 2/year
Circulation: 1,200
Pages/issue: 180
Readership: historians, scientists, libraries

Manuscripts
Query: no
Abstract: no
Style guide: *Harvard University Press*
Preferred length: open
Number of copies: 2 preferred
Notes: end of manuscript
Blind referee: no
Time to consider manuscript: 1–2 months
Proportion of manuscripts accepted: 3/10
Illustrations accepted: tables, graphs, charts, pictures
Foreign languages: no

Reviews
Seeking reviewers: yes (for review essays)
Unsolicited reviews accepted: no
How to apply: letter
Include in application: professional degrees, areas of expertise, current research
Materials reviewed: books, articles
Length of review: review essays 8–35 pages

Additional notes
The *Journal* averages approximately one review essay per issue. Short notes on books appear under "JHB Bookshelf" and are written in-house.

JOURNAL OF THE HISTORY OF IDEAS

Focus: intellectual and cultural history of pivotal ideas
Institutional affiliation: Temple University
Editor: K. S. Shin
Book review editor: Philip P. Wiener
Address: Temple University
Philadelphia, PA 19122
Frequency: 4/year
Circulation: 3,800
Pages/issue: 160
Readership: academics

Manuscripts
Abstract: no
Style guide: MOS
Preferred length: 4,000–9,000 words
Number of copies: 2
Notes: end of manuscript
Blind referee: yes
Time to consider manuscript: 2–3 months
Proportion of manuscripts accepted: 1/10
Illustrations accepted: pictures, one or two camera-ready black-and-white illustrations
Foreign languages: no

Reviews
Seeking reviewers: no
Unsolicited reviews accepted: no

Additional notes
Consult the *Journal's* inside rear cover for the statement of its aims and scope.

JOURNAL OF THE HISTORY OF THE BEHAVIORAL SCIENCES

Focus: interdisciplinary and international history of the behavioral and social sciences
Institutional affiliation: University of Massachusetts, Boston
Editor: Charles Jakiela
Book review editor: George Mora
Address: 4 Conant Square
Brandon, VT 05733
Frequency: 4/year
Circulation: 1,050
Pages/issue: 100
Readership: academics

Manuscripts
Query: no
Abstract: yes
Style guide: MOS
Preferred length: 6–10 pages
Number of copies: 3
Notes: end of manuscript
Blind referee: yes
Time to consider manuscript: 3 months
Illustrations accepted: occasionally
Foreign languages: no

Reviews
Seeking reviewers: no
Unsolicited reviews accepted: no
How to apply: letter
Include in application: institutional affiliation, areas of expertise
Materials reviewed: books

JOURNAL OF THE ILLINOIS STATE HISTORICAL SOCIETY

Focus: original research on Illinois subjects

Institutional affiliation: Illinois State Historical Society

Editor: Mary Ellen McElligott

Book review editor: same

Address: Illinois State Historical Library
Springfield, IL 62706

Frequency: 4/year

Circulation: 3,000

Pages/issue: 80

Readership: academics, general public, research and public libraries

Manuscripts

Query: preferred

Abstract: yes

Style guide: own

Preferred length: 25 pages

Number of copies: 2

Notes: end of manuscript

Blind referee: yes

Time to consider manuscript: 1–3 months

Proportion of manuscripts accepted: 1/6

Illustrations accepted: tables, graphs, charts, pictures (contributor must secure permission for nonoriginal matter; staff will assist in locating illustrations)

Foreign languages: no

Reviews

Seeking reviewers: yes

Unsolicited reviews accepted: rarely

How to apply: letter, vita

Include in application: areas of expertise

Materials reviewed: books

Length of review: 250–500 words

JOURNAL OF THE LANCASTER COUNTY HISTORICAL SOCIETY

Focus: Lancaster County and Southeastern Pennsylvania; biographical, economic, political, social, intellectual, and technological aspects

Institutional affiliation: Lancaster County Historical Society

Editor: John Ward Willson Loose

Book review editor: J. R. Gaintner

Address: Lancaster County Historical Society
230 N. President Ave.
Lancaster, PA 17603

Frequency: 4/year

Circulation: 2,100

Pages/issue: 60

Readership: academics, buffs

Manuscripts

Query: no

Abstract: encouraged

Style guide: MOS

Preferred length: 18–52 pages

Number of copies: 1

Notes: end of manuscript preferred

Blind referee: no

Time to consider manuscript: 2–4 months

Proportion of manuscripts accepted: 2/3

Illustrations accepted: tables, graphs, charts, pictures (no more than six photographs unless additional illustrations would contribute greatly to the article)

Foreign languages: no

(continued on next page)

JOURNAL OF THE LANCASTER COUNTY HISTORICAL SOCIETY
(continued)

Reviews
Seeking reviewers: yes
Unsolicited reviews accepted: yes, if pertinent
How to apply: letter
Include in application: areas of expertise, published works, current research, one or two copies of earlier reviews
Materials reviewed: books, trade books
Length of review: 300–500 words

Additional notes
The *Journal* publishes scholarly monographs (M.A. and Ph.D. dissertations included) as well as shorter pieces.

JOURNAL OF THE WEST

Focus: the West
Editor: Robin Higham
Book review editor: same
Address: P.O. Box 1009
      Manhattan, KS 66502
Frequency: 4/year
Circulation: 4,500
Pages/issue: 112
Readership: academics, general public

Manuscripts
Query: yes
Abstract: helpful
Style guide: own (see inside cover of any issue)
Preferred length: 20 pages maximum
Number of copies: 3
Notes: end of manuscript
Blind referee: yes
Time to consider manuscript: 3 months
Proportion of manuscripts accepted: low
Illustrations accepted: tables, graphs, charts, pictures (see inside front cover of journal; author responsible for costs and permissions)
Foreign languages: no

Reviews
Seeking reviewers: yes
Unsolicited reviews accepted: no
How to apply: letter, vita
Include in application: professional degrees, institutional affiliation, areas of expertise, published works, current research
Materials reviewed: books

JOURNAL OF URBAN HISTORY

Focus: cities and urban societies in all periods of human history and all geographical areas of the world
Editor: Blaine A. Brownell
Address: Center for Urban Affairs
University of Alabama
Birmingham, AL 35294
Frequency: 4/year
Pages/issue: 128
Readership: academics

Manuscripts
Query: no
Abstract: yes
Style guide: SAGE
Preferred length: 30 pages maximum
Number of copies: 3
Notes: end of manuscript
Blind referee: yes
Time to consider manuscript: 3 months
Illustrations accepted: original tables, graphs, charts
Foreign languages: no

JOURNALISM HISTORY

Focus: individuals, institutions, and events related to the history of journalism and mass communications, primarily in America
Institutional affiliation: California State University, Northridge
Editor: Tom Reilly
Address: Department of Journalism
California State University,
Northridge
Northridge, CA 91330
Book review editor: Thomas H. Heuterman
Address: Department of Communications
Washington State University
Pullman, WA 99164
Frequency: 4/year
Circulation: 1,000
Pages/issue: 32
Readership: academics, academic libraries

Manuscripts
Query: recommended
Abstract: no
Style guide: MFW
Preferred length: 15 pages
Number of copies: 3
Notes: end of manuscript
Blind referee: yes
Time to consider manuscript: 3–4 months
Proportion of manuscripts accepted: 1/5
Illustrations accepted: tables, graphs, charts, pictures
Foreign languages: no (except in citations)

Reviews
Seeking reviewers: yes
Unsolicited reviews accepted: no
How to apply: letter
Include in application: professional degrees, experience, background
Materials reviewed: all media
Length of review: 500 words maximum

KANSAS HISTORY: A JOURNAL OF THE CENTRAL PLAINS

Focus: Kansas and the West
Institutional affiliation: Kansas State Historical Society
Editor: Forrest R. Blackburn
Address: 120 West Tenth Street
Topeka, KS 66612
Frequency: 4/year
Circulation: 4,000
Pages/issue: 72
Readership: Society members, scholars, general public

Manuscripts
Query: no
Abstract: no
Preferred length: 10–50 pages
Number of copies: 1
Notes: end of manuscript
Time to consider manuscript: 1 month
Proportion of manuscripts accepted: 1/2
Illustrations accepted: tables, graphs, charts, pictures
Foreign languages: no

LABOR HISTORY

Focus: labor history
Editor: Daniel J. Leab
Address: Tamiment Institute
Bobst Library
New York University
New York, NY 10012
Frequency: 4/year
Circulation: 2,000
Pages/issue: 160
Readership: academics, general public

Manuscripts
Query: no
Abstract: no
Style guide: MLA
Preferred length: 25–30 pages
Number of copies: 2
Notes: bottom of page
Blind referee: yes
Time to consider manuscript: 3 months
Proportion of manuscripts accepted: 1/4
Illustrations accepted: tables, graphs, charts
Foreign languages: no

Reviews
Seeking reviewers: yes
Unsolicited reviews accepted: yes
How to apply: letter
Include in application: professional degrees, institutional affiliation, areas of expertise, published works, foreign languages, current research
Materials reviewed: books
Length of review: 800–1,000 words

LANDMARK

Focus: Waukesha County, Wisconsin
Institutional affiliation: Waukesha
County Historical Society
Editor: Libbie Nolan
Book review editor: same
Address: 20245 W. National Ave.
New Berlin, WI 53151
(from May 1 to Nov. 1)
617 Riverview Drive
Ellenton, FL 33532
(from Nov. 1 to May 1)
Frequency: 4/year
Circulation: 800
Pages/issue: 24
Readership: general public

Manuscripts

Query: yes
Abstract: no
Style guide: none
Preferred length: 1,000 words maximum
Number of copies: 2
Notes: end of manuscript
Blind referee: no
Time to consider manuscript: varies
**Proportion of manuscripts
accepted:** 2/5
Illustrations accepted: tables, graphs,
charts, pictures
Foreign languages: no

Reviews

Seeking reviewers: yes
**Unsolicited reviews
accepted:** occasionally
How to apply: letter
Include in application: areas of
expertise, current research
Materials reviewed: books, films, audio
Length of review: 1,000 words maximum

Additional notes

Landmark is also interested in general
stories about the Great Depression and the
Prohibition Era. It is not interested in
dryly handled treatises but in entertaining
and readable stories, interviews,
reminiscences, and researched articles.

LATIN AMERICAN DIGEST

Focus: news, culture, history, and
literature of Latin America
Institutional affiliation: Center for Latin
American Studies
Editor: Janet Smith
Book review editors: Noel J. Stowe,
Carmelo Virgillo
Address: Center for Latin American
Studies
Arizona State University
Tempe, AZ 85281
Frequency: 4/year
Circulation: 1,000
Pages/issue: 28–32
Readership: general public

Manuscripts

Query: no
Abstract: no
Style guide: MOS or MLA
Preferred length: 6–12 pages
Number of copies: 1
Notes: end of manuscript
Blind referee: yes
Time to consider manuscript: 1–3 weeks
**Proportion of manuscripts
accepted:** 4/5
Illustrations accepted: tables, graphs,
charts, black-and-white pictures
Foreign languages: no

Reviews

Seeking reviewers: yes
Unsolicited reviews accepted: yes
How to apply: letter
Include in application: professional
degrees, institutional affiliation, areas
of expertise
Materials reviewed: books
Length of review: 500 words

Additional notes

Articles should deal with significant
material, of interest to a general audience.
Style of presentation should be popular,
readily readable and understandable;
minimal documentation can be included.
Underlying scholarship should be sound.
Submissions may be extracts of longer
studies in progress. However, this fact
must be acknowledged in a footnote to the
text.

LATIN AMERICAN RESEARCH REVIEW

Focus: Latin America; politics and culture
Institutional affiliation: University of North Carolina at Chapel Hill
Editor: Leah Florence
Book review editor: Arturo Valenzuela
Address: Hamilton Hall 070A
University of North Carolina
Chapel Hill, NC 27514
Frequency: 3/year
Circulation: 3,200
Pages/issue: 300
Readership: academics, students

Manuscripts
Query: no
Abstract: no
Style guide: MOS
Preferred length: 50 pages maximum
Number of copies: 3
Notes: end of manuscript
Blind referee: yes
Time to consider manuscript: 3 months
Illustrations accepted: tables, graphs, charts, pictures (for very detailed or complex maps or charts, provide camera-ready copy in accordance with the *Review*'s page size)
Foreign languages: Spanish, Portuguese

Reviews
Seeking reviewers: no
Unsolicited reviews accepted: no
How to apply: letter
Include in application: professional degrees, institutional affiliation, areas of expertise, published works, foreign languages, current research
Materials reviewed: books
Length of review: see Additional notes

Additional notes
Review length varies with the size of the review package; reviews of single books are rarely published. Review essays discourse on thematically related volumes.

LINCOLN HERALD

Focus: Abraham Lincoln and the Civil War
Institutional affiliation: Lincoln Museum of Lincoln Memorial University
Editor: Edgar G. Archer
Address: Lincoln Memorial University Press
Lincoln Museum
Harrogate, TN 37752
Frequency: 4/year
Circulation: 1,000
Pages/issue: 50
Readership: general public, Civil War specialists

Manuscripts
Query: no
Abstract: no
Style guide: MLA
Preferred length: 12–16 pages
Number of copies: 2
Notes: end of manuscript
Blind referee: no
Time to consider manuscript: 2 months
Proportion of manuscripts accepted: 9/10
Foreign languages: no

Reviews
Seeking reviewers: yes
Unsolicited reviews accepted: yes
How to apply: letter
Include in application: institutional affiliation, areas of expertise, current research
Materials reviewed: books
Length of review: 1 page

LITTLE BIG HORN ASSOCIATES RESEARCH REVIEW

Focus: Custeriana (including the Civil War), Plains Indians, the 7th Cavalry
Editor: John F. McCormack, Jr.
Book review editor: same
Address: 1532 Bancroft Drive
West Chester, PA 19380
Frequency: 4/year
Circulation: 400
Pages/issue: 20
Readership: buffs

Manuscripts
Query: no
Abstract: no
Preferred length: varies
Number of copies: 1
Notes: end of manuscript
Blind referee: no
Time to consider manuscript: 2–3 months
Illustrations accepted: tables, graphs, charts, pictures
Foreign languages: no

Reviews
Seeking reviewers: no
Unsolicited reviews accepted: yes
How to apply: letter
Include in application: professional degrees, institutional affiliation, areas of expertise, published works, current research
Materials reviewed: books, films, audio
Length of review: variable

Additional notes
Articles by members are more likely to be accepted, but membership is not absolutely necessary if an article is especially good. Lengthy reviews are not wanted.

LONG ISLAND FORUM

Focus: Long Island, New York and its folklore
Institutional affiliation: Friends of the Nassau Museum
Editor: Carl A. Starace
Book review editor: same
Address: P.O. Box 215
West Islip, NY 11795
Frequency: 1/month
Circulation: 3,000
Pages/issue: 24
Readership: members of Friends, libraries

Manuscripts
Query: yes
Style guide: none
Preferred length: 3,000 words maximum
Number of copies: 1
Notes: end of manuscript
Time to consider manuscript: 2 weeks
Proportion of manuscripts accepted: 3/5
Illustrations accepted: tables, graphs, charts, pictures
Foreign languages: no

Reviews
Seeking reviewers: no
Unsolicited reviews accepted: no (all reviews done in-house)

Additional notes
Articles, other than reviews, must deal with some aspect of Long Island's local history not generally known or easily available in another publication. The *Forum*'s mission is to collect and preserve for the enjoyment of its readers and the convenience of researchers.

LOUISIANA HISTORY

Focus: colonial Louisiana, state of Louisiana
Institutional affiliation: University of Southwestern Louisiana
Editor: Glenn R. Conrad
Book review editor: same
Address: P.O. Box 831
University of Southwestern Louisiana
Lafayette, LA 70501
Frequency: 4/year
Circulation: 1,500
Pages/issue: 128
Readership: academics, general public

Manuscripts
Query: no
Abstract: no
Style guide: MOS (a few in-house usages)
Preferred length: 20–30 pages
Number of copies: 2
Notes: end of manuscript
Blind referee: yes
Time to consider manuscript: 3–6 months
Proportion of manuscripts accepted: 4/5
Illustrations accepted: tables, graphs, charts, pictures
Foreign languages: short items in French

Reviews
Seeking reviewers: yes
Unsolicited reviews accepted: no
How to apply: letter
Include in application: professional degrees, institutional affiliation, areas of expertise, published works, foreign languages, current research
Materials reviewed: books
Length of review: 500–750 words

THE LOYALIST GAZETTE

Focus: genealogy and education in the Loyalist period (1775–1800)
Institutional affiliation: The United Empire Loyalists' Association of Canada
Editor: E. J. Chard
Book review editor: same
Address: United Empire Loyalists' Association of Canada
23 Prince Arthur Avenue
Toronto, Ontario M5R 1B2
CANADA
Frequency: 2/year
Circulation: 2,500
Pages/issue: 28
Readership: academics, Association members, genealogists, general public

Manuscripts
Query: yes
Abstract: no
Preferred length: 1,000–2,000 words
Number of copies: 3
Notes: end of manuscript
Time to consider manuscript: 6 months
Illustrations accepted: charts, pictures
Foreign languages: no

Reviews
Seeking reviewers: yes
Unsolicited reviews accepted: yes
How to apply: letter
Include in application: professional degrees, institutional affiliation, areas of expertise, published works
Materials reviewed: books
Length of review: 100–1,000 words

Additional notes
Articles must be on authentic historical material, with detailed footnotes or bibliographical references. Articles must be mostly of Loyalist content or in the Loyalist period.

MAINE HISTORICAL SOCIETY QUARTERLY

Focus: Maine
Institutional affiliation: Maine Historical Society
Editor: Thomas L. Gaffney
Book review editor: Joel W. Eastman
Address: 485 Congress Street
　　　　Portland, ME 04111
Frequency: 4/year
Circulation: 1,500
Pages/issue: 50
Readership: general public

Manuscripts
Query: no
Abstract: no
Style guide: MOS
Preferred length: 6,000 words
Number of copies: 6
Notes: end of manuscript
Blind referee: no
Time to consider manuscript: 2 months
Proportion of manuscripts accepted: 3/10
Illustrations accepted: camera-ready tables, graphs, charts, pictures
Foreign languages: no

Reviews
Seeking reviewers: no
Unsolicited reviews accepted: no
How to apply: letter
Include in application: professional degrees, institutional affiliation, areas of expertise, published works
Materials reviewed: books
Length of review: 1,000 words maximum

Additional notes
Articles submitted to the *Quarterly* must reflect original research and make use of primary source material.

MANKIND MAGAZINE

Focus: general history
Editor: Jared Rutter
Book review editor: same
Address: 8060 Melrose Avenue
　　　　Los Angeles, CA 90046
Frequency: 4/year
Circulation: 50,000
Pages/issue: 50
Readership: general public

Manuscripts
Query: yes
Abstract: no
Style guide: MOS
Preferred length: 1,000–4,000 words
Number of copies: 1
Notes: end of manuscript
Blind referee: no
Time to consider manuscript: 2–3 weeks
Illustrations accepted: no
Foreign languages: no

Reviews
Seeking reviewers: no
Unsolicited reviews accepted: no

MANUSCRIPTA

Focus: manuscript research in the humanities and history of science
Institutional affiliation: St. Louis University, St. Louis, Missouri
Editor: Charles J. Ermatinger
Book review editor: Rev. Lowrie J. Daly, S.J.
Address: Pius XII Memorial Library
St. Louis University
3655 West Pine Boulevard
St. Louis, MO 63108
Frequency: 3/year
Circulation: 900
Pages/issue: 64
Readership: researchers, scholars

Manuscripts
Query: no
Abstract: no
Style guide: MLA
Preferred length: 25 pages maximum (pica); 21 pages maximum (elite)
Number of copies: 1
Notes: end of manuscript
Blind referee: no
Time to consider manuscript: 1 month average
Proportion of manuscripts accepted: varies
Illustrations accepted: very few
Foreign languages: German, Spanish, French (whenever financially possible)

Reviews
Seeking reviewers: yes
Unsolicited reviews accepted: no
How to apply: letter
Include in application: professional degrees, institutional affiliation, areas of expertise, published works, foreign languages, current research
Materials reviewed: books
Length of review: 800 words

Additional notes
Shorter contributions (1,500–2,000 words) are printed under the heading "Notes and Comments."

THE MARYLAND HISTORIAN

Focus: world history, of any time period
Institutional affiliation: Department of History, University of Maryland
Editor: William A. Gray
Book review editor: same
Address: Department of History
University of Maryland
College Park, MD 20742
Frequency: 2/year
Circulation: 600
Pages/issue: 65
Readership: academics

Manuscripts
Query: no
Abstract: no
Style guide: MOS (recommended)
Preferred length: 30 pages maximum
Number of copies: 2
Notes: end of manuscript
Blind referee: no
Time to consider manuscript: 1 month
Proportion of manuscripts accepted: 3/10
Illustrations accepted: camera-ready tables, graphs, charts, pictures; illustrations encouraged
Foreign languages: no

Reviews
Seeking reviewers: will consider
Unsolicited reviews accepted: encouraged
How to apply: letter
Include in application: professional degrees, institutional affiliation, areas of expertise, published works, foreign languages, current research
Materials reviewed: books
Length of review: 3–5 pages

Additional notes
Graduate students as well as junior and senior faculty are encouraged to submit articles and book reviews. Submit copies of photographs. Materials will be returned to the author upon request. Acceptance of articles is based on quality and not on subject matter.

MARYLAND HISTORICAL MAGAZINE

Focus: Maryland
Institutional affiliation: Maryland Historical Society
Editor: Gary L. Browne
Address: 201 West Monument Street Baltimore, MD 21201
Frequency: 4/year
Circulation: 6,500
Pages/issue: 112
Readership: academics, general public, Society members

Manuscripts
Query: yes
Abstract: no
Style guide: MOS
Preferred length: 25 pages
Number of copies: 2
Notes: end of manuscript
Blind referee: yes
Time to consider manuscript: 2 months
Proportion of manuscripts accepted: 1/5
Illustrations accepted: tables, graphs, charts, pictures
Foreign languages: no

Reviews
Seeking reviewers: no
Unsolicited reviews accepted: yes
How to apply: letter
Include in application: professional degrees, institutional affiliation, areas of expertise, published works
Materials reviewed: books
Length of review: 1,000–2,000 words

THE MAYFLOWER QUARTERLY

Focus: family history in Colonial New England (pre-1775, approximately)
Institutional affiliation: General Society of Mayflower Descendants
Editor: Elizabeth P. White
Book review editor: same
Address: P.O. Box 297 Winnetka, IL 60093
Frequency: 4/year
Circulation: 19,000
Pages/issue: 52–68
Readership: Society members, libraries, general public

Manuscripts
Query: no
Abstract: no
Style guide: MOS
Preferred length: 1,000–2,500 words
Number of copies: 1
Notes: end of manuscript
Blind referee: no
Time to consider manuscript: 2 months
Proportion of manuscripts accepted: 1/2
Illustrations accepted: tables, graphs, charts, pictures (black-and-white glossies)
Foreign languages: no

Reviews
Seeking reviewers: yes
Unsolicited reviews accepted: yes
How to apply: letter
Include in application: professional degrees, institutional affiliation, areas of expertise, published works, current research
Materials reviewed: books
Length of review: 250 words

MEDIAEVALIA

Focus: interdisciplinary focus on the Middle Ages as well as traditional disciplinary approaches
Institutional affiliation: Center for Medieval and Early Renaissance Studies
Editor: Bernard S. Levy
Address: Center for Medieval and Early Renaissance Studies
SUNY, Binghamton
Binghamton, NY 13901
Frequency: 1/year
Circulation: 500
Pages/issue: 300
Readership: scholars

Manuscripts
Query: no
Abstract: no
Style guide: MLA
Preferred length: 10–25 pages
Number of copies: 2
Notes: end of manuscript
Blind referee: no
Time to consider manuscript: 3 months
Proportion of manuscripts accepted: 1/5
Illustrations accepted: tables, graphs, charts, pictures
Foreign languages: no

MERIP REPORTS

Focus: political and economic developments in the Middle East, North Africa, and Horn of Africa; United States policy in the region
Editor: Joe Stork
Address: P.O. Box 3122
Columbia Heights Station
Washington, DC 20010
Book review editor: Philip Khoury
Address: P.O. Box 48
Cambridge, MA 02138
Frequency: 10/year
Circulation: 3,000
Pages/issue: 28
Readership: academic libraries, scholars, activists

Manuscripts
Query: no
Abstract: no
Style guide: own
Preferred length: see Additional notes
Number of copies: 2
Notes: end of manuscript
Blind referee: no
Time to consider manuscript: 1 month minimum
Proportion of manuscripts accepted: fairly high
Illustrations accepted: tables, graphs, charts, pictures
Foreign languages: French, Arabic, German, Spanish

Reviews
Seeking reviewers: yes
Unsolicited reviews accepted: yes
How to apply: letter
Include in application: areas of expertise, current research
Materials reviewed: books, films

(continued on next page)

MERIP REPORTS
(continued)

Additional notes
Articles should analyze in depth a theoretical question, an institution, a social class, a particular struggle, or a cultural or ideological production. Articles which take the form of "country studies" are less desirable. Articles should be original, not formulaic, and they should be based on considerable knowledge of the subject matter. Length of articles and reviews: analytical article (4,000–6,000 words), interview (1,500–3,000), review article (2,000–4,000), regular review (1,000–2,000), review notes (50–1,000), special reports (500–2,000), current events articles (400–1,000).

MID-AMERICA

Focus: United States, especially the nineteenth and twentieth centuries
Institutional affiliation: Loyola University
Editor: John Mentag
Address: 6525 Sheridan Road
Chicago, IL 60626
Frequency: 4/year
Circulation: 700
Pages/issue: 75
Readership: scholars, general public

Manuscripts
Query: no
Abstract: no
Preferred length: 30 pages maximum
Number of copies: 1
Notes: end of manuscript
Illustrations accepted: tables, graphs, charts, if necessary
Foreign languages: no

Reviews
Seeking reviewers: no
Unsolicited reviews accepted: no
Include in application: professional degrees, institutional affiliation, areas of expertise, foreign languages
Materials reviewed: books
Length of review: 250–450 words

THE MIDWEST QUARTERLY

Focus: literature, government, other arts and sciences
Institutional affiliation: Pittsburg State University
Editor: V. J. Emmett, Jr.
Book review editor: same
Address: Pittsburg State University
Pittsburg, KS 66762
Frequency: 4/year
Circulation: 1,000
Pages/issue: 110
Readership: academics

Manuscripts
Query: no
Abstract: no
Style guide: MLA
Preferred length: 15 pages
Number of copies: 1
Notes: see Additional notes
Blind referee: no
Time to consider manuscript: 6 months
Proportion of manuscripts accepted: 1/5
Illustrations accepted: tables
Foreign languages: no

Reviews
Seeking reviewers: no
Unsolicited reviews accepted: no

Additional notes
No notes. The Quarterly uses a minimum of parenthetical documentation within the text and a short bibliography at the end.

MILITARY AFFAIRS

Focus: military, naval, and air history, technology, and theory
Institutional affiliation: American Military Institute
Editor: Ann A. Warren
Book review editor: Jacob W. Kipp
Address: Eisenhower Hall
Kansas State University
Manhattan, KS 66506
Frequency: 4/year
Circulation: 2,100
Pages/issue: 50–60
Readership: academics, libraries, military personnel, general public

Manuscripts
Query: no
Abstract: no
Style guide: MLA
Preferred length: 20 pages maximum
Number of copies: 3
Notes: end of manuscript
Blind referee: no
Time to consider manuscript: 2–3 months
Illustrations accepted: captioned tables, graphs, charts, pictures
Foreign languages: no

Reviews
Unsolicited reviews accepted: no
How to apply: letter, vita
Include in application: professional degrees, institutional affiliation, areas of expertise, published works
Materials reviewed: books
Length of review: 250 words

MILITARY HISTORY OF TEXAS AND THE SOUTHWEST

Focus: military history of Texas and the Southwest
Editor: Jay A. Matthews, Jr.
Book review editor: same
Address: P.O. Box 5248
Austin, TX 78763
Frequency: 4/year
Circulation: 750
Pages/issue: 64
Readership: academics, military personnel

Manuscripts
Query: no
Abstract: no
Style guide: MOS or MFW
Preferred length: 30 pages
Number of copies: 1
Notes: end of manuscript
Blind referee: no
Time to consider manuscript: 1–6 months
Proportion of manuscripts accepted: 1/3
Illustrations accepted: camera-ready tables, charts, pictures
Foreign languages: with translations

Reviews
Seeking reviewers: yes
Unsolicited reviews accepted: no
How to apply: letter
Include in application: professional degrees, institutional affiliation, areas of expertise, published works
Materials reviewed: books
Length of review: 1–2 pages

Additional notes
All publications must be accompanied by illustrative matter; this *does* make a difference. The most readily-accepted articles are based entirely on primary source material. Studies based on secondary sources are rarely accepted unless the analysis or subject area is extremely unique.

THE MILITARY JOURNAL

Focus: 20th century military history and weapons, specializing in World War II
Editor: Ray Merriam
Book review editor: same
Address: 218 Beech Street
Bennington, VT 05201
Frequency: 4/year
Circulation: 3,000
Pages/issue: 56
Readership: buffs

Manuscripts
Query: yes
Abstract: yes
Style guide: own
Preferred length: 10–25 pages
Number of copies: 1
Notes: end of manuscript
Blind referee: no
Time to consider manuscript: 2–4 weeks
Illustrations accepted: high quality tables, graphs, charts, pictures, otherwise will be omitted or redone at author's expense
Foreign languages: no

Reviews
Seeking reviewers: yes
Unsolicited reviews accepted: yes
How to apply: letter
Include in application: professional degrees, institutional affiliation, areas of expertise, published works, foreign languages, current research
Materials reviewed: books
Length of review: 1,000 words maximum

MINNESOTA HISTORY

Focus: Minnesota and the Upper Midwest
Institutional affiliation: Minnesota
Historical Society
Editor: Kenneth A. Carley
Book review editor: Bruce M. White
Address: Minnesota Historical Society
690 Cedar Street
St. Paul, MN 55101
Frequency: 4/year
Circulation: 7,000
Pages/issue: 40
Readership: general public, academics

Manuscripts
Query: preferred
Abstract: no
Style guide: MOS (with own
modifications)
Preferred length: 1,500–7,000 words
Number of copies: 1
Notes: end of manuscript
Blind referee: no
Time to consider manuscript: 3–4
months
Illustrations accepted: tables, graphs,
charts, pictures in rough form
Foreign languages: no

Reviews
Seeking reviewers: occasionally
Unsolicited reviews accepted: rarely
How to apply: letter
Include in application: institutional
affiliation, areas of expertise
Materials reviewed: books
Length of review: 350–450 words

MISSISSIPPI QUARTERLY: THE JOURNAL OF SOUTHERN CULTURE

Focus: culture of the American South;
literature, sociology, folklore,
speechways, economics
Institutional affiliation: Mississippi State
University
Editor: Peyton W. Williams, Jr.
Book review editor: Robert L. Phillips
Address: P.O. Box 5273
Mississippi State University
State College, MS 39762
Frequency: 4/year
Circulation: 700
Pages/issue: 144–160
Readership: scholars, general public

Manuscripts
Query: no
Abstract: no
Style guide: MLA
Preferred length: 4,000 words maximum
Number of copies: 2 preferred
Notes: bottom of page
Blind referee: no
Time to consider manuscript: 1–3
months
**Proportion of manuscripts
accepted:** 1/5
Illustrations accepted: tables, graphs,
charts
Foreign languages: no

Reviews
Seeking reviewers: no
Unsolicited reviews accepted: no
Materials reviewed: books

MISSOURI HISTORICAL REVIEW

Focus: Missouri and the trans–Mississippi West
Institutional affiliation: State Historical Society of Missouri
Editor: Richard S. Brownlee
Book review editor: same
Address: The State Historical Society of Missouri
Corner Hitt and Lowry Streets
Columbia, MO 65201
Frequency: 4/year
Circulation: 14,000
Pages/issue: 128
Readership: academics, general public

Manuscripts
Query: no
Abstract: no
Style guide: MOS
Preferred length: 7,500 words maximum
Number of copies: 2
Notes: end of manuscript
Blind referee: yes
Time to consider manuscript: 6–12 weeks
Proportion of manuscripts accepted: 3/10
Illustrations accepted: tables, graphs, charts, pictures
Foreign languages: no

MODERN CHINA: AN INTERNATIONAL QUARTERLY OF HISTORY AND SOCIAL SCIENCE

Focus: China, from 1800 to the present (will consider work on 14th to 18th centuries)
Institutional affiliation: University of California, Los Angeles
Editor: Philip C. C. Huang
Book review editor: same
Address: Department of History
University of California, Los Angeles
Los Angeles, CA 90024
Frequency: 4/year
Circulation: 1,000
Pages/issue: 128
Readership: academics

Manuscripts
Query: no
Abstract: no
Style guide: own
Preferred length: 40 pages maximum
Number of copies: 3
Notes: end of manuscript
Blind referee: yes
Time to consider manuscript: 2 months
Proportion of manuscripts accepted: 1/5
Illustrations accepted: camera-ready tables, graphs, charts, pictures
Foreign languages: no

Reviews
Seeking reviewers: no
Unsolicited reviews accepted: no

Additional notes
Special emphasis placed on society, economy, and popular movements. Review essays are solicited; no short reviews.

MONTANA: THE MAGAZINE OF WESTERN HISTORY

Focus: documented articles and verified reminiscences of Montana and the American West
Institutional affiliation: Montana Historical Society
Editor: William L. Lang
Book review editor: Michael P. Malone
Address: Montana Historical Society
225 North Roberts Street
Helena, MT 59601
Frequency: 4/year
Circulation: 10,000
Pages/issue: 80
Readership: academics, general public

Manuscripts
Query: no
Abstract: no
Style guide: MOS
Preferred length: 3,000–6,000 words
Number of copies: 2
Notes: end of manuscript
Blind referee: no
Time to consider manuscript: 4–6 weeks
Illustrations accepted: black-and-white glossies
Foreign languages: no

Reviews
Seeking reviewers: yes
Unsolicited reviews accepted: no
How to apply: letter
Include in application: professional degrees, institutional affiliation, areas of expertise, current research
Materials reviewed: books
Length of review: 300–400 words

Additional notes
Montana publishes a wide range of articles. First priority is accuracy and solid research for local, regional, and national topics. Reminiscences, memoirs, and the like must be verified. Illustrations are second priority, but each article must be illustrated. Editors aid in securing photographs, engravings, etc. Captions are written by editors.

MUSEUM OF THE CONFEDERACY NEWSLETTER

Focus: United States, 1850–1877, the Confederacy
Institutional affiliation: Museum of the Confederacy
Editor: Edward D. C. Campbell, Jr.
Book review editor: same
Address: 1201 East Clay Street
Richmond, VA 23219
Frequency: 4/year
Circulation: 2,000
Pages/issue: 10–12
Readership: members of the Museum, general public

Manuscripts
Query: yes
Abstract: yes
Style guide: MOS
Preferred length: 3–6 pages
Number of copies: 2
Notes: end of manuscript
Blind referee: no
Time to consider manuscript: 1 month
Proportion of manuscripts accepted: 1/10
Illustrations accepted: pictures
Foreign languages: no

Reviews
Seeking reviewers: no
Unsolicited reviews accepted: no

MUSEUM OF THE FUR TRADE QUARTERLY

Focus: the North American fur trade
Institutional affiliation: Museum of the Fur Trade
Editor: Charles E. Hanson, Jr.
Book review editor: same
Address: Route 2, Box 18
Chadron, NB 69337
Frequency: 4/year
Circulation: 1,200
Pages/issue: 12
Readership: historians, curators, antiquarians, buffs

Manuscripts

Query: yes
Abstract: no
Style guide: none
Preferred length: 2,000–3,500 words
Number of copies: 1
Notes: end of manuscript
Blind referee: no
Time to consider manuscript: 1 month
Proportion of manuscripts accepted: 2/5
Illustrations accepted: tables, charts, pictures
Foreign languages: no

Reviews

Seeking reviewers: no
Unsolicited reviews accepted: yes
How to apply: letter
Include in application: professional degrees, institutional affiliation, areas of expertise, foreign languages
Materials reviewed: books
Length of review: 300–400 words

THE MUSK-OX

Focus: scientific, cultural, economic, and historical aspects of northern Canada and other parts of the circumpolar world
Institutional affiliation: Institute for Northern Studies, University of Saskatchewan
Editor: Shirley Milligan
Address: Institute for Northern Studies, University of Saskatchewan
Saskatoon, Saskatchewan
S7N 0W0
CANADA
Frequency: 2/year
Circulation: 800
Pages/issue: 96
Readership: libraries, general public

Manuscripts

Query: yes
Abstract: yes, 250 words (in English and also in French, if possible)
Preferred length: 80 pages maximum
Number of copies: 2
Notes: (see Additional notes)
Blind referee: yes
Illustrations accepted: tables, graphs, charts, pictures (see Additional notes)
Foreign languages: French

Reviews

Seeking reviewers: yes
Unsolicited reviews accepted: yes
How to apply: letter
Include in application: professional degrees, institutional affiliation, areas of expertise, published works, foreign languages, current research
Materials reviewed: books
Length of review: 1,000 words

Additional notes

The preferred referencing procedure is the author-date-page system incorporated into the text. References cited in the article follow at the conclusion, and are listed alphabetically by author. If this system is followed, footnotes are not required; however, if the article lends itself to footnotes rather than the author-date-page

(continued on next page)

THE MUSK-OX
(continued)

system, then the footnotes should be numbered and listed as notes at the conclusion of the article, followed by a complete list of references cited.

All illustrations, whether line drawings or photographs, should be called figures. Both illustrations and tables should be numbered consecutively and referred to in the text. The most favorable positions of insertion should be indicated in the margins of the text.

In addition to articles, the *Musk-Ox* carries a section entitled "Notes." These latter are less exhaustive than articles but should conform to the general objectives of the journal. Notes do not require external reviewing but will be subjected to internal review. Notes need not be accompanied by an abstract.

THE MUSLIM WORLD

Focus: study of Islam and Christian–Muslim relationship in past and present
Institutional affiliation: The Hartford Seminary Foundation
Editors: Willem A. Bijlefeld, Issa J. Boullata
Book review editor: Issa J. Boullata
Address: 77 Sherman Street
Hartford, CT 06105
Frequency: 4/year
Pages/issue: 80
Readership: academics, persons concerned with Christian–Muslim relations, missionaries

Manuscripts
Query: no
Abstract: no
Style guide: MOS
Preferred length: 6,000–6,500 words
Number of copies: 2
Notes: end of manuscript
Blind referee: no
Time to consider manuscript: 2 months
Illustrations accepted: tables, charts
Foreign languages: no, except for short passages in Arabic and Persian, if necessary

Reviews
Seeking reviewers: no
Unsolicited reviews accepted: no

Additional notes
Follow the transliteration system used by the *Encyclopaedia Islamica, New Edition,* but omit underlining with th, kh, dh, sh, and gh; use j instead of *dj*; and use q instead of k.

NATIONAL GENEALOGICAL SOCIETY QUARTERLY

Focus: genealogy
Institutional affiliation: National Genealogical Society
Editor: George Ely Russell
Address: 3 Lombardy Drive
Middletown, MD 21769
Book review editor: Milton Rubincam
Address: 6303 20th Avenue
West Hyattsville, MD 20782
Frequency: 4/year
Circulation: 5,000
Pages/issue: 80
Readership: Society members, libraries

Manuscripts

Query: no
Abstract: no
Style guide: MOS
Preferred length: 16 pages maximum
Number of copies: 2
Notes: end of manuscript
Blind referee: no
Time to consider manuscript: 1 week
Proportion of manuscripts accepted: 1/4
Illustrations accepted: tables, graphs, charts, pictures
Foreign languages: no

Reviews

Seeking reviewers: yes
Unsolicited reviews accepted: yes
Materials reviewed: books, films
Length of review: 2 pages maximum

NEBRASKA HISTORY

Focus: the Midwest
Institutional affiliation: Nebraska State Historical Society
Editor: Marvin F. Kivett
Address: Nebraska State Historical Society
1500 R Street
Lincoln, NB 68508
Frequency: 4/year
Circulation: 5,500
Pages/issue: 135
Readership: Society members, general public

Manuscripts

Query: no
Abstract: no
Style guide: MOS
Preferred length: 10,000 words
Number of copies: 1
Notes: end of manuscript
Blind referee: no
Time to consider manuscript: 2 months
Proportion of manuscripts accepted: 1/2
Illustrations accepted: tables, graphs, charts, pictures
Foreign languages: no

Reviews

Seeking reviewers: no
Unsolicited reviews accepted: no
Materials reviewed: books
Length of review: 800 words

NEVADA HISTORICAL SOCIETY QUARTERLY

Focus: Nevada, the Great Basin, and the West; anthropological and cultural aspects
Institutional affiliation: Nevada Historical Society, Reno and Las Vegas
Editor: Gary K. Roberts
Address: 1555 East Flamingo, No. 253 Las Vegas, NV 89109
Frequency: 4/year
Circulation: 1,000
Pages/issue: 78
Readership: academics, general public

Manuscripts
Query: no
Abstract: no
Style guide: MOS
Preferred length: 2,500–7,500 words
Number of copies: 2
Notes: end of manuscript
Blind referee: yes
Time to consider manuscript: 6–8 weeks
Illustrations accepted: tables, graphs, charts, pictures
Foreign languages: no

Reviews
Seeking reviewers: yes
Unsolicited reviews accepted: no
How to apply: letter
Include in application: professional degrees, institutional affiliation, areas of expertise, published works, current research
Materials reviewed: books
Length of review: 700–900 words

NEW ENGLAND HISTORICAL AND GENEALOGICAL REGISTER

Focus: New England family and local history
Institutional affiliation: New England Historic Genealogical Society
Assistant editor: Catherine L. Slichter
Book review editor: same
Address: 101 Newbury Street Boston, MA 02116
Frequency: 4/year
Circulation: 6,000
Pages/issue: 80
Readership: academics, general public

Manuscripts
Query: no
Abstract: no
Style guide: MOS, own
Preferred length: 15–20 pages
Number of copies: 2
Notes: end of manuscript
Blind referee: no
Time to consider manuscript: 1 month
Illustrations accepted: tables, graphs, charts
Foreign languages: no

Reviews
Seeking reviewers: yes
Unsolicited reviews accepted: no
How to apply: letter
Include in application: professional degrees, institutional affiliation, areas of expertise, current research
Materials reviewed: books
Length of review: 500–800 words

THE NEW ENGLAND QUARTERLY

Focus: New England life and letters
Institutional affiliation: Colonial Society of Massachusetts
Editor: Herbert Brown
Book review editor: John D. Cushing
Address: Hubbard Hall
Bowdoin College
Brunswick, ME 04011
Frequency: 4/year
Circulation: 3,000
Pages/issue: 164
Readership: academics, general public

Manuscripts
Query: no
Preferred length: 25 pages
Number of copies: 2
Notes: bottom of page
Blind referee: no
Time to consider manuscript: 2 months
Proportion of manuscripts accepted: 1/10
Illustrations accepted: no
Foreign languages: no

Reviews
Seeking reviewers: yes
Unsolicited reviews accepted: no
How to apply: letter
Include in application: institutional affiliation
Materials reviewed: trade books

NEW JERSEY HISTORICAL COMMISSION NEWSLETTER

Focus: New Jersey
Institutional affiliation: New Jersey Historical Commission, New Jersey Department of Education
Editor: Peggy Lewis
Book review editor: same
Address: 113 W. State St.
Trenton, NJ 08530
Frequency: 10/year
Circulation: 10,000
Pages/issue: 8
Readership: academics, historical societies, general public

Manuscripts
Query: yes
Abstract: no
Style guide: MOS
Preferred length: open
Number of copies: 1
Notes: end of manuscript
Blind referee: no
Time to consider manuscript: 3 months
Illustrations accepted: pictures (black-and-white glossies preferable)
Foreign languages: no

Reviews
Seeking reviewers: yes
Unsolicited reviews accepted: no
How to apply: letter
Include in application: areas of expertise, current research
Materials reviewed: books, films, audio, articles
Length of review: 250–500 words

NEW JERSEY HISTORY

Focus: New Jersey
Institutional affiliation: New Jersey
    Historical Society
Editor: Joseph F. Mahoney
Book review editor: Morris Garber
Address: 230 Broadway
         Newark, NJ 07104
Frequency: 4/year
Circulation: 3,300
Pages/issue: 80
Readership: academics, general public

Manuscripts
Query: no
Abstract: no
Style guide: MLA
Number of copies: 1
Notes: end of manuscript
Blind referee: yes
Time to consider manuscript: 4–5
    months
**Proportion of manuscripts
    accepted:** 1/2
Illustrations accepted: tables, graphs,
    charts, pictures
Foreign languages: no

Reviews
Seeking reviewers: yes
Unsolicited reviews accepted: no
How to apply: letter
Include in application: professional
    degrees, institutional affiliation, areas
    of expertise
Materials reviewed: books
Length of review: 400 words

NEW MEXICO HISTORICAL REVIEW

Focus: New Mexico and Borderlands
Institutional affiliation: University of New
    Mexico, Albuquerque
Editor: Richard W. Etulain
Book review editor: Richard N. Ellis
Address: University of New Mexico
         Mesa Vista 1013
         Albuquerque, NM 87131
Frequency: 4/year
Circulation: 1,100
Pages/issue: 80–100
Readership: academics, general public

Manuscripts
Query: no
Abstract: no
Style guide: MOS
Preferred length: 10–30 pages
Number of copies: 2
Notes: end of manuscript
Blind referee: yes
Time to consider manuscript: 6–8
    weeks
**Proportion of manuscripts
    accepted:** 1/2
Illustrations accepted: tables, graphs,
    charts, pictures (2 or 3)
Foreign languages: Spanish in text, if
    applicable, with accompanying
    translation

Reviews
Seeking reviewers: yes
Unsolicited reviews accepted: no
How to apply: letter
Include in application: professional
    degrees, institutional affiliation, areas
    of expertise, published works, foreign
    languages, current research
Materials reviewed: books
Length of review: 400–600 words

NEW SCHOLAR

Focus: the Americas, especially Latin America; Chicanos, Native Americans, Blacks
Institutional affiliation: University of California, San Diego and Santa Barbara
Editor: Michael T. Arguello
Address: South Hall 4607
University of California, Santa Barbara
Santa Barbara, CA 93106
Book review editor: Phil Brian Johnson
Address: Department of History
San Francisco State University
San Francisco, CA 94132
Frequency: 2/year
Circulation: 650
Pages/issue: 225
Readership: academics

Manuscripts
Query: yes
Abstract: yes
Style guide: MOS
Number of copies: 3
Notes: end of manuscript
Blind referee: yes
Time to consider manuscript: 3 months
Proportion of manuscripts accepted: 3/10
Illustrations accepted: tables, charts, pictures
Foreign languages: translations should be arranged by the author and the editors

Reviews
Seeking reviewers: yes
Unsolicited reviews accepted: yes
How to apply: letter
Include in application: professional degrees, institutional affiliation, areas of expertise, published works, foreign languages, current research
Materials reviewed: books, films
Length of review: by arrangement

Additional notes
Special emphasis is placed on review essays, reviews of literature in the social sciences, etc.

THE NEW-YORK HISTORICAL SOCIETY QUARTERLY

Focus: New York State and New York City; American history in general, but not foreign policy
Institutional affiliation: The New-York Historical Society
Editor: Elaine Andrews
Book review editor: Bruce F. Krueger
Address: 170 Central Park West
New York, NY 10024
Frequency: 4/year
Circulation: 2,200
Pages/issue: 96
Readership: historians, academics, Society members

Manuscripts
Query: no
Abstract: yes
Style guide: MOS
Preferred length: 15–30 pages
Number of copies: 1
Notes: end of manuscript
Blind referee: no
Time to consider manuscript: 2–6 weeks
Proportion of manuscripts accepted: 1/5
Illustrations accepted: pictures
Foreign languages: no

Reviews
Seeking reviewers: yes
Unsolicited reviews accepted: rarely
How to apply: letter
Include in application: professional degrees, institutional affiliation, areas of expertise, published works, current research
Materials reviewed: books
Length of review: 500–600 words

Additional notes
Manuscripts may be from professional as well as amateur historians and from established scholars as well as promising students. Careful documentation, original research, a thesis or point of view, analysis, interpretation, and conclusions are essential. The *Quarterly* does not publish dissertations or verbatim addresses.

NEW YORK HISTORY

Focus: all aspects of New York
Institutional affiliation: New York State Historical Association
Editor: Wendell Tripp
Book review editor: Langdon G. Wright
Address: New York State Historical Association
Cooperstown, NY 13326
Frequency: 4/year
Circulation: 2,500
Pages/issue: 128
Readership: academics, scholars, buffs

Manuscripts
Query: no
Abstract: no
Style guide: MOS
Preferred length: 4,000–5,000 words
Number of copies: 1
Notes: end of manuscript
Blind referee: no
Time to consider manuscript: 3 months
Proportion of manuscripts accepted: 1/4
Illustrations accepted: tables, graphs, charts, pictures
Foreign languages: no

Reviews
Seeking reviewers: no
Unsolicited reviews accepted: no
How to apply: letter
Include in application: professional degrees, institutional affiliation, areas of expertise, published works
Materials reviewed: books
Length of review: 500 words

NEWPORT HISTORY

Focus: the City of Newport, Newport County, and the State of Rhode Island
Institutional affiliation: Newport Historical Society
Editor: Howard Browne
Book review editor: William Reitzel
Address: 82 Touro Street
Newport, RI 02840
Frequency: 4/year
Circulation: 1,000
Pages/issue: 35–40
Readership: general public, institutions

Manuscripts
Query: no
Abstract: no
Number of copies: 1
Notes: end of manuscript
Blind referee: no
Proportion of manuscripts accepted: high
Illustrations accepted: tables, charts, pictures
Foreign languages: no

Reviews
Seeking reviewers: no
Unsolicited reviews accepted: yes
Materials reviewed: trade books

NEWSLETTER: WHOOP-UP COUNTRY CHAPTER, HISTORICAL SOCIETY OF ALBERTA

Focus: local and regional history
Institutional affiliation: Historical Society of Alberta
Editor: Alex Johnston
Address: Research Station
Lethbridge, Alberta T1J 4B1
CANADA
Frequency: 6/year
Circulation: 300
Pages/issue: 6
Readership: general public

Manuscripts
Query: no
Abstract: no
Style guide: none
Preferred length: 250–1,000 words
Number of copies: 1
Notes: end of manuscript
Blind referee: no
Proportion of manuscripts accepted: 9/10
Illustrations accepted: preferably not
Foreign languages: no

NIAGARA FRONTIER

Focus: western New York
Institutional affiliation: Buffalo and Erie County Historical Society
Editor: vacant
Address: Buffalo and Erie County
Historical Society
25 Nottingham Court
Buffalo, NY 14216
Frequency: 4/year
Circulation: 1,300
Pages/issue: 28
Readership: Society members, academics

Manuscripts
Query: no
Abstract: no
Preferred length: 8,000 words maximum
Number of copies: 1
Notes: end of manuscript
Blind referee: no
Time to consider manuscript: varies
Illustrations accepted: tables, graphs, charts, pictures
Foreign languages: no

Reviews
Seeking reviewers: no
Unsolicited reviews accepted: no
Materials reviewed: books

NORTH CAROLINA HISTORICAL REVIEW

Focus: North Carolina; the South or other southern states as they relate to North Carolina

Institutional affiliation: Division of Archives and History, North Carolina Department of Cultural Resources

Editor: Memory F. Mitchell

Book review editor: same

Address: 109 East Jones Street
Raleigh, NC 27611

Frequency: 4/year

Circulation: 2,150

Pages/issue: 110

Readership: academics, general public

Manuscripts

Query: no

Abstract: no

Style guide: MOS

Preferred length: 20–25 pages

Number of copies: 2

Notes: end of manuscript

Blind referee: yes

Time to consider manuscript: 8–10 weeks

Proportion of manuscripts accepted: 1/10–1/7

Illustrations accepted: tables, pictures (black-and-white only)

Foreign languages: no

Reviews

Seeking reviewers: yes

Unsolicited reviews accepted: no

How to apply: letter

Include in application: professional degrees, institutional affiliation, areas of expertise

Materials reviewed: books

Length of review: 350–400 words

Additional notes

Articles should be based on primary sources; do not rehash previously published material.

NORTH DAKOTA HISTORY: JOURNAL OF THE NORTHERN PLAINS

Focus: culture of North Dakota and northern Great Plains

Institutional affiliation: State Historical Society of North Dakota

Editor: Larry Remele

Address: State Historical Society of North Dakota
North Dakota Heritage Center
Capitol Grounds
Bismarck, ND 58505

Frequency: 4/year

Circulation: 1,500

Pages/issue: 40

Readership: academics, general public

Manuscripts

Query: no

Abstract: no

Style guide: MFW

Preferred length: 20–30 pages

Number of copies: 1

Notes: end of manuscript

Blind referee: no

Time to consider manuscript: 3 months

Proportion of manuscripts accepted: 1/2

Illustrations accepted: photos/illustrations will be copied and originals returned; tables, charts, graphs should be in black ink and large enough to transpose to print

Foreign languages: no

Reviews

Seeking reviewers: yes

Unsolicited reviews accepted: no

How to apply: letter

Include in application: resume

Materials reviewed: books, films, audio

Length of review: 2–3 pages

Additional notes

The *Journal* provides galleys for perusal prior to publication and supplies authors with copies of the issue.

NORTH JERSEY HIGHLANDER

Focus: northern New Jersey, southern New York, and eastern Pennsylvania
Institutional affiliation: North Jersey Highlands Historical Society
Editor: W. Mead Stapler
Book review editor: Frederick Talasco
Address: P.O. Box 1
Newfoundland, NJ 07435
Frequency: 4/year
Circulation: 250
Pages/issue: 36
Readership: historians

Manuscripts
Query: yes
Abstract: yes
Style guide: none
Preferred length: open
Number of copies: 1
Notes: bottom of page
Blind referee: no
Time to consider manuscript: 3 weeks
Proportion of manuscripts accepted: 1/2
Illustrations accepted: camera-ready tables, graphs, charts, pictures
Foreign languages: no

NORTH WIND

Focus: medieval cultures before 1650 and their recreation
Institutional affiliation: Northern Society for Creative Anachronism
Editors: Sue Walsh, Pam Martin
Address: Box 65583
Vancouver 12, B.C. V5N 5K5
CANADA
Frequency: 1/month
Circulation: 200
Pages/issue: 20
Readership: academics, general public, buffs

Manuscripts
Query: no
Abstract: useful
Style guide: MLA suggested
Preferred length: 750–5,000 words
Number of copies: 1
Notes: end of manuscript
Blind referee: no
Time to consider manuscript: 1 month
Illustrations accepted: tables, graphs, charts, pictures
Foreign languages: French (with English abstract)

Reviews
Seeking reviewers: yes
Unsolicited reviews accepted: yes
Materials reviewed: books, films
Length of review: 200 words minimum

Additional notes
North Wind does not want narrow historical accounts, except intercultural ones; instead, it asks for rigorous articles of a practical cultural nature (cooking, clothing, fighting, behavior, etc.), from all cultures in the medieval period.

NORTHEAST AFRICAN STUDIES

Focus: scholarly accounts of northeast Africa including Ethiopia, Somalia, the Horn of Africa, the Sudan, Kenya
Institutional affiliation: African Studies Center, Michigan State University
Editor: Harold G. Marcus
Address: African Studies Center
Michigan State University
East Lansing, MI 48824
Frequency: 3/year
Circulation: 157
Pages/issue: 80
Readership: academics, area specialists

Manuscripts
Query: no
Abstract: no
Style guide: MOS
Preferred length: 30 pages (but will do two- and three-part items up to 90 pages)
Number of copies: 1
Notes: end of manuscript
Blind referee: no
Time to consider manuscript: depends on material
Proportion of manuscripts accepted: 1/2
Illustrations accepted: tables, camera-ready graphs, charts, line illustrations

Reviews
Seeking reviewers: yes
Unsolicited reviews accepted: no
How to apply: letter
Include in application: professional degrees, areas of expertise, published works, foreign languages, current research, experience in northeast Africa
Materials reviewed: books, films
Length of review: variable

Additional notes
A journal of opinion as well as scholarship.

NORTHEASTERN NEVADA HISTORICAL SOCIETY QUARTERLY

Focus: northeastern Nevada
Institutional affiliation: Northeastern Nevada Historical Society
Editor: Howard Hickson
Book review editor: same
Address: P.O. Box 503
Elko, NV 89801
Frequency: 4/year
Circulation: 1,700
Pages/issue: 28–40
Readership: Society members, general public

Manuscripts
Query: no
Abstract: no
Style guide: Associated Press
Preferred length: 20–30 pages
Number of copies: 2
Notes: end of manuscript
Blind referee: no
Time to consider manuscript: 1 month
Proportion of manuscripts accepted: 1/4
Illustrations accepted: tables, graphs, charts, pictures
Foreign languages: no

Reviews
Seeking reviewers: no
Unsolicited reviews accepted: yes
How to apply: letter
Include in application: areas of expertise
Materials reviewed: books
Length of review: 3 pages

Additional notes
Articles selected for publication must be written for the layman. Footnotes and accuracy are researched by the editor and a museum researcher. Articles' rights and copyrights remain with author.

NORTHWEST OHIO QUARTERLY

Focus: Maumee Valley region, which consists of northwest Ohio, southwest Michigan, and northeast Indiana
Institutional affiliation: Maumee Valley Historical Society; Bowling Green State University
Editor: Richard J. Wright
Address: Wolcott Howe Museum
1031 River Road
Maumee, OH 43537
Frequency: 4/year
Circulation: 700–800
Pages/issue: 36–42
Readership: general public, historians

Manuscripts
Query: no
Abstract: no
Style guide: none
Preferred length: 20–30 pages
Number of copies: 2
Notes: end of manuscript
Blind referee: no
Time to consider manuscript: 2 months
Proportion of manuscripts accepted: 3/4
Illustrations accepted: tables, graphs, charts, pictures
Foreign languages: no

NOVA SCOTIA HISTORICAL QUARTERLY

Focus: Nova Scotia
Editor: W. H. McCurdy
Book review editor: Lorna Inness
Address: Petheric Press, Ltd.
Box 1102
Halifax, Nova Scotia
CANADA
Frequency: 4/year
Pages/issue: 100
Readership: general public

Manuscripts
Query: yes
Abstract: no
Preferred length: 2,500–5,000 words
Number of copies: 1
Notes: end of manuscript
Blind referee: no
Time to consider manuscript: 3 months
Illustrations accepted: no
Foreign languages: no

Reviews
Seeking reviewers: no
Unsolicited reviews accepted: no

OHIO HISTORY

Focus: Ohio
Editor: Robert L. Daugherty
Book review editor: Laura Russell
Address: Ohio Historical Society
I–71 and 17th Avenue
Columbus, OH 43211
Frequency: 4/year
Circulation: 3,500
Pages/issue: 100
Readership: scholars

Manuscripts

Query: no
Abstract: no
Style guide: MOS
Preferred length: 20 pages
Number of copies: 2
Notes: end of manuscript
Blind referee: no
Time to consider manuscript: 6 months
**Proportion of manuscripts
accepted:** 1/4
Illustrations accepted: tables, graphs,
charts, pictures
Foreign languages: no

Reviews

Seeking reviewers: yes
Unsolicited reviews accepted: no
How to apply: special form
Include in application: institutional
affiliation, areas of expertise,
published works, current research
Materials reviewed: books
Length of review: 600 words

THE OLD NORTHWEST: A JOURNAL OF REGIONAL LIFE AND LETTERS

Focus: interdisciplinary studies of the Old
Northwest Territory and the states
which developed from it: Ohio,
Indiana, Michigan, Wisconsin, Illinois
Institutional affiliation: Miami University
Editor: Robert R. Kettler
Book review editor: John N. Dickinson
Address: Bachelor Hall
Miami University
Oxford, OH 45056
Frequency: 4/year
Circulation: 3,500
Readership: general public, libraries

Manuscripts

Query: no
Abstract: no
Style guide: MLA
Preferred length: 5,000–7,000 words
Number of copies: 1
Notes: end of manuscript
Blind referee: no
Time to consider manuscript: 3–6
months
**Proportion of manuscripts
accepted:** 1/4
Illustrations accepted: tables, graphs,
charts, pictures
Foreign languages: no

Reviews

Seeking reviewers: yes
Unsolicited reviews accepted: no
How to apply: letter
Include in application: institutional
affiliation
Materials reviewed: books, fiction
Length of review: 600–1,000 words

OLD-TIME NEW ENGLAND

Focus: architecture, decorative arts, social and cultural characteristics of New England
Institutional affiliation: Society for the Preservation of New England Antiquities
Executive editor: Abbott Lowell Cummings
Address: 141 Cambridge Street
Boston, MA 02114
Frequency: 4/year
Circulation: 5,000
Pages/issue: 60–96
Readership: Society members, academics

Manuscripts
Query: no
Abstract: no
Style guide: MOS
Preferred length: 15 pages
Number of copies: 1
Notes: end of manuscript
Blind referee: no
Time to consider manuscript: varies
Illustrations accepted: tables, graphs, charts, pictures (black-and-white glossy photographs only; other illustrations in clear-cut outline)
Foreign languages: no

OLD WEST

Focus: events and lives in the Old West, preferably 1840–1905
Editor: Pat Wagner
Address: P.O. Box 3338
Austin, TX 78764
Frequency: 4/year
Circulation: 60,000
Pages/issue: 64
Readership: general public

Manuscripts
Query: yes
Abstract: no
Style guide: own
Preferred length: 1,500–4,000 words
Number of copies: 1
Notes: no notes; list sources separately
Time to consider manuscript: 6 weeks
Illustrations accepted: pictures
Foreign languages: no

Reviews
Seeking reviewers: no

Additional notes
Old West does not use fiction based on fact or a lot of dialogue that cannot be substantiated. Its editors are not looking for the dry textbook approach, but do insist that the material be researched and accurate. *Old West* pays 2¢ a word minimum on acceptance, plus an allowance for pictures.

ONTARIO HISTORY

Focus: Province of Ontario from earliest times to present
Institutional affiliation: Ontario Historical Society
Editor: Royce MacGillivray
Book review editor: Roger Hall
Address: Department of History
University of Waterloo
Waterloo, Ontario, N2L 3G1
CANADA
Frequency: 4/year
Circulation: 2,100
Pages/issue: 64
Readership: academics, general public

Manuscripts
Query: no
Abstract: no
Style guide: R. M. Wiles, *Scholarly Reporting in the Humanities*
Preferred length: 6,000–7,000 words
Number of copies: 2 preferred
Notes: end of manuscript
Blind referee: no
Time to consider manuscript: 3 months
Illustrations accepted: yes, but most articles are better without them
Foreign languages: French

Reviews
Materials reviewed: books

ORAL HISTORY REVIEW

Focus: articles of substance which use oral history methodology or deal with problems of methodology
Institutional affiliation: Oral History Association
Editor: Richard Sweterlitsch
Book review editor: John Neuenschwander
Address: 307 Old Mill
University of Vermont
Burlington, VT 05405
Frequency: 1/year
Circulation: 1,400
Pages/issue: 96–124
Readership: academics

Manuscripts
Query: no
Abstract: no
Style guide: MLA
Number of copies: 2
Notes: end of manuscript
Blind referee: yes
Time to consider manuscript: 3–6 months
Proportion of manuscripts accepted: 3/5
Illustrations accepted: tables, graphs, charts, pictures

Foreign languages: no

Reviews
Seeking reviewers: yes
Unsolicited reviews accepted: yes
How to apply: letter
Include in application: institutional affiliation, areas of expertise
Materials reviewed: books, films, audio

OREGON HISTORICAL QUARTERLY

Focus: life in the Oregon Country and its relationship to national and world events
Institutional affiliation: Oregon Historical Society
Editor: Priscilla Knuth
Address: 1230 S.W. Park Avenue
Portland, OR 97205
Frequency: 4/year
Circulation: 6,200
Pages/issue: 96–112
Readership: academics, general public

Manuscripts
Query: no
Abstract: no
Style guide: MOS or MLA
Preferred length: 8,000–10,000 words
Number of copies: 1
Notes: end of manuscript
Blind referee: no
Time to consider manuscript: 6 weeks
Proportion of manuscripts accepted: 1/3
Illustrations accepted: camera-ready tables, graphs, charts, pictures
Foreign languages: no

Reviews
Unsolicited reviews accepted: no
How to apply: letter
Include in application: professional degrees, institutional affiliation, areas of expertise, published works
Materials reviewed: material pertinent to the region

THE OZARKER

Focus: Shannon County, Missouri, surrounding area, and interesting people of today
Editors: James G. and Vada Chilton
Address: P.O. Box A
Eminence, MO 65466
Frequency: 8/year
Circulation: 656
Pages/issue: 20
Readership: general public

Manuscripts
Query: no
Abstract: no
Style guide: none
Preferred length: open
Number of copies: 1
Notes: end of manuscript
Blind referee: no
Proportion of manuscripts accepted: 4/5
Illustrations accepted: tables, graphs, charts, pictures
Foreign languages: no

PACIFIC AFFAIRS: AN INTERNATIONAL REVIEW OF ASIA AND THE PACIFIC

Focus: political, economic, social, and diplomatic problems of Eastern and Southern Asia and the South Pacific
Institutional affiliation: University of British Columbia
Editor: H. B. Chamberlain
Book review editor: Hazel Ackner
Address: 2075 Westbrook Mall
Vancouver, B.C. V6T 1W5
CANADA
Frequency: 4/year
Circulation: 3,000
Pages/issue: 180
Readership: libraries, academic and government institutions, academics

Manuscripts
Query: preferred
Abstract: no
Style guide: MLA
Preferred length: 6,500 words
Number of copies: 2 (1 blind review)
Notes: end of manuscript
Blind referee: yes
Time to consider manuscript: 4–6 weeks
Illustrations accepted: some tables
Foreign languages: English preferred but can translate if necessary

Reviews
Seeking reviewers: yes
Unsolicited reviews accepted: rarely
How to apply: letter
Include in application: professional degrees, institutional affiliation, areas of expertise, published works, foreign languages, current research, anything relevant
Materials reviewed: books
Length of review: variable

THE PACIFIC HISTORIAN

Focus: Western history and ideas
Institutional affiliation: University of the Pacific
Editor: Martha O'Bryon
Book review editor: Ernestine Smutny
Address: University of the Pacific
Stockton, CA 95204
Frequency: 4/year
Circulation: 2,000
Pages/issue: 125
Readership: academics, buffs

Manuscripts
Query: no
Abstract: yes
Style guide: MOS
Preferred length: 1,500–3,000 words
Number of copies: 2
Notes: end of manuscript
Blind referee: no
Time to consider manuscript: 3 months
Illustrations accepted: tables, graphs, charts, pictures (black-and-white glossies)
Foreign languages: no

Reviews
Seeking reviewers: yes
Unsolicited reviews accepted: no
How to apply: letter
Include in application: professional degrees, institutional affiliation, areas of expertise, published work, foreign languages, current research
Materials reviewed: books
Length of review: 1 page

PACIFIC HISTORICAL REVIEW

Focus: American diplomatic history, frontier history, and the western states in the twentieth century
Editor: Norris Hundley, Jr.
Book review editor: Craig Cunningham
Address: Ralph Bunche Hall
University of California
Los Angeles, CA 90024
Frequency: 4/year
Circulation: 3,000
Pages/issue: 150
Readership: academics

Manuscripts
Query: no
Abstract: no
Style guide: MOS
Preferred length: 25 pages
Number of copies: 3
Notes: end of manuscript
Blind referee: yes
Time to consider manuscript: 2–5 months
Proportion of manuscripts accepted: 1/7
Illustrations accepted: camera-ready tables, graphs, charts, pictures
Foreign languages: no

Reviews
Seeking reviewers: no
Unsolicited reviews accepted: no

THE PACIFIC NORTHWEST FORUM

Focus: environment, biographies, documents, photos, drawings, fiction, poetry of the Pacific Northwest
Institutional affiliation: Eastern Washington University
Editor: J. William T. Youngs, Jr.
Book review editors: same, Robert B. Olafson
Address: Department of History
Eastern Washington University
Cheney, WA 99004
Frequency: 4/year
Circulation: 500
Pages/issue: 28–30
Readership: academics, schools, general public

Manuscripts
Query: no
Abstract: no
Number of copies: 1
Notes: end of manuscript
Blind referee: no
Time to consider manuscript: 1 month
Proportion of manuscripts accepted: 3/5
Illustrations accepted: tables, graphs, charts, pictures
Foreign languages: no

Reviews
Seeking reviewers: no
Unsolicited reviews accepted: yes
How to apply: letter
Include in application: professional degrees, institutional affiliation, areas of expertise, published works, current research
Materials reviewed: books
Length of review: 300–600 words

Additional notes
The Pacific Northwest includes Washington, Oregon, Idaho, Montana, Canada and Alaska.

PACIFIC NORTHWEST QUARTERLY

Focus: the Pacific Northwest, including Alaska and western Canada
Institutional affiliation: University of Washington
Editor: Robert E. Burke
Book review editor: same
Address: 4045 Brooklyn Avenue NE
Seattle, WA 98105
Frequency: 4/year
Circulation: 1,700
Pages/issue: 36–40
Readership: scholars, libraries, members of the Washington State Historical Society

Manuscripts
Query: no
Abstract: no
Style guide: MOS
Preferred length: 6,000–7,000 words
Number of copies: 2
Notes: end of manuscript
Blind referee: yes
Time to consider manuscript: 3 months
Proportion of manuscripts accepted: 1/6–1/5
Illustrations accepted: tables, graphs, charts, pictures (illustrations are eagerly sought)
Foreign languages: no

Reviews
Seeking reviewers: yes
Unsolicited reviews accepted: rarely
How to apply: letter
Include in application: professional degrees, institutional affiliation, areas of expertise, published works, foreign languages, current research
Materials reviewed: books
Length of review: 350–400 words

Additional notes
The *Quarterly* is interested in scholarly writings and edited reminiscences.

THE PALIMPSEST

Focus: Iowa
Institutional affiliation: State Historical Society of Iowa
Editor: Charles Phillips
Address: 402 Iowa Avenue
Iowa City, IA 52240
Frequency: 6/year
Pages/issue: 30
Readership: general public, historians

Manuscripts
Query: no
Abstract: no
Style guide: MLA
Preferred length: 15–25 pages
Number of copies: 1
Notes: end of manuscript
Blind referee: no
Time to consider manuscript: 3 months
Proportion of manuscripts accepted: 1/5
Illustrations accepted: pictures
Foreign languages: no

PASSWORD

Focus: El Paso, Texas Southwest
Institutional affiliation: El Paso County
   Historical Society
Editor: Conrey Bryson
Book review editor: same
Address: 600 Gregory Way
   El Paso, TX 79902
Frequency: 4/year
Circulation: 1,000
Pages/issue: 48
Readership: general public

Manuscripts
Query: no
Abstract: no
Preferred length: 3,000–5,000 words
Number of copies: 1
Notes: end of manuscript
Blind referee: no
Time to consider manuscript: 1 month
Illustrations accepted: simple tables,
   graphs, charts, pictures
Foreign languages: no

Reviews
Seeking reviewers: yes
Unsolicited reviews accepted: yes
How to apply: letter
Include in application: institutional
   affiliation, areas of expertise,
   published works, current research
Materials reviewed: books
Length of review: 300–500 words

PEA RIVER TRAILS

Focus: Alabama; genealogy
Institutional affiliation: Pea River
   Historical and Genealogical Society,
   Alabama
Editor: James B. Jolley
Book review editor: Faye Grimmer
Address: Box 628
   Enterprise, AL 36330
Frequency: 2/year
Circulation: 250
Pages/issue: 40–45
Readership: general public

Manuscripts
Query: no
Abstract: no
Style guide: none
Preferred length: open
Number of copies: 1
Notes: no preference
Blind referee: no
Time to consider manuscript: varies
**Proportion of manuscripts
   accepted:** 9/10
Illustrations accepted: tables, graphs,
   charts, pictures
Foreign languages: no

Reviews
Seeking reviewers: no
Unsolicited reviews accepted: no

PEASANT STUDIES NEWSLETTER

Focus: interdisciplinary study of rural peoples
Institutional affiliation: University of Pittsburgh
Editors: Murdo McCleod, David Sabean
Book review editors: same
Address: Department of History
University of Pittsburgh
3K30
Forbes Quadrangle
Pittsburgh, PA 15260
Frequency: 4/year
Circulation: 550
Pages/issue: 62
Readership: scholars, academic libraries

Manuscripts

Query: no
Abstract: no
Style guide: MOS
Preferred length: 25–35 pages
Number of copies: 1
Notes: end of manuscript
Blind referee: no
Time to consider manuscript: 3 months
Proportion of manuscripts accepted: 2/5
Illustrations accepted: tables, graphs, charts, maps
Foreign languages: accepted with reluctance

Reviews

Seeking reviewers: yes
Unsolicited reviews accepted: yes
How to apply: letter
Include in application: professional degrees, published works
Materials reviewed: books
Length of review: 25 pages, only essay reviews

PENNSYLVANIA FOLKLIFE

Focus: folklife and folk culture of any and all ethnic groups in Pennsylvania, particularly of a comparative nature; crafts, personalities, folk heritage from settlement to the present
Institutional affiliation: Ursinus College and Pennsylvania Folklife Society
Editor: William T. Parsons
Address: P.O. Box 92
Collegeville, PA 19426
Frequency: 4/year
Pages/issue: 48
Readership: institutional libraries, museums, academics, general public

Manuscripts

Query: no
Abstract: helpful
Style guide: MOS preferred
Preferred length: 1,500–5,000 words
Number of copies: 2
Notes: end of manuscript
Blind referee: no
Time to consider manuscript:
5 weeks–3 months
Proportion of manuscripts accepted: 1/4–1/3
Illustrations accepted: tables, graphs, charts, pictures (photos or line drawings equally acceptable; 6–10 illustrations minimum)
Foreign languages: yes, if relevant: Pennsylvania Deitsch, South German, Welsh, Slovak, French dialects, or language transliteration but always with English translations.

Additional notes

Articles which attempt comparative studies of neighboring cultures or which compare folk cultural traits as they vary and change over several generations are especially welcome. If the work contains dialect or brogue or folkspeech, strive for consistency in use since the experts have not yet agreed on standard spellings.

PENNSYLVANIA HERITAGE

Focus: Pennsylvania
Institutional affiliation: Quarterly of the Pennsylvania Historical and Museum Commission
Editor: Douglas H. West
Address: Pennsylvania Historical and Museum Commission
Box 1026
Harrisburg, PA 17120
Frequency: 4/year
Circulation: 3,800
Pages/issue: 32
Readership: scholars, preservationists, historical society members, oral historians, general public

Manuscripts
Query: no
Abstract: yes
Style guide: MOS
Preferred length: 12 pages
Number of copies: 2
Notes: end of manuscript
Blind referee: no
Time to consider manuscript: 2 months
Proportion of manuscripts accepted: 1/6
Illustrations accepted: tables, graphs, charts, pictures (submit with article)
Foreign languages: no

PENNSYLVANIA HISTORY

Focus: Pennsylvania
Institutional affiliation: Pennsylvania Historical Association
Editor: Harold E. Cox
Book review editor: Charles D. Cashdollar
Address: Wilkes College
Wilkes Barre, PA 18766
Frequency: 4/year
Circulation: 1,100
Pages/issue: 96
Readership: academics, general public

Manuscripts
Query: no
Abstract: no
Style guide: MOS
Preferred length: 10–30 pages
Number of copies: 1
Notes: end of manuscript
Blind referee: no
Time to consider manuscript: 1–3 months
Proportion of manuscripts accepted: 1/3–1/2
Illustrations accepted: tables, graphs, charts, pictures
Foreign languages: no

Reviews
Seeking reviewers: yes
Unsolicited reviews accepted: no
How to apply: letter
Include in application: professional degrees, institutional affiliation, areas of expertise, published works, current research
Materials reviewed: books

THE PENNSYLVANIA MAGAZINE OF HISTORY AND BIOGRAPHY

Focus: Pennsylvania
Institutional affiliation: The Historical Society of Pennsylvania
Editor: Nicholas B. Wainwright
Book review editor: same
Address: 1300 Locust Street
Philadelphia, PA 19107
Frequency: 4/year
Circulation: 3,800
Pages/issue: 140
Readership: academics, general public

Manuscripts

Query: no
Abstract: no
Style guide: MOS preferred
Preferred length: 30–35 pages
Number of copies: 1
Notes: end of manuscript
Blind referee: no
Time to consider manuscript: 1 month
Illustrations accepted: no halftone illustrations; tables, graphs, and charts discouraged
Foreign languages: no

Reviews

Seeking reviewers: no
Unsolicited reviews accepted: no
Materials reviewed: books
Length of review: 600 words

PENNSYLVANIA MENNONITE HERITAGE

Focus: religious thought and expression, culture, and genealogy of Mennonite-related groups originating in Pennsylvania
Institutional affiliation: Lancaster Mennonite Historical Society
Editor: Carolyn C. Wenger
Book review editor: same
Address: 2215 Millstream Road
Lancaster, PA 17602
Frequency: 4/year
Circulation: 1,400
Pages/issue: 36
Readership: general public, academics

Manuscripts

Query: no
Abstract: no
Style guide: MOS
Preferred length: 2,000–4,000 words
Number of copies: 2 preferred
Notes: end of manuscript
Blind referee: no
Time to consider manuscript: 1 month
Illustrations accepted: tables, graphs, charts, pictures
Foreign languages: Pennsylvania Dutch dialect and German

Reviews

Seeking reviewers: yes
Unsolicited reviews accepted: yes
How to apply: letter
Include in application: professional degrees, institutional affiliation, areas of expertise, published works, current research
Materials reviewed: books
Length of review: 250–500 words

PERSIMMON HILL

Focus: cowboys, cattlemen, and rodeos of the American West; the West in literature, art, and film
Institutional affiliation: National Cowboy Hall of Fame
Editor: Dean Krakel
Book review editor: same
Address: 1700 N.E. 63rd Street
Oklahoma City, OK 73111
Frequency: 4/year
Circulation: 25,000
Pages/issue: 80–90
Readership: general public

Manuscripts
Query: yes
Abstract: sometimes
Style guide: MOS
Preferred length: 2,000–3,000 words
Number of copies: 1
Notes: end of manuscript
Blind referee: no
Time to consider manuscript: 3 months
Illustrations accepted: pictures
Foreign languages: no

Reviews
Seeking reviewers. no
Unsolicited reviews accepted: no

PHARMACY IN HISTORY

Focus: pharmacy and drugs
Institutional affiliation: American Institute of the History of Pharmacy
Editor: George Bender
Book review editor: David L. Cowen
Address: American Institute of the History of Pharmacy
Pharmacy Building
Madison, WI 53706
Frequency: 4/year
Circulation: 1,400
Readership: pharmacists, historians

Manuscripts
Query: no
Abstract: no
Style guide: none
Preferred length: 30 pages maximum
Number of copies: 2
Notes: end of manuscript
Blind referee: no
Time to consider manuscript: 1–2 months
Proportion of manuscripts accepted: 2/5
Illustrations accepted: tables, graphs, charts, pictures
Foreign languages: no

Reviews
Seeking reviewers: yes
Unsolicited reviews accepted: no
How to apply: letter
Include in application: professional degrees, institutional affiliation, areas of expertise, foreign languages
Materials reviewed: books
Length of review: variable

PHYLON: THE ATLANTA UNIVERSITY REVIEW OF RACE AND CULTURE

Focus: sociology, social sciences, some literature
Institutional affiliation: Atlanta University
Editor: Charles F. Duncan, Jr. (Acting)
Address: 223 Chestnut Street, S.W.
Atlanta University
Atlanta, GA 30314
Frequency: 4/year
Circulation: 2,000
Pages/issue: 96–100
Readership: academics, school libraries, other agencies, general public

Manuscripts
Query: no
Abstract: no
Style guide: MOS
Preferred length: 20 pages maximum
Number of copies: 3
Notes: end of manuscript
Blind referee: yes
Time to consider manuscript: 4–6 weeks
Illustrations accepted: tables, charts (conforming to MOS)
Foreign languages: no

Reviews
Seeking reviewers: no
Unsolicited reviews accepted: yes
How to apply: letter
Include in application: institutional affiliation
Materials reviewed: books
Length of review: 5–6 pages

Additional notes
Phylon does not publish articles that are too specialized or too journalistic. It attempts to publish articles that will appeal to social scientists and/or humanists in general.

PICKAWAY QUARTERLY

Focus: Pickaway County, Ohio
Institutional affiliation: Pickaway County Historical Society
Editor: Johnda T. Davis
Address: 120 Montclair Avenue
Circleville, OH 43113
Frequency: 4/year
Circulation: 900
Pages/issue: 24–32
Readership: general public

Manuscripts
Query: yes
Abstract: no
Preferred length: 2,000 words
Number of copies: 1
Notes: end of manuscript
Blind referee: no
Time to consider manuscript: 1 month
Illustrations accepted: tables, graphs, charts, pictures
Foreign languages: no

Reviews
Seeking reviewers: no
Unsolicited reviews accepted: yes
How to apply: letter
Include in application: areas of expertise, current research
Materials reviewed: books

PICKET POST

Focus: American Revolutionary War era
Institutional affiliation: Valley Forge
Historical Society
Editor: Carole Smith
Address: The Valley Forge Historical
Society
Valley Forge, PA 19481
Frequency: 4/year
Circulation: 1,200
Pages/issue: 45
Readership: general public

Manuscripts
Query: no
Abstract: no
Preferred length: 600–4,000 words
Number of copies: 1
Blind referee: no
Time to consider manuscript: 3 weeks
**Proportion of manuscripts
accepted:** good
Illustrations accepted: tables, graphs,
charts, pictures
Foreign languages: no

Reviews
Seeking reviewers: yes
Unsolicited reviews accepted: yes
How to apply: letter
Include in application: professional
degrees, institutional affiliation, areas
of expertise
Materials reviewed: books
Length of review: 400 words maximum

PIONEER AMERICA

Focus: Americana before 1840
Institutional affiliations: Louisiana State
University Department of Geography
and Anthropology; Pioneer America
Society
Editor: Larisa Rathburn
Book review editor: Jay D. Edwards
Address: Louisiana State University
Box 22230
Baton Rouge, LA 70893
Frequency: 4/year
Circulation: 400
Pages/issue: 100
Readership: academics, buffs

Manuscripts
Query: no
Abstract: no
Style guide: MOS
Preferred length: 20 pages
Number of copies: 2
Notes: end of manuscript
Blind referee: yes
Time to consider manuscript: 2–3
months
**Proportion of manuscripts
accepted:** 3/5
Illustrations accepted: tables, graphs,
charts, pictures (editor makes final
decision)
Foreign languages: no

Reviews
Seeking reviewers: yes
Unsolicited reviews accepted: yes
How to apply: letter
Include in application: qualifications
Materials reviewed: books, films, audio,
agency reports
Length of review: 500 words

Additional notes
Reviews may be illustrated. Reserve
footnotes for substantive diversions, for
asides that are worth reading in their own
right. References to other works take the
form used by anthropologists, *viz.,*
(Kroeber 1956:108–23), and References
Cited (at the end of the article) also follows
anthropological form.

PROCEEDINGS OF THE AMERICAN ANTIQUARIAN SOCIETY

Focus: American culture through 1876
Institutional affiliation: American Antiquarian Society
Editor: John B. Hench
Address: 185 Salisbury Street
Worcester, MA 01609
Frequency: 2/year
Circulation: 900
Pages/issue: 200
Readership: academics, bibliographers, librarians, book dealers, book collectors

Manuscripts
Query: no
Abstract: no
Style guide: MOS (with modifications: see Additional notes)
Preferred length: 10–120 pages
Number of copies: 2
Notes: end of manuscript
Blind referee: yes
Time to consider manuscript: 1 month
Proportion of manuscripts accepted: 1/4
Illustrations accepted: tables, graphs, charts, pictures (editor makes final decision)
Foreign languages: no

Additional notes
Proceedings is more receptive to longer articles than are many journals. Brief notes ("American Bibliographical Notes") are regularly published. *Proceedings* emphasizes publication of bibliographies, previously unpublished primary materials, and other tools for scholarship in American history and culture through 1876, but also welcomes narrative or interpretive articles in the same fields. The journal particularly favors pieces that are closely related to or derived from the collections in the Society's library.

Proceedings uses single quotation marks in place of double and prefers the month-day-year order for dates (e.g., February 21, 1743).

PROLOGUE: THE JOURNAL OF THE NATIONAL ARCHIVES

Focus: American history and national archives
Institutional affiliation: National Archives and Records Service
Editor: John J. Rumbarger
Address: National Archives and Records Service
Washington, DC 20408
Frequency: 4/year
Circulation: 8,500
Pages/issue: 72
Readership: historians, general public

Manuscripts
Query: no
Abstract: no
Style guide: MOS
Preferred length: 20–30 pages
Number of copies: 1
Notes: end of manuscript
Blind referee: yes
Time to consider manuscript: 8–10 weeks
Proportion of manuscripts accepted: 1/5
Illustrations accepted: tables, graphs, charts, pictures (keep separate from text)
Foreign languages: no

THE PUBLIC HISTORIAN

Focus: applied history in government, business, cultural resources management, and planning
Institutional affiliation: University of California, Santa Barbara
Editor: Thomas Fuller
Book review editor: Rebecca Conard
Address: Department of History
University of California
Santa Barbara, CA 93106
Frequency: 4/year
Circulation: 1,000
Pages/issue: 96
Readership: historians, policy analysts, archivists, cultural resource managers, museum personnel, administrators in government and business

Manuscripts
Query: no
Abstract: no
Style guide: MOS
Preferred length: issue and analysis, 8–12 pages; research and case studies, 15–20 pages
Number of copies: 2
Notes: end of manuscript
Blind referee: yes
Time to consider manuscript: 6–10 weeks
Illustrations accepted: camera-ready tables, graphs, charts, pictures (two per article average; only those vital to the article are accepted)
Foreign languages: no

Reviews
Seeking reviewers: yes
Unsolicited reviews accepted: no
How to apply: letter
Include in application: professional degrees, institutional affiliation, areas of expertise, published works, current research
Materials reviewed: books, films
Length of review: 2–3 pages

RAILROAD HISTORY

Focus: United States railroad
Institutional affiliations: Railway and Locomotive Historical Society; Harvard Business School
Editor: John H. White
Address: Division of Transportation
Smithsonian Institution
Washington, DC 20560
Frequency: 2/year
Circulation: 2,500
Pages/issue: 120
Readership: hobbyists, historians

Manuscripts
Query: no
Abstract: no
Style guide: MOS
Preferred length: 25 pages maximum
Number of copies: 1
Notes: end of manuscript
Blind referee: no
Time to consider manuscript: 6 months
Proportion of manuscripts accepted: 1/5
Illustrations accepted: tables, graphs, charts, pictures
Foreign languages: no

Reviews
Seeking reviewers: yes
Unsolicited reviews accepted: yes
How to apply: letter
Include in application: professional degrees, institutional affiliation, areas of expertise
Materials reviewed: books
Length of review: 2 pages maximum

RAINCOAST CHRONICLES

Focus: coast of British Columbia
Editor: M. L. White
Book review editor: H. White
Address: Box 119
Madeira Park, B.C. V0N 2H0
CANADA
Frequency: irregular
Circulation: 5,000
Pages/issue: 56
Readership: general public

Manuscripts
Query: no
Abstract: no
Style guide: none
Preferred length: 5,000 words maximum
Number of copies: 1
Notes: end of manuscript
Blind referee: no
Time to consider manuscript: 3 weeks
Illustrations accepted: pictures
Foreign languages: no

Reviews
Seeking reviewers: yes
Unsolicited reviews accepted: yes
How to apply: letter
Include in application: areas of
expertise, published works
Materials reviewed: trade books
Length of review: 750 words maximum

RED RIVER VALLEY HISTORICAL JOURNAL OF WORLD HISTORY

Focus: world history, excluding the
United States
Institutional affiliation: Southeastern
Oklahoma State University
Editor: Edward L. Byrd, Jr.
Book review editor: L. David Norris
Address: Department of Social Sciences
Southeastern Oklahoma State
University
Durant, OK 74701
Frequency: 4/year
Circulation: 500
Pages/issue: 100
Readership: academics

Manuscripts
Query: no
Abstract: no
Style guide: MOS
Preferred length: variable
Number of copies: 1
Notes: end of manuscript
Blind referee: yes
Time to consider manuscript: 6–8
weeks
**Proportion of manuscripts
accepted:** 1/5–1/4
Illustrations accepted: tables, graphs,
charts, pictures
Foreign languages: no

Reviews
Seeking reviewers: yes
Unsolicited reviews accepted: yes
How to apply: letter
Include in application: professional
degrees, institutional affiliation, areas
of expertise, published works, foreign
languages, current research
Materials reviewed: books
Length of review: 400–500 words

RED RIVER VALLEY HISTORICAL REVIEW

Focus: the American Southwest
Institutional affiliation: Southeastern
Oklahoma State University
Editor: Charles W. Goss
Book review editor: James C. Milligan
Address: Department of Social Sciences
Southeastern Oklahoma State
University
Durant, OK 74701
Frequency: 4/year
Circulation: 1,000
Pages/issue: 100
Readership: academics, libraries,
general public

Manuscripts

Query: no
Abstract: no
Style guide: MOS
Preferred length: variable
Number of copies: 1
Notes: end of manuscript
Blind referee: yes
Time to consider manuscript: 6–8
weeks
**Proportion of manuscripts
accepted:** 1/5–1/4
Illustrations accepted: tables, graphs,
charts, pictures
Foreign languages: no

Reviews

Seeking reviewers: yes
Unsolicited reviews accepted: yes
How to apply: letter
Include in application: professional
degrees, institutional affiliation, areas
of expertise, published works, foreign
languages, current research
Materials reviewed: books
Length of review: 400–500 words

THE REGISTER OF THE KENTUCKY HISTORICAL SOCIETY

Focus: Kentucky
Institutional affiliation: Kentucky
Historical Society
Editor: James C. Klotter
Address: Old State House
P.O. Box H
Frankfort, KY 40602
Frequency: 4/year
Circulation: 9,656
Pages/issue: 90
Readership: academics, general public

Manuscripts

Query: no
Abstract: no
Style guide: MOS
Preferred length: 15–30 pages
Number of copies: 1
Notes: bottom of page
Time to consider manuscript: 1 month
**Proportion of manuscripts
accepted:** 1/3
Illustrations accepted: tables, graphs,
charts, pictures
Foreign languages: no

Reviews

Seeking reviewers: yes
Unsolicited reviews accepted: no
How to apply: letter
Include in application: professional
degrees, institutional affiliation, areas
of expertise, published works, current
research
Materials reviewed: books
Length of review: 500–750 words

RENAISSANCE AND REFORMATION
RENAISSANCE ET REFORME

Focus: Renaissance and Reformation
Institutional affiliation: Canadian
Society for Renaissance Studies,
North Central Conference of the
Renaissance Society of America
Editor: R. W. Van Fossen
Book review editor: Thomas Martone
Address: University of Toronto
Erindale College
Mississauga, Ontario L5L 1C6
CANADA
Frequency: 2/year
Circulation: 500
Pages/issue: 112
Readership: academics

Manuscripts
Query: no
Abstract: no
Style guide: MLA
Preferred length: 10–20 pages
Number of copies: 2
Notes: end of manuscript
Blind referee: no
Time to consider manuscript: 1–3
months
**Proportion of manuscripts
accepted:** 1/10
Illustrations accepted: camera-ready
tables, graphs, charts, pictures
Foreign languages: French sought

Reviews
Seeking reviewers: yes
Unsolicited reviews accepted: no
How to apply: letter
Include in application: professional
degrees, institutional affiliation, areas
of expertise, published works, foreign
languages
Materials reviewed: books
Length of review: variable

Additional notes
New reviewers literate in French are
particularly welcome. They should contact
Claude Sutto, Université de Montréal.

RENAISSANCE QUARTERLY

Focus: Renaissance period, 1399–1660
Editors: Bridget Gellert Lyons, Edward P.
Mahoney
Book review editor: Bridget Gellert
Lyons
Address: Renaissance Society of
America
1161 Amsterdam Avenue
New York, NY 10027
Frequency: 4/year
Circulation: 2,800
Pages/issue: 170
Readership: academics

Manuscripts
Query: no
Abstract: no
Style guide: own (based on MLA)
Preferred length: 35 pages maximum
Number of copies: 1
Notes: end of manuscript
Blind referee: no
Time to consider manuscript: 3 months
Illustrations accepted: tables, graphs,
charts, pictures (glossy halftones)
Foreign languages: no

Reviews
Seeking reviewers: occasionally
Unsolicited reviews accepted: no
How to apply: letter
Include in application: professional
degrees, institutional affiliation, areas
of expertise, published works, foreign
languages, current research
Materials reviewed: books
Length of review: 600–800 words

REVIEWS IN AMERICAN HISTORY

Focus: United States and current affairs
Institutional affiliation: Johns Hopkins
  University Press
Editor: Stanley I. Kutler
Address: Department of History
  University of Wisconsin
  Madison, WI 53706
Frequency: 4/year
Circulation: 2,200
Pages/issue: 160
Readership: academics, general public

Reviews

Seeking reviewers: yes
Unsolicited reviews accepted: yes
Materials reviewed: books, films, audio
Length of review: 2,000–3,000 words
  (essay reviews)
Style guide: MOS
Number of copies: 2
Notes: end of manuscript

Additional notes

This journal is devoted exclusively to essay
reviews, with occasional retrospective
bibliographical essays.

REVUE D'HISTOIRE DE L'AMERIQUE FRANÇAISE

Focus: French American history
Editor: Jean-Paul Bernard
Book review editor: René Hardy
Address: 261, Avenue Bloomfield
  Outremont, Quebec H2V 3R6
  CANADA
Frequency: 4/year
Circulation: 1,600
Pages/issue: 160
Readership: academics, general public

Manuscripts

Query: no
Abstract: no
Preferred length: 25–30 pages
Number of copies: 3
Notes: bottom of page
Blind referee: no
Time to consider manuscript: 2–3
  months
**Proportion of manuscripts
  accepted:** 3/4
Illustrations accepted: tables, graphs,
  charts (submit with article)
Foreign languages: published in French;
  manuscripts submitted in English are
  translated at author's expense

Reviews

Seeking reviewers: yes
Unsolicited reviews accepted: yes
How to apply: special form
Materials reviewed: books
Length of review: 2–3 pages

LA REVUE D'HISTOIRE DE LA SOCIETE HISTORIQUE NICOLAS-DENYS

Focus: local history
Editor: Sr. Corinne La Plante
Address: C.P. 3000
Tracadie, New Brunswick
E0C 2B0
CANADA
Frequency: 3/year
Circulation: 350
Pages/issue: 80
Readership: general public, historians

Manuscripts
Abstract: no
Style guide: none
Preferred length: 5–10 pages
Notes: end of manuscript
Illustrations accepted: tables, graphs, pictures
Foreign languages: French only, no English

Reviews
Unsolicited reviews accepted: yes
Materials reviewed: books

RHODE ISLAND HISTORY

Focus: Rhode Island, prominent local figures
Institutional affiliation: Rhode Island Historical Society
Editor: Glenn Warren LaFantasie
Address: Aldrich House
110 Benevolent Street
Providence, RI 02906
Frequency: 4/year
Circulation: 3,000
Pages/issue: 32
Readership: academics, Society members

Manuscripts
Query: no
Abstract: no
Style guide: MOS
Preferred length: 18–25 pages
Number of copies: 1
Notes: end of manuscript
Blind referee: no
Time to consider manuscript: 3–5 weeks
Proportion of manuscripts accepted: 3/10
Illustrations accepted: tables, graphs, charts, pictures (give proper sources and include permission to print)
Foreign languages: no

RICHMOND COUNTY HISTORY

Focus: Richmond County, Georgia; some genealogy, if locally oriented
Institutional affiliation: Richmond County, Georgia, Historical Society
Editors: A. Ray Rowland, Virginia E. deTreville
Address: Augusta College Library
2500 Walton Way
Augusta, GA 30904
Frequency: 2/year
Circulation: 400
Pages/issue: 40
Readership: Society members, students

Manuscripts
Query: no
Abstract: no
Preferred length: 12–18 pages
Number of copies: 1
Notes: end of manuscript
Blind referee: no
Time to consider manuscript: 1 month
Illustrations accepted: tables, graphs, charts, pictures
Foreign languages: no

RIO GRANDE HISTORY

Focus: New Mexico
Institutional affiliation: New Mexico State University Library
Editor: Austin Hoover
Address: University Library
New Mexico State University
Box 3475
Las Cruces, NM 88003
Frequency: 2/year
Circulation: 500
Pages/issue: 24
Readership: general public, buffs

Manuscripts
Query: no
Abstract: no
Style guide: MOS
Preferred length: 2,500–4,000 words
Number of copies: 1
Notes: end of manuscript
Blind referee: no
Time to consider manuscript: 2 months
Proportion of manuscripts accepted: 2/5
Illustrations accepted: tables, graphs, charts, pictures
Foreign languages: no

Reviews
Seeking reviewers: yes
Unsolicited reviews accepted: yes
How to apply: letter
Include in application: professional degrees, institutional affiliation, areas of expertise, published works, current research
Materials reviewed: books
Length of review: 250–500 words

Additional notes
Rio Grande History promotes the utilization of source materials contained in manuscript collections and archival repositories by printing manuscripts, photographs, documents, and articles of interest to the history enthusiast.

ROCHESTER HISTORY

Focus: Rochester and western New York
Institutional affiliation: Rochester Public
   Library
Editor: Joseph W. Barnes
Address: Public Library
   115 South Avenue
   Rochester, NY 14604
Frequency: 4/year
Circulation: 900
Pages/issue: 24
Readership: academics, buffs

Manuscripts
Query: no
Abstract: no
Preferred length: 28 pages
Number of copies: 1
Notes: end of manuscript
Blind referee: no
Time to consider manuscript: 6 months
**Proportion of manuscripts
   accepted:** 2/5
Illustrations accepted: tables, graphs,
   charts, pictures
Foreign languages: no

Additional notes
Subject or theme must have a strong
Rochester connection. Although academic
monographs are acceptable and have
been published, the general reader is our
audience—i.e., no largely quantitative
study or essay written in the idiom of a
peculiar scholastic ideology would be
appropriate.

RURAL AFRICANA

Focus: scholarly social science research
   on sub-Saharan Africa
Institutional affiliation: African Studies
   Center, Michigan State University
Editors: Assefa Mehretu, David Wiley
Address: African Studies Center
   Michigan State University
   East Lansing, MI 48824
Frequency: 3/year
Circulation: 250
Pages/issue: 90
Readership: academics, research and
   government agencies

Manuscripts
Query: no
Abstract: no
Style guide: MOS
Preferred length: 30 pages maximum
Number of copies: 1
Notes: end of manuscript
Blind referee: no
Time to consider manuscript: 2 weeks
**Proportion of manuscripts
   accepted:** 1/2
Illustrations accepted: tables,
   camera-ready graphs, charts, line
   illustrations
Foreign languages: no—will consider
   French

Reviews
Seeking reviewers: no
Unsolicited reviews accepted: yes
How to apply: letter
Include in application: institutional
   affiliation
Materials reviewed: books, films, audio
Length of review: 3 pages

RURAL FOLIO

Focus: Rensselaerville, Albany County, New York
Institutional affiliation: Rensselaerville Historical Society
Editor: Kate Storms
Address: Box 8
Rensselaerville, NY 12147
Frequency: 4/year
Pages/issue: 24
Readership: Society members, libraries, general public

Manuscripts
Query: no
Abstract: no
Preferred length: 12 pages maximum
Number of copies: 2
Notes: end of manuscript
Blind referee: no
Time to consider manuscript: 1 month
Proportion of manuscripts accepted: most
Illustrations accepted: tables, graphs, charts, pictures
Foreign languages: no

Reviews
Seeking reviewers: no
Unsolicited reviews accepted: yes
How to apply: letter
Materials reviewed: books
Length of review: short

RUSSIAN HISTORY

Focus: medieval, imperial, Soviet history; bibliography and historiography
Institutional affiliation: Arizona State University
Editor: Charles Schlacks, Jr.
Address: Arizona State University
Russian and East European Publications
120B McAllister Office Complex
Tempe, AZ 85281
Book review editor: W. A. Kohls
Address: Department of History
Moravian College
Bethlehem, PA 18018
Frequency: 2–4/year
Pages/issue: 128–160
Readership: academics

Manuscripts
Query: no
Abstract: no
Style guide: MLA
Preferred length: 20–30 pages
Number of copies: 3
Notes: end of manuscript
Blind referee: no
Time to consider manuscript: 3 months
Illustrations accepted: tables, graphs, charts, pictures
Foreign languages: French, German, Russian

Reviews
Seeking reviewers: yes
Unsolicited reviews accepted: no
How to apply: letter
Include in application: areas of expertise
Materials reviewed: books
Length of review: 600–800 words

THE RUSSIAN REVIEW

Focus: Russia, past and present
Institutional affiliation: Hoover
  Institution, Stanford, California
Editor: Terence Emmons
Address: Hoover Institution
        Stanford, CA 94305
Frequency: 4/year
Circulation: 1,850
Pages/issue: 140
Readership: academics, general public

Manuscripts
Query: no
Abstract: no
Style guide: MOS
Preferred length: 25 pages
Number of copies: 2
Notes: end of manuscript
Blind referee: no
Time to consider manuscript: 6–8
  weeks
Illustrations accepted: tables, graphs,
  charts, pictures
Foreign languages: occasionally
  Russian and French

Reviews
Unsolicited reviews accepted: no
How to apply: letter
Include in application: professional
  degrees, institutional affiliation, areas
  of expertise, published works, foreign
  languages, current research
Materials reviewed: books
Length of review: 150–800 words

SAGUENAYENSIA

Focus: Saguenay-Lac St-Jean, Quebec,
  and genealogy
Institutional affiliation: Société
  historique du Saguenay
Editor: Gaston Gagnon
Address: C.P. 456
        Chicoutimi, Quebec G7H 5C8
        CANADA
Frequency: 6/year
Pages/issue: 30
Readership: academics, libraries,
  general public

Manuscripts
Query: yes
Abstract: yes
Style guide: MOS
Preferred length: 15–20 pages
Number of copies: 2
Notes: end of manuscript
Blind referee: no
Time to consider manuscript: 1 month
Illustrations accepted: tables, graphs,
  charts, pictures (limited)
Foreign languages: French preferred

THE SAN LUIS VALLEY HISTORIAN

Focus: San Luis Valley, Colorado
Institutional affiliation: Adams State College
Editor: Jeanne Leader
Address: Box 982
Alamosa, CO 81101
Frequency: 4/year
Circulation: 500
Pages/issue: 26
Readership: general public

Manuscripts
Query: yes
Abstract: no
Style guide: none
Preferred length: open
Number of copies: 1
Notes: end of manuscript
Blind referee: no
Time to consider manuscript: 2 months
Illustrations accepted: whatever is needed for article
Foreign languages: Spanish (with English translation)

SARAPIS: THE AMERICAN JOURNAL OF EGYPTOLOGY

Focus: studies on Pharaonic, Persian, Hellenistic, Roman, and Byzantine Egypt; related studies
Institutional affiliation: The Sarapis Society
Editors: Eugene Cruz-Uribe; Peter A. Piccione
Address: The Oriental Institute of the University of Chicago
1155 E. 58th St.
Chicago, IL 60677
Frequency: 2/year
Circulation: 500
Pages/issue: 32–40
Readership: scholars

Manuscripts
Query: no
Abstract: no
Style guide: *American Journal of Archaeology*
Preferred length: open
Number of copies: 1
Notes: end of manuscript
Blind referee: no
Time to consider manuscript: 1 month
Illustrations accepted: tables, graphs, charts, pictures
Foreign languages: yes, although English preferred

Reviews
Seeking reviewers: yes
How to apply: letter
Include in application: professional degrees, institutional affiliation, areas of expertise, published works, foreign languages, current research
Materials reviewed: books
Length of review: open

SCANDINAVIAN STUDIES

Focus: Scandinavian literature, philology, and linguistics; society and culture of the North

Institutional affiliation: Society for the Advancement of Scandinavian Study

Editor: Paul Schach

Address: Department of Modern Languages
University of Nebraska
Lincoln, NB 68588

Book review editor: George C. Schoolfield

Address: Yale University
New Haven, CT

Frequency: 4/year

Circulation: 1,000

Pages/issue: 125

Readership: academics, general public

Manuscripts

Query: no

Abstract: no

Style guide: MOS

Preferred length: 30 pages maximum

Number of copies: 2

Notes: end of manuscript

Blind referee: no

Time to consider manuscript: 2–3 months

Proportion of manuscripts accepted: 3/10–4/10

Illustrations accepted: tables, graphs, charts, pictures (only when necessary)

Foreign languages: no, but literary quotations must be in the original language

Reviews

Seeking reviewers: yes

Unsolicited reviews accepted: no

How to apply: letter

Include in application: areas of expertise

Materials reviewed: books

Length of review: variable

Additional notes

Only articles based on original sources in the original languages are considered for publication.

SCHATZKAMMER

Focus: interdisciplinary: teaching German; creative writing; historical and cultural contributions of Germans to America

Book review editors: W. Lee Nahrgang, D. V. Keilstrup

Address: Department of Foreign Languages
University of Texas at Arlington
Arlington, TX 76019

Frequency: 1/year

Circulation: 500

Readership: teachers, all levels

Manuscripts

Query: no

Abstract: yes

Style guide: MLA

Preferred length: 15 pages maximum

Number of copies: 3

Notes: end of manuscript

Blind referee: no

Time to consider manuscript: 2 months

Proportion of manuscripts accepted: 1/2

Foreign languages: German

Reviews

Seeking reviewers: yes

Unsolicited reviews accepted: yes

How to apply: letter

Include in application: professional degrees, institutional affiliation, areas of expertise, published works, foreign languages, current research

Materials reviewed: books, films, audio, German-American creative writing

Length of review: 2–4 pages

THE SCHUYLERITE

Focus: Schuyler County, Illinois, and its people from 1825 to the present
Institutional affiliation: Schuyler-Brown Historical and Genealogical Society
Editor: Lavina Walton
Address: Schuyler Jail Museum
Congress and Madison Streets
Rushville, IL 62681
Frequency: 4/year
Circulation: 300
Pages/issue: 32–40
Readership: general public

Manuscripts
Query: no
Style guide: none
Preferred length: 4–6 pages
Number of copies: 1
Notes: end of manuscript
Blind referee: no
Proportion of manuscripts accepted: all
Foreign languages: no

Additional notes
The Schuylerite also publishes old letters and diaries.

SCOTTISH TRADITION

Focus: Scottish literature, politics, and culture; the Scots overseas, particularly in Canada
Institutional affiliation: Canadian Association for Scottish Studies
Editor: W. W. Straka
Book review editor: same
Address: Chairman, Department of History
University of Guelph
Guelph, Ontario
CANADA
Frequency: 1–2/year
Circulation: 250
Pages/issue: 100
Readership: academics, general public

Manuscripts
Query: yes
Abstract: no
Preferred length: 20–35 pages
Number of copies: 2
Notes: end of manuscript
Blind referee: no
Time to consider manuscript: 3–6 months
Proportion of manuscripts accepted: 2/3
Illustrations accepted: tables, graphs, charts (maps and diagrams should be India ink on white paper and camera-ready)
Foreign languages: French

THE SEA CHEST

Focus: maritime history pertinent to Pacific Northwest and Alaskan waters
Institutional affiliation: Puget Sound Maritime Historical Society
Editor: Hal H. Will (temporary)
Book review editor: Editorial Board
Address: 2161 East Hamlin Street
Seattle, WA 98102
Frequency: 4/year
Circulation: 800
Pages/issue: 40
Readership: Society members, libraries, museums

Manuscripts

Query: no
Abstract: no
Style guide: none (fully capitalize all vessel names)
Preferred length: 1,500–5,000 words
Number of copies: 2
Notes: end of manuscript
Blind referee: no
Time to consider manuscript: 2–3 months
Proportion of manuscripts accepted: 3/4
Illustrations accepted: black-and-white photos, charts, or sketches (no color)
Foreign languages: no

Reviews

Seeking reviewers: no
Unsolicited reviews accepted: yes (maritime history *only)*
How to apply: letter
Include in application: areas of expertise
Length of review: 200 words maximum

Additional notes

Articles must be factual and, hopefully, light reading.

SEAPORT

Focus: New York Harbor
Institutional affiliation: South Street Seaport Museum
Editor: Katharine Downer
Book review editor: same
Address: 203 Front Street
New York, NY 10038
Frequency: 4/year
Circulation: 15,000
Pages/issue: 36
Readership: members of the Museum

Manuscripts

Query: suggested
Abstract: no
Preferred length: 2,000–3,000 words
Number of copies: 1
Blind referee: no
Time to consider manuscript: 2–4 weeks
Illustrations accepted: no
Foreign languages: no

Reviews

Seeking reviewers: no
Unsolicited reviews accepted: no

SIGNS: JOURNAL OF WOMEN IN CULTURE AND SOCIETY

Focus: new scholarship about women
Institutional affiliation: Barnard College
Editor: Elsa Dixler
Book review editor: Joan Burstyn
Address: Barnard Hall
Barnard College
New York, NY 10027
Frequency: 4/year
Circulation: 7,500
Pages/issue: 200
Readership: academics

Manuscripts
Query: advised
Abstract: no
Style guide: own (based on MOS)
Preferred length: 35 pages
Number of copies: 3
Notes: end of manuscript
Blind referee: yes
Time to consider manuscript: 4–6 months
Illustrations accepted: tables, graphs, charts, pictures
Foreign languages: occasionally, but only Western European languages

Reviews
Seeking reviewers: no
Unsolicited reviews accepted: rarely
How to apply: letter
Include in application: professional degrees, institutional affiliation, areas of expertise, published works, foreign languages, current research
Materials reviewed: books
Length of review: 300 words

THE SIXTEENTH CENTURY JOURNAL

Focus: literature and other intellectual, social, economic, and cultural currents in the 16th century
Institutional affiliation: Center for Reformation Research and Sixteenth Century Studies Conference, with sponsorship from Northeast Missouri State University
Editor: Robert V. Schnucker
Book review editor: same
Address: Concordia College
Hamline and Marshall Avenue
St. Paul, MN 55104
Frequency: 3–4/year
Circulation: 1,300
Pages/issue: 128
Readership: academics

Manuscripts
Query: no
Abstract: no
Style guide: MOS
Preferred length: 40 pages
Number of copies: 2
Notes: end of manuscript
Blind referee: yes
Time to consider manuscript: 3–4 months
Proportion of manuscripts accepted: 1/3
Illustrations accepted: tables, graphs, charts, pictures
Foreign languages: no

Reviews
Seeking reviewers: yes
Unsolicited reviews accepted: no
How to apply: letter
Include in application: professional degrees, institutional affiliation, areas of expertise, foreign languages, current research
Materials reviewed: books
Length of review: 500 words

SLAVIC REVIEW

Focus: Slavic and East European studies
Institutional affiliation: University of Illinois
Editor: James R. Millar
Book review editor: same
Address: 911 West High Street
Room 200
University of Illinois at
Urbana-Champaign
Urbana, IL 61801
Frequency: 4/year
Circulation: 3,500
Pages/issue: 192
Readership: academics

Manuscripts

Query: no
Abstract: no
Style guide: MOS
Preferred length: 25 pages
Number of copies: 3
Notes: end of manuscript
Blind referee: no (manuscript can be reviewed anonymously if requested and prepared accordingly)
Time to consider manuscript: 3–4 months
Proportion of manuscripts accepted: 1/10
Illustrations accepted: camera-ready tables, graphs, charts, pictures
Foreign languages: no

Reviews

Seeking reviewers: yes
Unsolicited reviews accepted: no
How to apply: letter, plus letter of recommendation
Include in application: professional degrees, institutional affiliation, areas of expertise, published works, current research
Materials reviewed: books
Length of review: varies

SLOVENE STUDIES: JOURNAL OF THE SOCIETY FOR SLOVENE STUDIES

Focus: Slovene literature, linguistics, and comparative topics involving Slovene, Slovenes, or Slovenia
Institutional affiliation: Society for Slovene Studies, New York
Editor: Henry R. Cooper, Jr.
Book review editor: same
Address: Slavic Department
Northwestern University
Evanston, IL 60201
Frequency: 2/year
Circulation: 200
Pages/issue: 40–50
Readership: academics, general public

Manuscripts

Query: no
Abstract: no
Style guide: MLA
Preferred length: 10 pages
Number of copies: 1
Notes: end of manuscript
Blind referee: no
Time to consider manuscript: 1 month
Illustrations accepted: tables, graphs, charts
Foreign languages: no

Reviews

Seeking reviewers: yes
Unsolicited reviews accepted: yes
How to apply: letter
Include in application: professional degrees, institutional affiliation, areas of expertise
Materials reviewed: books; publications from Slovenia in any scholarly field; publications about Slovene things
Length of review: 1 page; review articles may be up to 5 pages

Additional notes

Contributions to *Slovene Studies* must possess scholarly worth in their respective fields. Articles of general or popular interest, or belle-lettristic offerings, cannot be considered.

SNAKE RIVER ECHOES

Focus: Idaho
Institutional affiliation: Upper Snake River Valley Historical Society
Editor: Ralph Thompson
Book review editor: Jerry L. Glenn
Address: Box 244
Rexburg, ID 83440
Frequency: 4/year
Circulation: 1,000
Pages/issue: 24
Readership: general public, libraries, historical societies

Manuscripts
Query: no
Abstract: no
Style guide: none
Preferred length: 1,200–5,000 words
Number of copies: 1
Notes: end of manuscript
Blind referee: no
Time to consider manuscript: 2 weeks
Proportion of manuscripts accepted: 3/4
Illustrations accepted: tables, graphs, charts, pictures (photographs preferred)
Foreign languages: no

Reviews
Seeking reviewers: no
Unsolicited reviews accepted: yes
How to apply: letter
Include in application: areas of expertise, current research
Materials reviewed: books
Length of review: 1,200 words

Additional notes
Snake River Echoes is a local quarterly aimed at the armchair historian. It is not a scholarly historical journal. Its editors are not interested in long, footnoted articles. They are looking for well-written, interesting historical articles on the Upper Snake River Valley.

SOCIAL HISTORY
HISTOIRE SOCIALE

Focus: social history; Canadian, American, British, French, and German subjects given priority
Institutional affiliation: University of Ottawa and Carleton University
Editors: Fernand Ouellet, Julian Gwyn, D. A. Muise
Book review editor: R. B. Goheen
Address: Department of History
University of Ottawa
Ottawa K1N 6N5
CANADA
Frequency: 2/year
Circulation: 1,100
Pages/issue: 250
Readership: academics

Manuscripts
Query: no
Abstract: no
Style guide: MOS (Canadian spelling)
Preferred length: 30–45 pages
Number of copies: 3
Notes: end of manuscript
Blind referee: no
Time to consider manuscript: 3 months
Proportion of manuscripts accepted: 1/4–1/3
Illustrations accepted: tables, pictures, professionally drawn graphs, maps, and charts (illustrations in black-and-white glossy at least 4 x 6)
Foreign languages: French

Reviews
Seeking reviewers: yes
Unsolicited reviews accepted: no
How to apply: letter
Include in application: professional degrees, institutional affiliation, areas of expertise, published works, foreign languages, current research
Materials reviewed: books
Length of review: 3 pages

Additional notes
Social History also publishes "Notes de recherche" on methodological, historiographical, or archival aspects of social history.

SOCIAL SCIENCE

Focus: economics, political science, sociology
Institutional affiliation: Pi Gamma Mu
Editor: Panos D. Bardis
Book review editor: same
Address: Department of Sociology
Toledo University
Toledo, OH 43606
Frequency: 4/year
Circulation: 10,000
Pages/issue: 64
Readership: academics, general public

Manuscripts
Query: no
Abstract: yes
Style guide: own
Preferred length: 10–20 pages
Number of copies: 1
Notes: end of manuscript
Blind referee: no
Time to consider manuscript: 2 weeks
**Proportion of manuscripts
accepted:** 2/5
Illustrations accepted: tables, graphs, charts, pictures (not many)
Foreign languages: no

Reviews
Seeking reviewers: yes
Unsolicited reviews accepted: yes
How to apply: letter
Include in application: professional degrees, institutional affiliation, areas of expertise, published works
Materials reviewed: books
Length of review: 500–1,500 words

Additional notes
Social Science is an interdisciplinary journal which stresses both the present and the past, and seeks qualitative as well as quantitative studies.

SOCIAL SCIENCE HISTORY

Focus: the study of social theory within an empirical, historical context to make a valuable contribution to understanding of societies past and present
Editors: James O. Graham, Jr., Robert P. Swierenga
Address: Department of History
Bowling Green State
University
111 Williams Hall
Bowling Green, OH 43403
Book review editor: Alan M. Kraut
Address: Department of History
American University
Washington, DC 20016
Frequency: 4/year
Circulation: 1,000
Pages/issue: 128
Readership: academics

Manuscripts
Query: no
Abstract: no
Style guide: own
Preferred length: 15–30 pages, including references and notes
Number of copies: 3
Notes: in-text citations; references at end
Blind referee: yes
Time to consider manuscript: 4 months
**Proportion of manuscripts
accepted:** 1/3
Illustrations accepted: tables, graphs, charts, pictures (see *SSH* "Guide for Authors" for instructions)

Reviews
Seeking reviewers: yes
Unsolicited reviews accepted: no
How to apply: letter
Include in application: professional degrees, institutional affiliation, areas of expertise, published works, foreign languages, current research
Length of review: 500 words maximum

THE SOCIAL SCIENCE JOURNAL

Focus: interdisciplinary social sciences
Institutional affiliation: Colorado State University
Editor: Stanley Eitzen
Address: Social Science Building
Colorado State University
Fort Collins, CO 80523
Book review editor: Fred Eissman
Address: Department of English
Texas Christian University
Fort Worth, TX 76129
Frequency: 3/year
Circulation: 1,300
Pages/issue: 140
Readership: academics

Manuscripts
Query: no
Abstract: no
Style guide: MOS
Preferred length: 25 pages maximum
Number of copies: 3
Notes: end of manuscript
Blind referee: yes
Time to consider manuscript: 7 weeks
Proportion of manuscripts accepted: 1/7
Illustrations accepted: camera-ready tables, graphs, charts, pictures
Foreign languages: no

Reviews
Seeking reviewers: yes
Unsolicited reviews accepted: no
How to apply: letter
Include in application: professional degrees, institutional affiliation, areas of expertise, published works, current research
Materials reviewed: books
Length of review: review essays, 10 pages; single books, 3–4 pages

SOCIAL SCIENCE QUARTERLY

Focus: interdisciplinary sociology, economics, political science, geography, history
Institutional affiliation: The University of Texas at Austin
Editor: Charles M. Bonjean
Book review editor: H. Malcolm Macdonald
Address: The University of Texas at Austin
Austin, TX 78712
Frequency: 4/year
Circulation: 3,000
Pages/issue: 180
Readership: academics

Manuscripts
Query: no
Abstract: yes
Style guide: own
Preferred length: 14–23 pages, 30 pages maximum
Number of copies: 4
Notes: end of manuscript
Blind referee: yes
Time to consider manuscript: 2 months
Proportion of manuscripts accepted: 1/10
Illustrations accepted: tables, graphs, charts, pictures
Foreign languages: no

Reviews
Seeking reviewers: yes
Unsolicited reviews accepted: no
How to apply: letter
Include in application: professional degrees, institutional affiliation, areas of expertise, published works
Materials reviewed: books
Length of review: variable

SOUND HERITAGE

Focus: British Columbia and aural history
Institutional affiliation: Provincial Archives of British Columbia
Editor: Derek Reimer
Address: Provincial Archives, Aural History
Victoria, B.C. V8V 1X4
CANADA
Frequency: 4/year
Circulation: 7,000
Pages/issue: 80
Readership: general public

Manuscripts
Query: yes
Abstract: no
Style guide: none
Preferred length: 25,000–35,000 words
Number of copies: 1
Notes: bottom of page
Blind referee: no
Time to consider manuscript: 4 weeks
Proportion of manuscripts accepted: nearly all
Illustrations accepted: charts, pictures

Additional notes
Sound Heritage is a magazine aimed at a popular audience but tries to maintain a high level of academic respectability by presenting new and interesting information via the techniques of aural history. Manuscripts submitted must have a significant amount of their content derived from aural sources, either oral history interviews or historical sound recordings. Payment is made for some manuscripts at a rate negotiated with the editors.

SOUTH ATLANTIC QUARTERLY

Focus: humanities, social sciences, general interest
Institutional affiliation: Duke University
Editor: Oliver W. Ferguson
Book review editor: same
Address: P.O. Box 6697
College Station
Durham, NC 27706
Frequency: 4/year
Circulation: 1,200
Pages/issue: 150
Readership: academics

Manuscripts
Query: no
Abstract: no
Preferred length: 4,500 words maximum
Number of copies: 1
Notes: end of manuscript
Blind referee: no
Time to consider manuscript: 4–6 weeks
Proportion of manuscripts accepted: 1/15
Illustrations accepted: tables, graphs, charts, pictures, but discouraged
Foreign languages: no

Reviews
Seeking reviewers: no
Unsolicited reviews accepted: no
How to apply: letter
Materials reviewed: books
Length of review: 100–350 words

SOUTH CAROLINA HISTORICAL MAGAZINE

Focus: South Carolina
Institutional affiliation: South Carolina Historical Society
Editor: Gene Waddell
Book review editor: Elisa Pinckney
Address: Fireproof Building
Charleston, SC 29401
Frequency: 4/year
Circulation: 3,000
Pages/issue: 90
Readership: scholars

Manuscripts
Query: no
Abstract: no
Style guide: MLA or MOS
Preferred length: 3,000–4,000 words
Number of copies: 3
Notes: either at bottom of page or at end of manuscript
Blind referee: no
Time to consider manuscript: 3 months
Proportion of manuscripts accepted: 1/2
Illustrations accepted: tables, graphs, charts, pictures (limited)
Foreign languages: no

Reviews
Seeking reviewers: no
Unsolicited reviews accepted: no
Length of review: 300 words

SOUTH DAKOTA HISTORY

Focus: South Dakota
Institutional affiliation: South Dakota Historical Society and South Dakota Board of Cultural Preservation
Editor: Nancy Tystad Koupal
Book review editor: same
Address: Memorial Building
Pierre, SD 57501
Frequency: 4/year
Circulation: 2,200
Pages/issue: 108
Readership: academics, general public

Manuscripts
Query: no
Abstract: no
Style guide: own (variation of MFW) or MOS
Preferred length: 20 pages
Number of copies: 2 preferred
Notes: end of manuscript
Blind referee: no
Time to consider manuscript: 6–8 weeks or longer
Illustrations accepted: tables, graphs, charts, pictures with source notes (illustrations should be explained on an extra sheet or on a strip of paper taped to the back and folded over the front of the illustration; any permissions for use should be obtained by the author or the necessity of such brought to the attention of the editor)
Foreign languages: no

Reviews
Seeking reviewers: yes
Unsolicited reviews accepted: no
How to apply: letter
Include in application: professional degrees, institutional affiliation, areas of expertise
Materials reviewed: books
Length of review: 2–3 pages

SOUTHEASTERN EUROPE

Focus: humanities and social sciences pertaining to the Balkans, Yugoslavia, Romania, Bulgaria, Albania, Greece, and European Turkey
Institutional affiliation: Arizona State University
Editor: Charles Schlacks, Jr.
Book review editor: same
Address: Arizona State University
Russian and East European Publications
120 B McAllister Office Complex
Tempe, AZ 85281
Frequency: 2–4/year
Circulation: 500
Pages/issue: 128–160
Readership: academics, diplomats

Manuscripts
Query: no
Abstract: no
Style guide: MLA
Preferred length: 20–30 pages
Number of copies: 3
Notes: end of manuscript
Blind referee: no
Time to consider manuscript: 3 months
Illustrations accepted: tables, graphs, charts, pictures
Foreign languages: French, German, Russian

Reviews
Seeking reviewers: yes
Unsolicited reviews accepted: no
How to apply: letter
Include in application: areas of expertise
Materials reviewed: books
Length of review: 600–800 words

Additional notes
Southeastern Europe publishes frequent contributions by foreign scholars.

SOUTHERN CALIFORNIA QUARTERLY

Focus: California, near regions
Institutional affiliation: Historical Society of Southern California
Editor: Doyce B. Nunis, Jr.
Book review editor: same
Address: Department of History
University of Southern California
Los Angeles, CA 90007
Frequency: 4/year
Circulation: 1,100
Pages/issue: 120
Readership: Society members

Manuscripts
Query: no
Abstract: no
Style guide: MOS
Preferred length: open
Number of copies: 2
Notes: end of manuscript
Blind referee: yes
Time to consider manuscript: 3–6 months
Illustrations accepted: tables, graphs, charts, pictures
Foreign languages: no

Reviews
Seeking reviewers: yes
Unsolicited reviews accepted: no
How to apply: letter
Include in application: professional degrees, institutional affiliation, areas of expertise, published works, foreign languages, current research
Materials reviewed: books
Length of review: assigned

SOUTHERN STUDIES: AN INTERDISCIPLINARY JOURNAL OF THE SOUTH

Focus: interdisciplinary (mostly history and literature) articles about Louisiana, the South, and Southern writers
Institutional affiliation: Northwestern State University of Louisiana
Editor: John M. Price
Book review editor: C. Wells
Address: Southern Studies Institute
Northwestern State University of Louisiana
Natchitoches, LA 71457
Frequency: 4/year
Circulation: 500
Pages/issue: 128
Readership: academics

Manuscripts
Query: no
Abstract: no
Style guide: MOS
Number of copies: 1
Notes: end of manuscript
Blind referee: no
Time to consider manuscript: 6 months
Proportion of manuscripts accepted: 3/4
Illustrations accepted: tables, graphs, charts
Foreign languages: no

Reviews
Seeking reviewers: yes
Unsolicited reviews accepted: no
How to apply: letter
Include in application: professional degrees, institutional affiliation, areas of expertise, published works, foreign languages, current research
Length of review: 2 pages

SOUTHWESTERN HISTORICAL QUARTERLY

Focus: Texas and the Southwest
Institutional affiliation: University of Texas at Austin
Editor: L. Tuffly Ellis
Book review editor: Robert Calvert
Address: Texas State Historical Association
2.306 Sid Richardson Hall,
University Station
Austin, TX 78712
Frequency: 4/year
Circulation: 3,000
Pages/issue: 110
Readership: academics, buffs

Manuscripts
Query: no
Abstract: no
Style guide: MOS
Preferred length: 30 pages
Number of copies: 1
Notes: end of manuscript
Blind referee: yes
Time to consider manuscript: 4–8 weeks
Proportion of manuscripts accepted: 1/3
Illustrations accepted: tables, graphs, charts, pictures
Foreign languages: no

Reviews
Seeking reviewers: yes
Unsolicited reviews accepted: no
How to apply: letter
Include in application: areas of expertise
Materials reviewed: books
Length of review: 350–500 words

SOUTHWESTERN STUDIES

Focus: culture and art of southwest United States and northern Mexico
Institutional affiliation: University of Texas at El Paso
Editor: E. H. Antone
Address: Texas Western Press
University of Texas at El Paso
El Paso, TX 79968
Frequency: 4/year
Circulation: 1,500
Pages/issue: 56
Readership: general public

Manuscripts
Query: yes
Abstract: no
Style guide: MLA
Preferred length: 60 pages
Number of copies: 1
Notes: end of manuscript
Blind referee: no
Time to consider manuscript: 4 months
Illustrations accepted: tables, graphs, charts, pictures
Foreign languages: no

Additional notes
Southwestern Studies is a series of separate monographs dealing with the Southwest.

SPANISH RIVER PAPERS

Focus: Boca Raton, Florida
Institutional affiliation: Boca Raton Historical Society
Editor: D. W. Curl
Address: Department of History
Florida Atlantic University
Boca Raton, FL 33431
Frequency: 3/year
Circulation: 250
Pages/issue: 24
Readership: general public, Society members

Manuscripts
Query: yes
Abstract: no
Style guide: MOS
Preferred length: 20 pages maximum
Number of copies: 1
Notes: end of manuscript
Blind referee: no
Foreign languages: no

Additional notes
Only material specifically related to Boca Raton history is published.

SPECULUM: A JOURNAL OF MEDIEVAL STUDIES

Focus: all aspects of medieval studies
Institutional affiliation: The Mediaeval Academy of America
Editor: Paul Meyvaert
Book review editors: Larry Benson, Fredric Cheyette, Nathaniel Smith
Address: 1430 Massachusetts Avenue Cambridge, MA 02138
Frequency: 4/year
Circulation: 6,000
Pages/issue: 240
Readership: academics

Manuscripts
Query: no
Abstract: no
Style guide: own
Preferred length: 50 pages maximum
Number of copies: 1
Notes: end of manuscript
Blind referee: no
Time to consider manuscript: 3 months
Proportion of manuscripts accepted: 1/6
Illustrations accepted: tables, graphs, charts, pictures (only if strictly necessary)
Foreign languages: no

Reviews
Seeking reviewers: yes
Unsolicited reviews accepted: no
How to apply: letter
Include in application: professional degrees, institutional affiliation, areas of expertise, published works, foreign languages, current research
Materials reviewed: books
Length of review: 1,500 words maximum

Additional notes
Articles must offer substantial new findings, carefully documented to convince other scholars.

STATEN ISLAND HISTORIAN

Focus: Staten Island
Institutional affiliation: Staten Island Historical Society
Editor: Norma Siebenheller
Book review editor: same
Address: 267 Edinboro Road Staten Island, NY 10306
Frequency: 4/year
Circulation: 1,200
Pages/issue: 12
Readership: general public

Manuscripts
Query: no
Abstract: no
Style guide: none
Preferred length: open
Number of copies: 1
Notes: end of manuscript
Blind referee: no
Proportion of manuscripts accepted: 3/4
Illustrations accepted: tables, graphs, charts, pictures
Foreign languages: no

STEAMBOAT BILL

Focus: self-propelled vessels
Institutional affiliation: University of
  Baltimore
Editor: Peter T. Eisele
Book review editor: William H. Tantum, IV
Address: 74 Chatham Street
  Chatham, NJ 07928
Frequency: 4/year
Circulation: 3,500
Pages/issue: 68
Readership: historians

Manuscripts
Query: yes
Abstract: no
Preferred length: 20 pages maximum
Number of copies: 1
Time to consider manuscript: 3 months
Illustrations accepted: tables, pictures
Foreign languages: no

Reviews
Seeking reviewers: no
Unsolicited reviews accepted: yes
Materials reviewed: books on shipping

THE STREAM OF HISTORY

Focus: Northeast Arkansas; White River
  transportation
Institutional affiliation: Jackson County
  Historical Society
Editor: James Logan Morgan
Book review editor: same
Address: 314 Vine Street
  Newport, AR 72112
Frequency: 4/year
Circulation: 450
Pages/issue: 40
Readership: general public

Manuscripts
Query: no
Abstract: no
Preferred length: open
Number of copies: 1
Notes: end of manuscript
Blind referee: no
Time to consider manuscript: short
**Proportion of manuscripts
  accepted:** high
Illustrations accepted: tables, graphs,
  charts, pictures
Foreign languages: no

Reviews
Seeking reviewers: yes
Unsolicited reviews accepted: yes
How to apply: letter
Materials reviewed: books
Length of review: variable

Additional notes
Books reviewed must have some bearing
on Arkansas history. Articles must relate to
the history of the northeastern part of
Arkansas, or to the history of transportation
on White River.

SWEDISH PIONEER HISTORICAL QUARTERLY

Focus: Swedish emigration and the Swedish element in North America
Institutional affiliation: Swedish Pioneer Historical Society, Chicago
Editor: H. Arnold Barton
Book review editor: Walter Johnson
Address: Department of History
Southern Illinois University
Carbondale, IL 62901
Frequency: 4/year
Circulation: 2,000
Pages/issue: 72–80
Readership: academics, general public

Manuscripts
Query: no
Abstract: no
Style guide: MLA
Preferred length: 3,000–6,000 words
Number of copies: 2
Notes: end of manuscript
Blind referee: no
Time to consider manuscript: 1–2 months
Proportion of manuscripts accepted: 1/2
Illustrations accepted: tables, pictures, occasionally camera-ready graphs or charts
Foreign languages: Swedish

Reviews
Seeking reviewers: no
Unsolicited reviews accepted: no
How to apply: letter
Include in application: professional degrees, institutional affiliation, areas of expertise, published works, foreign languages, current research
Materials reviewed: books
Length of review: 300–600 words

Additional notes
The *Quarterly* seeks monographic articles, interesting letters, diaries, and other documentary material dealing with its area of concern, as well as relevant personal reminiscences.

SWISS AMERICAN HISTORICAL SOCIETY NEWSLETTER

Focus: Swiss in America; United States–Swiss relations
Institutional affiliation: Swiss American Historical Society
Editor: Heinz K. Meier
Book review editor: same
Address: School of Arts and Letters
Old Dominion University
Norfolk, VA 23508
Frequency: 3/year
Circulation: 250
Pages/issue: 30
Readership: academics, general public

Manuscripts
Query: no
Abstract: no
Preferred length: open
Number of copies: 1
Notes: no preference
Blind referee: no
Time to consider manuscript: 2 weeks
Proportion of manuscripts accepted: 1/2
Illustrations accepted: tables, graphs, charts, pictures
Foreign languages: no

Reviews
Seeking reviewers: no
Unsolicited reviews accepted: yes
How to apply: letter
Include in application: professional degrees, institutional affiliation, areas of expertise, published works, foreign languages, current research
Materials reviewed: books, films
Length of review: open

TECHNOLOGY AND CULTURE

Focus: technology and relations of technology with society and culture
Institutional affiliation: Society for the History of Technology
Editor: Melvin Kranzberg
Book review editor: same
Address: Georgia Institute of Technology Atlanta, GA 30332
Frequency: 4/year
Circulation: 2,400
Pages/issue: 225
Readership: academics

Manuscripts

Query: no
Abstract: no
Style guide: MOS
Preferred length: 3,000 words
Number of copies: 2
Notes: end of manuscript
Blind referee: yes
Time to consider manuscript: 4 months
Proportion of manuscripts accepted: 3/10
Illustrations accepted: tables, graphs, charts, pictures
Foreign languages: no

Reviews

Seeking reviewers: yes
Unsolicited reviews accepted: yes
How to apply: letter
Include in application: professional degrees, institutional affiliation, areas of expertise, published works, foreign languages, current research
Materials reviewed: books, museum exhibits
Length of review: 800 words

TENNESSEE HISTORICAL QUARTERLY

Focus: Tennessee
Institutional affiliation: Tennessee Historical Society
Editor: Robert M. McBride
Book review editor: Robert L. Taylor, Jr.
Address: 403 Seventh Avenue North Nashville, TN 37219
Frequency: 4/year
Circulation: 3,400
Pages/issue: 110
Readership: general public

Manuscripts

Query: no
Abstract: no
Style guide: MOS
Preferred length: 20 pages maximum
Number of copies: 2 preferred
Notes: bottom of page
Blind referee: no
Time to consider manuscript: 3 months
Proportion of manuscripts accepted: 1/2
Illustrations accepted: not in all cases
Foreign languages: no

Reviews

Seeking reviewers: no
Unsolicited reviews accepted: yes
How to apply: letter
Include in application: professional degrees, institutional affiliation, areas of expertise, published works, current research
Materials reviewed: books
Length of review: 1–1½ pages

THEODORE ROOSEVELT ASSOCIATION JOURNAL

Focus: life and times of Theodore Roosevelt
Institutional affiliation: Theodore Roosevelt Association
Editor: John Allen Gable
Book review editor:
Address: Theodore Roosevelt
Association
P.O. Box 720
Oyster Bay, NY 11771
Frequency: 4/year
Circulation: 2,000
Pages/issue: 16–24
Readership: general public, TRA members, academics

Manuscripts
Query: no
Abstract: no
Style guide: any standard guide
Preferred length: 5–25 pages
Number of copies: 2 preferred
Notes: end of manuscript
Blind referee: no
Time to consider manuscript: prompt decision
Proportion of manuscripts accepted: high
Illustrations accepted: tables, graphs, charts, pictures (glossy prints, any size, helpful)
Foreign languages: no

Reviews
Seeking reviewers: yes
Unsolicited reviews accepted: yes (check first)
How to apply: letter
Materials reviewed: books, films, audio
Length of review: 3–10 pages

Additional notes
Please include short biography of the writer.

THIRD REPUBLIC TROISIEME REPUBLIQUE

Focus: French history, 1870–1940
Institutional affiliation: Northern Illinois University (strictly informal affiliation)
Editor: William Logue
Address: Department of History
Northern Illinois University
De Kalb, IL 60115
Frequency: 2/year
Circulation: 110
Pages/issue: 200
Readership: scholars

Manuscripts
Query: no
Abstract: yes
Style guide: MOS
Number of copies: 1, but 2–3 welcomed
Notes: end of manuscript
Blind referee: no
Time to consider manuscript: 2–6 months
Illustrations accepted: tables, graphs, charts, pictures (must be adaptable to format)
Foreign languages: French

THE THIRD WORLD REVIEW

Focus: interdisciplinary: sociological, economic, political, historical, interface of developing and developed societies
Institutional affiliation: SUNY at Cortland
Editor: Ilyas Ba-Yunus
Book review editor: Nicolas Gavrielides
Address: Department of Sociology
SUNY, Cortland
Cortland, NY 13045
Frequency: 2/year
Circulation: 700
Pages/issue: 100
Readership: academics

Manuscripts
Query: no
Abstract: yes
Style guide: MOS
Preferred length: 20 pages
Number of copies: 3
Notes: end of manuscript
Blind referee: yes
Time to consider manuscript: 3 months
Proportion of manuscripts accepted: 1/2
Illustrations accepted: tables, graphs, charts, pictures
Foreign languages: no

Reviews
Seeking reviewers: yes
Unsolicited reviews accepted: yes
How to apply: letter
Include in application: professional degrees, institutional affiliation, areas of expertise, published works, current research
Materials reviewed: books
Length of review: 4 pages (longer for review essay)

THE TOMBSTONE EPITAPH

Focus: Western history of the later nineteenth century
Editor: Wallace E. Clayton
Address: Box 1880
Tombstone, AZ 85638
Frequency: 1/month
Circulation: 6,000
Pages/issue: 20
Readership: general public, buffs, libraries

Manuscripts
Query: no
Abstract: no
Preferred length: 3,000–5,000 words
Number of copies: 1
Notes: end of manuscript
Blind referee: no
Time to consider manuscript: 3 weeks
Proportion of manuscripts accepted: high
Illustrations accepted: pictures
Foreign languages: no

THE TRAIL GUIDE

Focus: Western Americana
Institutional affiliation: Kansas City
    Posse of the Westerners
Editor: Payson Lowell
Address: 1815 East 76th Terrace
    Kansas City, MO 64132
Frequency: 2/year
Circulation: 300
Pages/issue: 24–32
Readership: historians, libraries,
    historical societies

Manuscripts
Query: yes
Abstract: yes
Style guide: MOS
Preferred length: 100–200 pages
Number of copies: 1
Notes: end of manuscript
Blind referee: no
Time to consider manuscript: 1–2
    months
**Proportion of manuscripts
    accepted:** 1/10–1/5
Illustrations accepted: tables, graphs,
    charts, pictures
Foreign languages: no

Reviews
Seeking reviewers: no
Unsolicited reviews accepted: no
How to apply: letter
Include in application: areas of
    expertise, published works, current
    research

Additional notes
Each issue is an independent issue
concentrating on some particular topic of
Western Americana history.

THE TRAINMASTER

Focus: railroad history and current events
Institutional affiliation: Pacific
    Northwest Chapter, National Railway
    Historical Society
Editor: Bryan Leeder
Book review editor: Walter Grande
Address: Room 1
    Union Station
    Portland, OR 97209
Frequency: 9/year
Circulation: 350
Pages/issue: 6
Readership: buffs, libraries

Manuscripts
Query: yes
Abstract: no
Number of copies: 1
Blind referee: no
Time to consider manuscript: 3 months
Illustrations accepted: no
Foreign languages: no

Reviews
Seeking reviewers: no
Unsolicited reviews accepted: yes
How to apply: letter
Include in application: areas of expertise
Materials reviewed: books, audio
Length of review: ½-1 page

TRUE WEST

Focus: events and lives in the Old West, preferably 1840–1905
Editor: Pat Wagner
Address: P.O. Box 3338
Austin, TX 78764
Frequency: 6/year
Circulation: 85,000
Pages/issue: 64
Readership: general public

Manuscripts
Query: yes
Abstract: no
Style guide: own
Preferred length: 1,500–4,000 words
Number of copies: 1
Notes: no notes; list sources separate from text
Time to consider manuscript: 6 weeks
Illustrations accepted: pictures
Foreign languages: no

Reviews
Seeking reviewers: no

Additional notes:
True West does not use fiction based on fact or a lot of dialogue that cannot be substantiated. Its editors are not looking for the dry textbook approach, but do insist that the material be researched and accurate. *True West* pays 2¢ a word minimum on acceptance, plus an allowance for pictures.

THE UKRAINIAN QUARTERLY

Focus: the USSR, the Ukraine in particular; captive nations, eastern Europe, Asia
Institutional affiliation: Ukrainian Congress Committee of America
Editor: Walter Dushnyck
Book review editor: same
Address: 203 Second Avenue
New York, NY 10003
Frequency: 4/year
Circulation: 3,500–4,000
Pages/issue: 112
Readership: academics, research institutions, government offices, libraries

Manuscripts
Query: no
Abstract: no
Style guide: none
Preferred length: 14–24 pages
Number of copies: 2
Notes: bottom of page
Blind referee: no
Time to consider manuscript: 1–3 months
Proportion of manuscripts accepted: 9/10
Illustrations accepted: tables, charts
Foreign languages: preferably in English

Reviews
Seeking reviewers: yes
Unsolicited reviews accepted: yes
How to apply: letter
Include in application: professional degrees, institutional affiliation, areas of expertise, published works
Materials reviewed: books
Length of review: 2–5 pages

UMPQUA TRAPPER

Focus: Douglas County, Oregon
Institutional affiliation: Douglas County
    Historical Society
Editor: G. B. Abdill
Book review editor: same
Address: Douglas County Museum
        Box 1550
        Roseburg, OR 97470
Frequency: 4/year
Circulation: 500
Pages/issue: 24
Readership: general public

Manuscripts
Query: yes
Preferred length: 6–10 pages
Number of copies: 1
Notes: end of manuscript
Blind referee: no
Time to consider manuscript: 1 month
Illustrations accepted: pictures
Foreign languages: no

Reviews
Seeking reviewers: no
Unsolicited reviews accepted: yes

URBAN HISTORY REVIEW
REVUE D'HISTOIRE URBAINE

Focus: urban history in Canada and
    overviews of similar studies elsewhere
Institutional affiliation: National
    Museum of Man, Ottawa
Editor: A. F. J. Artibise
Book review editor: John Weaver
Address: Department of History
        University of Victoria
        Victoria, B.C., V8W 2Y2
        CANADA
Frequency: 3/year
Circulation: 600
Pages/issue: 140
Readership: academics

Manuscripts
Query: no
Abstract: yes
Style guide: MOS
Preferred length: 20 pages
Number of copies: 1
Notes: bottom of page
Blind referee: no
Time to consider manuscript: 3 months
**Proportion of manuscripts
    accepted:** over half
Illustrations accepted: tables, graphs,
    charts, pictures
Foreign languages: French

Reviews
Seeking reviewers: yes
Unsolicited reviews accepted: yes
How to apply: letter
Include in application: professional
    degrees, institutional affiliation, areas
    of expertise, current research, review
    interests
Materials reviewed: books, conferences
Length of review: 600–850 words

Additional notes:
The *Review* is designed to inform and
accepts notes, comments, shorter articles,
and notices of events, as well as longer
articles and book reviews.

UTAH HISTORICAL QUARTERLY

Focus: Utah and folklore
Institutional affiliation: Utah State Historical Society
Editor: Stanford J. Layton
Book review editor: same
Address: 307 West Second South
Salt Lake City, UT 84101
Frequency: 4/year
Circulation: 3,500
Pages/issue: 104
Readership: academics, Society members, general public

Manuscripts
Query: no
Abstract: no
Style guide: MOS
Preferred length: 4,000–5,000 words
Number of copies: 2
Notes: end of manuscript
Blind referee: no
Time to consider manuscript: 8 weeks
Proportion of manuscripts accepted: 1/5
Illustrations accepted: tables, graphs, charts, pictures
Foreign languages: no

Reviews
Seeking reviewers: yes
Unsolicited reviews accepted: no
How to apply: letter
Include in application: professional degrees, institutional affiliation, areas of expertise, current research
Materials reviewed: books
Length of review: 500–750 words

VENTURA COUNTY HISTORICAL SOCIETY QUARTERLY

Focus: Ventura County, California
Institutional affiliation: Ventura County Historical Society
Editor: Grant W. Heil
Address: 221 North Katherine Drive
Ventura, CA 93003
Frequency: 4/year
Circulation: 1,250
Pages/issue: 32
Readership: general public

Manuscripts
Preferred length: 16 pages
Number of copies: 1
Notes: end of manuscript
Blind referee: no
Illustrations accepted: black-and-white tables, graphs, charts
Foreign languages: no

VERMONT HISTORY

Focus: Vermont's past, with preference given to items which present new ideas or information
Institutional affiliation: Vermont Historical Society
Editor: H. N. Muller, III
Address: Pavilion Building
Montpelier, VT 05602
Frequency: 4/year
Circulation: 2,800
Pages/issue: 64
Readership: Society members, scholars, buffs

Manuscripts
Query: no
Abstract: no
Style guide: MLA
Preferred length: 5–35 pages
Number of copies: 1
Notes: end of manuscript
Blind referee: yes
**Proportion of manuscripts
accepted:** 1/5
Illustrations accepted: clean, camera-ready tables, graphs, charts, pictures
Foreign languages: no

Reviews
Seeking reviewers: yes
**Unsolicited reviews
accepted:** occasionally
How to apply: letter
Include in application: institutional affiliation, areas of expertise, published works, current research
Materials reviewed: books
Length of review: variable

VICTORIAN STUDIES

Focus: all aspects of Victorian Britain
Editor: Martha Vicinus
Book review editor: Patrick Brantlinger
Address: Ballantine Hall 338
Indiana University
Bloomington, IN 47405
Frequency: 4/year
Circulation: 3,000
Pages/issue: 128–136
Readership: academics

Manuscripts
Query: no
Abstract: no
Style guide: MOS
Preferred length: 35 pages maximum
Number of copies: 2
Notes: end of manuscript
Blind referee: yes
Time to consider manuscript: 3–4 months
**Proportion of manuscripts
accepted:** 1/15
Illustrations accepted: clear copies of tables, graphs, charts, pictures
Foreign languages: not usually

Reviews
Seeking reviewers: yes
Unsolicited reviews accepted: no
How to apply: form
Materials reviewed: books
Length of review: assigned

VIRGINIA CAVALCADE

Focus: Virginia
Institutional affiliation: Virginia State
Library
Editor: W. Donald Rhinesmith
Address: Virginia State Library
Richmond, VA 23219
Frequency: 4/year
Circulation: 12,000
Pages/issue: 48
Readership: general public, academics

Manuscripts
Query: no
Abstract: no
Style guide: MOS
Preferred length: 15 pages
Number of copies: 1
Notes: end of manuscript
Blind referee: no
Time to consider manuscript: 3–4
months
**Proportion of manuscripts
accepted:** 1/4
Illustrations accepted: tables, graphs,
charts, pictures
Foreign languages: no

THE VIRGINIA MAGAZINE OF HISTORY AND BIOGRAPHY

Focus: Virginia
Institutional affiliation: The Virginia
Historical Society
Editor: William M. E. Rachal
Book review editor: same
Address: P.O. Box 7311
Richmond, VA 23221
Frequency: 4/year
Circulation: 2,900
Pages/issue: 128
Readership: academics, Society
members, general public

Manuscripts
Query: no
Abstract: no
Style guide: MOS
Preferred length: 4,000–10,000 words
Number of copies: 1
Notes: end of manuscript
Blind referee: no
Time to consider manuscript: 2 months
**Proportion of manuscripts
accepted:** 1/4
Illustrations accepted: tables, graphs,
charts, pictures
Foreign languages: no

Reviews
Seeking reviewers: no
Unsolicited reviews accepted: no
How to apply: letter
Include in application: professional
degrees, institutional affiliation, areas
of expertise, published works
Materials reviewed: books
Length of review: 600 words

WE PROCEEDED ON

Focus: the heritage of the Lewis and Clark Expedition, 1803–1806, and news items related to the activities of the Lewis and Clark Trail Heritage Foundation, Inc.
Institutional affiliation: Lewis and Clark Trail Heritage Foundation, Inc.
Editor: Robert E. Lange
Address: 5054 S.W. 26th Place
Portland, OR 97201
Frequency: 4/year
Circulation: 450
Pages/issue: 16–20
Readership: academics, buffs, general public

Manuscripts
Query: yes
Abstract: no
Preferred length: 5,000 words maximum
Number of copies: 1, if suitable for copy machine
Notes: end of manuscript
Time to consider manuscript: 3 weeks
Illustrations accepted: tables, graphs, charts, pictures (only black-and-white glossy photographs)
Foreign languages: no

Reviews
Seeking reviewers: no
Unsolicited reviews accepted: no

WEST VIRGINIA HILLBILLY

Focus: West Virginia and Appalachia, past and present
Editor: Jim Comstock
Address: Richmond, WV 26261
Frequency: 1/week
Circulation: 16,000
Pages/issue: 24
Readership: general public

Manuscripts
Query: yes
Abstract: no
Style guide: MOS
Number of copies: 1
Notes: end of manuscript
Blind referee: no
Time to consider manuscript: 1 week
Illustrations accepted: tables, graphs, charts, pictures
Foreign languages: no

Reviews
Seeking reviewers: yes
Unsolicited reviews accepted: no
How to apply: form
Include in application: professional degrees
Materials reviewed: books, films, audio
Length of review: varies

Additional notes:
West Virginia Hillbilly is an offset-printed tabloid.

WEST VIRGINIA HISTORY

Focus: biography, bibliography of West Virginia and adjacent regions
Institutional affiliation: Department of Culture and History, Archives and History Division
Editor: Rodney A. Pyles
Book review editor: Otis K. Rice
Address: Department of Culture and History
Archives and History Division
Cultural Center
Charleston, WV 25305
Frequency: 4/year
Circulation: 900
Pages/issue: 100–120
Readership: academics, general public

Manuscripts

Query: no
Abstract: no
Style guide: MOS
Preferred length: 25–35 pages
Number of copies: 2
Notes: end of manuscript
Blind referee: no
Time to consider manuscript: 6 weeks
Proportion of manuscripts accepted: 6/10–7/10
Illustrations accepted: tables, graphs, charts, pictures
Foreign languages: no

Reviews

Seeking reviewers: no
Unsolicited reviews accepted: no
How to apply: letter
Include in application: professional degrees, institutional affiliation, areas of expertise, published works, current research
Materials reviewed: books
Length of review: 2–2½ pages

WESTCHESTER HISTORIAN

Focus: Westchester County, New York
Institutional affiliation: Westchester County Historical Society
Editor: Renoda Hoffman
Address: 5 Belmont Street
White Plains, NY 10605
Frequency: 4/year
Circulation: 1,000
Pages/issue: 28
Readership: general public

Manuscripts

Query: no
Abstract: no
Style guide: none
Preferred length: 500–3,000 words
Number of copies: 1
Notes: end of manuscript
Blind referee: no
Time to consider manuscript: 1 month
Proportion of manuscripts accepted: 4/5
Illustrations accepted: pictures must be reproducible
Foreign languages: no

Reviews

Seeking reviewers: no
Unsolicited reviews accepted: only those concerning Westchester County
Materials reviewed: only that which concerns Westchester County

WESTERN HISTORICAL QUARTERLY

Focus: American West
Institutional affiliation: Utah State University
Editor: Charles S. Peterson
Book review editor: Paul A. Hutton
Address: Utah State University, UMC 07 Logan, UT 84322
Frequency: 4/year
Circulation: 3,000
Pages/issue: 136
Readership: scholars, buffs

Manuscripts
Query: no
Abstract: no
Style guide: MOS
Preferred length: 7,500 words
Number of copies: 2
Notes: end of manuscript
Blind referee: no
Time to consider manuscript: 2–8 weeks
Proportion of manuscripts accepted: 1/10
Illustrations accepted: tables, graphs, charts, pictures (cost of printing is always considered)
Foreign languages: no

Reviews
Seeking reviewers: yes
Unsolicited reviews accepted: no
How to apply: form
Length of review: 300 words

Additional notes
Primary consideration for publication is given to narrative, descriptive, interpretative, and analytical essays which deal with broad movements, themes, or problems, based on primary sources and distinguished monographic literature. Originality of treatment, general interest of the article, and the style in which it is written are also criteria for acceptance. Particularly welcome are contributions setting forth new interpretations, reporting new discoveries, or synthesizing knowledge on major themes or subjects.

WESTERN PENNSYLVANIA HISTORICAL MAGAZINE

Focus: western Pennsylvania
Institutional affiliation: Historical Society of Western Pennsylvania
Editor: William F. Trimble
Address: 4338 Bigelow Boulevard Pittsburgh, PA 15213
Frequency: 4/year
Circulation: 1,200
Pages/issue: 100
Readership: academics, buffs, Society members

Manuscripts
Query: no
Abstract: yes
Style guide: MOS
Preferred length: 30–35 pages
Number of copies: 2
Notes: end of manuscript
Blind referee: yes
Time to consider manuscript: 10–12 weeks
Proportion of manuscripts accepted: 2/5
Illustrations accepted: tables, graphs, charts, pictures
Foreign languages: no

Reviews
Seeking reviewers: yes
Unsolicited reviews accepted: no
How to apply: letter
Include in application: professional degrees, institutional affiliation, areas of expertise, published works, current research
Materials reviewed: books
Length of review: 500–600 words

Additional notes
The *Magazine* is especially interested in receiving articles on nineteenth and twentieth century urban history, as well as manuscripts dealing with blacks and other ethnic groups.

WILLIAM AND MARY QUARTERLY

Focus: early America to 1815, and related history of the British Isles, the European continent, and other areas of the New World
Institutional affiliation: College of William and Mary; Colonial Williamsburg Foundation
Editor: Michael McGiffert
Book review editor: John E. Selby
Address: Box 220
Williamsburg, VA 23185
Frequency: 4/year
Circulation: 3,900
Pages/issue: 190
Readership: scholars, academic libraries

Manuscripts
Query: no
Abstract: no
Style guide: MOS, own
Preferred length: 40 pages
Number of copies: 2
Notes: end of manuscript
Blind referee: yes
Time to consider manuscript: 2–3 months
Proportion of manuscripts accepted: 1/10
Illustrations accepted: limited number of camera-ready tables, graphs, charts, pictures
Foreign languages: no

Reviews
Seeking reviewers: yes
Unsolicited reviews accepted: no
How to apply: letter
Include in application: professional degrees, institutional affiliation, areas of expertise, published works, foreign languages, current research
Materials reviewed: books
Length of review: assigned

WISCONSIN MAGAZINE OF HISTORY

Focus: biography and documentation of Upper Midwest, focusing on Wisconsin but including the United States generally
Institutional affiliation: State Historical Society of Wisconsin
Editor: Paul H. Hass
Book review editor: Mary Lou Schulz
Address: 816 State Street
Madison, WI 53706
Frequency: 4/year
Circulation: 7,000
Pages/issue: 80
Readership: Society members, academics, libraries

Manuscripts
Query: no
Abstract: no
Style guide: *Words Into Type*
Preferred length: 25–35 pages
Number of copies: 1
Notes: end of manuscript
Blind referee: no
Time to consider manuscript: 3–4 weeks
Proportion of manuscripts accepted: 1/10–1/7
Illustrations accepted: tables, graphs, charts, pictures, if necessary (a lot of photographs used)
Foreign languages: no

Reviews
Seeking reviewers: yes
Unsolicited reviews accepted: rarely
How to apply: letter
Include in application: institutional affiliation, areas of expertise
Materials reviewed: books, trade books, pamphlets
Length of review: 3 pages maximum

THE WRANGLER

Focus: all phases of western history: travels, personalities, entrepreneurs, ranching or mining enterprises
Institutional affiliation: San Diego Corral of the Westerners
Editor: Ray Tetzlaff
Address: P.O. Box 7174
              San Diego, CA 92102
Frequency: 4/year
Circulation: 250
Pages/issue: 8–12
Readership: Society members, libraries, historical societies

Manuscripts
Query: no
Abstract: no
Style guide: MOS
Preferred length: 2,000–2,500 words
Number of copies: 1
Notes: end of manuscript
Blind referee: no
Time to consider manuscript: immediate
Proportion of manuscripts accepted: 4/5
Illustrations accepted: tables, graphs, charts, pictures (line drawings and photos are produced in each issue)
Foreign languages: no

Reviews
Seeking reviewers: no
Unsolicited reviews accepted: yes
How to apply: letter
Include in application: professional degrees, institutional affiliation, areas of expertise, published works, current research
Length of review: 300 words

Additional notes
The history buff as well as the professional is encouraged to submit substantiated articles.

WYTHE COUNTY HISTORICAL REVIEW

Focus: Wythe County, Virginia
Institutional affiliation: Wythe County Historical Society
Editor: Mrs. William R. Grove
Address: 1635 West Main Street
              Wytheville, VA 24382
Frequency: 2/year
Circulation: 250
Pages/issue: 30
Readership: Society members, libraries

Manuscripts
Query: no
Abstract: no
Style guide: MOS
Preferred length: 2,500–3,500 words
Number of copies: 1
Notes: end of manuscript
Blind referee: no
Time to consider manuscript: 1 month
Illustrations accepted: tables, graphs, charts, pictures
Foreign languages: no

Subject Index

Africa
Africa Today
African Urban Studies
Canadian Journal of African Studies
History in Africa: A Journal of Method
International Journal of African Historical
    Studies
Journal of African Studies
Journal of Black Studies
MERIP Reports
Northeast African Studies
Rural Africana

Agriculture
Agricultural History

America, also see American Revolution, Civil War/Confederacy, Local, State/Provincial/Regional, The West/Frontier
American Heritage
American History Illustrated
American Quarterly
American Studies
Canadian Review of American History
Civil War History
Good Old Days
Journal of American Culture
Mid-America
The New-York Historical Society Quarterly
Proceedings of the American Antiquarian
    Society
Prologue: The Journal of the National
    Archives
Reviews in American History
William and Mary Quarterly

American Revolution
Daughters of the American Revolution
    Magazine
The Loyalist Gazette
Picket Post

Ancient, see Classical

Archaeology
American Journal of Archaeology
Historical Archaeology

Archives
The American Archivist
Archivaria
Georgia Archive
Prologue: The Journal of the National
    Archives

Asia
Asian Affairs, An American Review
Asian Survey
Bulletin of Concerned Asian Scholars
Harvard Journal of Asiatic Studies
Journal of Asian Studies
Journal of Japanese Studies
Modern China: An International Quarterly
    of History and Social Sciences
Pacific Affairs: An International Review of
    Asia and the Pacific

Aviation
Aerospace Historian
Cross and Cockade
Historical Aviation Album

Biography
Hayes Historical Journal
Lincoln Herald
The Pennsylvania Magazine of History and
    Biography
Theodore Roosevelt Association Journal
The Virginia Magazine of History and
    Biography

British Isles
Albion
Eire-Ireland: A Journal of Irish Studies
Journal of British Studies
Scottish Tradition
Victorian Studies

Business
Business History Review

Canada, also see Local, State/Provincial/Regional

American Review of Canadian Studies
Bulletin du Centre de Recherche en
    Civilisation Canadienne-Française
Canadian Historic Sites
Canadian Historical Review
Journal of Canadian Studies
Revue d'Histoire de l'Amerique Française

Civil War/Confederacy

Civil War History
Civil War Round Table Digest
Civil War Times Illustrated
The Journal of Mississippi History
The Journal of Southern History
Lincoln Herald
Museum of the Confederacy Newsletter

Classical, also see Archaeology

American Journal of Ancient History
The Ancient World
Byzantine Studies
The Classical Journal
Classical Philology
The Classical World
Greek, Roman and Byzantine Studies
Journal of Near Eastern Studies
Manuscripta
Sarapis: The American Journal of
    Egyptology

Communication, also see Oral History

Film and History
Journalism History

Current History

Current History

Diplomatic/International Affairs

Diplomatic History
International Journal
Journal of Interamerican Studies and World
    Affairs
MERIP Reports
Pacific Historical Review

Eastern Europe

Canadian-American Review of Hungarian
    Studies
Canadian-American Slavic Studies
Canadian Slavonic Papers
East Central Europe
East European Quarterly
Russian History
The Russian Review
Slavic Review
Slovene Studies: Journal of the Society for
    Slovene Studies
Southeastern Europe
The Ukrainian Quarterly

Economic History

Explorations in Economic History
History of Political Economy
Journal of Economic History

Eighteenth Century

Eighteenth Century Studies
The Eighteenth Century: Theory and
    Interpretations

Environment

Environmental Review
Journal of Forest History

Ethnic Minorities (Canada and the United States)

Afro-Americans in New York Life and
    History
Amerasia Journal
American Jewish History
Les Cahiers: La Société Historique
    Acadienne
Canadian Ethnic Studies
Immigration History Newsletter
Journal of Black Studies
The Journal of Ethnic Studies
Journal of Negro History
New Scholar
Pennsylvania Folklife
Phylon: The Atlanta University Review of
    Race and Culture
Schatzkammer
Scottish Tradition
Swedish Pioneer Historical Quarterly
Swiss American Historical Society
    Newsletter

Europe, also see British Isles, Eastern Europe, France

Central European History
Europa: A Journal of Interdisciplinary
    Studies
European Studies Newsletter
Journal of Modern History
Scandinavian Studies
Swedish Pioneer Historical Studies

Folklore

Journal of American Folklore
Pennsylvania Folklife

France

Contemporary French Civilization
French Historical Studies
Third Republic

Frontier, see The West/Frontier

Genealogy/Family

Genealogical Journal
The Loyalist Gazette
The Mayflower Quarterly
National Genealogical Society Quarterly
New England Historical and Genealogical
    Register

General

American Historical Review
Canada and the World
Canadian Journal of History
Clio
The Historian
Historical Reflections
The History Book Club Review
The Journal of Historical Studies
Mankind Magazine
The Maryland Historian
The Public Historian
Red River Valley Historical Journal of World
    History

Intellectual History

History of Education Quarterly
Journal of the History of Ideas

Interdisciplinary, also see Social Science

American Review of Canadian Studies
American Studies

Appalachian Journal: A Regional Studies
    Review
Canadian Review of American Studies
Centerpoint: A Journal of Interdisciplinary
    Studies
Clio
Comparative Frontier Studies
Daedalus
Eighteenth Century Studies
Ethnohistory
Europa: A Journal of Interdisciplinary
    Studies
Feminist Studies
The Greater Llano Estacado Southwest
    Heritage
The Humanities Association Review
Journal of Black Studies
Journal of Conflict Resolution
The Journal of Ethnic Studies
Journal of Interdisciplinary History
Journal of Near Eastern Studies
Journal of the History of the Behavioral
    Sciences
Manuscripta
Mediaevalia
The Musk-Ox
The Old Northwest: A Journal of Regional
    Life and Letters
Phylon: The Atlanta Review of Race and
    Culture
Renaissance and Reformation
Schatzkammer
Signs: Journal of Women in Culture and
    Society
South Atlantic Quarterly
Southern Studies: An Interdisciplinary
    Journal of the South
The Third World Review

Latin America

The Americas
Hispanic American Historical Review
Journal of Interamerican Studies and World
    Affairs
Latin American Digest
Latin American Research Review
New Scholar
Southwestern Studies

Legal

The American Journal of Legal History

Local

Afro-Americans in New York Life and
History (New York)
The Allen County Reporter (Ohio)
Attakapas Gazette (Louisiana)
Le Brayon: Revue de la Société Historique
du Madawaska (New Brunswick)
The Bronx County Historical Society
Journal (New York)
Bulletin of the Historical Society of
Montgomery County (Pennsylvania)
Chicago History (Illinois)
Diggin's (California)
El Escribano (Florida)
Essex Institute Historical Collections
(Massachusetts)
Flashback (Arkansas)
Franklin County Historical Review
(Tennessee)
Franklin Flyer (Washington)
Fulton County Historical and
Genealogical Society Newsletter
Quarterly (Illinois)
The Glades Star (Maryland)
Historic Kern (California)
Huntsville Historical Review (Alabama)
Journal of Erie Studies (Pennsylvania)
The Journal of San Diego History
(California)
Journal of the Lancaster County Historical
Society (Pennsylvania)
Landmark (Wisconsin)
Long Island Forum (New York)
Newport History (Rhode Island)
Newsletter: Whoop-Up Country Chapter,
Historical Society of Alberta (Alberta)
Niagara Frontier (New York)
Northeastern Nevada Historical Society
Quarterly (Nevada)
The Ozarker (Missouri)
Password (Texas)
Pea River Trails (Alabama)
Pickaway Quarterly (Ohio)
Raincoast Chronicles (British Columbia)
La Revue d'Histoire de la Société
Historique Nicolas-Denys (New
Brunswick)
Richmond County History (Georgia)
Rochester History (New York)
Rural Folio (New York)
Saguenayensia (Quebec)
The San Luis Valley Historian (Colorado)
The Schuylerite (Illinois)
Seaport (New York)
Spanish River Papers (Florida)
Staten Island Historian (New York)

The Stream of History (Arkansas)
Umpqua Trapper (Oregon)
Ventura County Historical Society Quarterly
(California)
Westchester Historian (New York)
Western Pennsylvania Historical Magazine
(Pennsylvania)
Wythe County Historical Review (Virginia)

Maritime

American Neptune
Inland Seas
The Sea Chest
Seaport
Steamboat Bill

Medieval/Renaissance/ Reformation

Byzantine Studies
Journal of Medieval and Renaissance
Studies
Manuscripta
Mediaevalia
North Wind
Renaissance and Reformation
Renaissance Quarterly
The Sixteenth Century Journal
Speculum: A Journal of Medieval Studies

Methodology/Theory, also see Teaching

Film and History
Historical Methods
History and Theory: Studies in the
Philosophy of History
History in Africa: A Journal of Method
History News
International Journal of Oral History
Oral History Review
Prologue: The Journal of the National
Archives
The Public Historian
Sound Heritage

Middle East

Journal of Near Eastern Studies
The Muslim World

Military/War and Peace, also see American Revolution, Civil War

Army Museum Newsletter
Council on Abandoned Military Posts
Periodical
Cross and Cockade

History, Numbers and War
Journal of Conflict Resolution
Military Affairs
Military History of Texas and the Southwest
The Military Journal

Nationalism
Canadian Review of Studies in Nationalism

Oral History
International Journal of Oral History
Oral History Review

Preservation/Collections
Americana Magazine
Army Museum Newsletter
The Connecticut Antiquarian
Council on Abandoned Military Posts
    Periodical
Historic Preservation
Historically Speaking
Old-Time New England
Proceedings of the American Antiquarian
    Society

Provincial, see
State/Provincial/Regional

Psychohistory
The Journal of Psychohistory

Public History, also see
Archives,
Preservation/Collections
The Public Historian

Railroads
Railroad History
The Trainmaster

Reformation, see
Medieval/Renaissance/
Reformation

Regional, see
State/Provincial/Regional

Religion
The Alabama Baptist Historian
Baptist History and Heritage

Catholic Historical Review
Church History
Fides et Historia
Foundations
The Greek Orthodox Theological Review
Historical Magazine of the Episcopal
    Church
The Historical Messenger
History of Religions
Journal of Presbyterian History
The Muslim World
Pennsylvania Mennonite Heritage

Renaissance, see
Medieval/Renaissance/
Reformation

Russia, see Eastern Europe

Science/Technology
Historia Mathematica
Isis
Journal of the History of Biology
Pharmacy in History
Technology and Culture

Social History, also see Sport
History of Education Quarterly
International Labor and Working Class
    History
Journal of American Culture
Journal of Popular Culture
The Journal of Social History
Journal of Urban History
Labor History
Peasant Studies Newsletter
Social History
Urban History Review

Social Science
Historical Methods
Indiana Social Studies Quarterly
Social Science
Social Science History
The Social Science Journal
Social Science Quarterly

Sport
Canadian Journal of History of Sport and
    Physical Education
Journal of Sport History

State/Provincial/Regional

Acadiensis: Journal of the History of the
    Atlantic Region
Alabama Historical Quarterly
Alabama Review
The Alaska Journal
Alberta History
The Annals of Iowa
Annals of Wyoming
Appalachian Journal: A Regional Studies
    Review
Arizona and the West
Arkansas Historical Quarterly
B.C. Historical News
Bulletin of Historic Sites and Properties
The Bulletin of the Missouri Historical
    Society
California History
The Chronicles of Oklahoma
Cincinnati Historical Society Quarterly
The Colorado Magazine
La Confluencia
Detroit in Perspective: A Journal of
    Regional History
East Tennessee Historical Society
    Publications
Echoes
The Filson Club History Quarterly
Florida Historical Quarterly
Georgia Historical Quarterly
Great Plains Journal
The Greater Llano Estacado Southwest
    Heritage
The High Country
Historical New Hampshire
Historical Society of Michigan Chronicle
Idaho Yesterdays
Indiana History Bulletin
Indiana Magazine of History
The Journal of Arizona History
The Journal of Mississippi History
Journal of Southern History
The Journal of the Illinois State Historical
    Society
Kansas History: A Journal of the Central
    Plains
Louisiana History
Maine Historical Society Quarterly
Maryland Historical Magazine
The Mayflower Quarterly
The Midwest Quarterly
Minnesota History
Mississippi Quarterly: The Journal of
    Southern Culture

Missouri Historical Review
Montana: The Magazine of Western History
The Musk-Ox
Nebraska History
Nevada Historical Society Quarterly
New England Historical and Genealogical
    Register
The New England Quarterly
New Jersey Historical Commission
    Newsletter
New Jersey History
New Mexico Historical Review
The New-York Historical Society Quarterly
New York History
North Carolina Historical Review
North Dakota History: Journal of the
    Northern Plains
North Jersey Highlander
Northwest Ohio Quarterly
Nova Scotia Historical Quarterly
Ohio History
The Old Northwest: A Journal of Regional
    Life and Letters
Old-Time New England
Ontario History
Oregon Historical Quarterly
Pacific Historical Review
The Pacific Northwest Forum
The Pacific Northwest Quarterly
The Palimpsest
Pennsylvania Folklife
Pennsylvania Heritage
Pennsylvania History
The Pennsylvania Magazine of History and
    Biography
Red River Valley Historical Review
The Register of the Kentucky Historical
    Society
Rhode Island History
Rio Grande History
Snake River Echoes
Sound Heritage
South Carolina Historical Magazine
South Dakota History
Southern California Quarterly
Southern Studies: An Interdisciplinary
    Journal of the South
Southwestern Historical Quarterly
Southwestern Studies
Tennessee Historical Quarterly
Utah Historical Quarterly
Vermont History
Virginia Cavalcade
The Virginia Magazine of History and
    Biography

West Virginia Hillbilly
West Virginia History
Western Historical Quarterly
Wisconsin Magazine of History

Teaching
The History and Social Science Teacher
The History Teacher

Third World, also see Africa, Asia, Latin America, Middle East
Journal of Developing Areas
The Third World Review

Transportation, see Aviation, Maritime, Railroad

The West/Frontier
The American West
Annals of Wyoming
Arizona and the West
The Branding Iron
The Bulletin of the Missouri Historical Society
The Chronicles of Oklahoma
The Colorado Magazine

Comparative Frontier Studies
Frontier Times
The High Country
Journal of the West
Kansas History: A Journal of the Central Plains
Little Big Horn Associates Research Review
Missouri Historical Review
Montana: The Magazine of Western History
Museum of the Fur Trade Quarterly
Old West
The Pacific Historian
Pacific Historical Review
Persimmon Hill
Pioneer America
The Tombstone Epitaph
The Trail Guide
True West
We Proceeded On
Western Historical Quarterly
The Wrangler

Women
Feminist Studies
Signs: Journal of Women in Culture and Society

Edited by Elizabeth McNamara.
Composed by McAdams Type of Santa
Barbara. Printed and bound by
BookCrafters of Chelsea, Michigan. Text
and cover designed by Tom Reeg.